INTRODUCING QUALITATIVE METHODS provides a series of volumes which introduce qualitative research to the student and beginning researcher. The approach is interdisciplinary and international. A distinctive feature of these volumes is the helpful student exercises.

One stream of the series provides texts on the key methodologies used in qualitative research. The other stream contains books on qualitative research for different disciplines or occupations. Both streams cover the basic literature in a clear and accessible style, but also cover the 'cutting edge' issues in the area.

SERIES EDITOR
David Silverman (Goldsmiths College)

EDITORIAL BOARD
Michael Bloor (University of Wales, Cardiff)
Barbara Czarniawska-Joerges (University of Gothenburg)
Norman Denzin (University of Illinois, Champaign)
Barry Glassner (University of Southern California)
Jaber Gubrium (University of Missouri)
Anne Murcott (South Bank University)
Jonathan Potter (Loughborough University)

TITLES IN SERIES

Doing Conversational Analysis: A Practical Guide
Paul ten Have

Using Foucault's Methods
Gavin Kendall and Gary Wickham

The Quality of Qualitative Research
Clive Seale

Qualitative Evaluation
Ian Shaw

Researching Life Stories and Family Histories
Robert L. Miller

Categories in Text and Talk: A Practical Introduction to Categorization Analysis
Georgia Lepper

Focus Groups in Social Research
Michael Bloor, Jane Frankland, Michelle Thomas, Kate Robson

Qualitative Research Through Case Studies
Max Travers

Methods of Critical Discourse Analysis
Ruth Wodak and Michael Meyer

Qualitative Research in Social Work
Ian Shaw and Nick Gould

Qualitative Research in Information Systems
Michael D. Myers and David Avison

Documents in Social Research
Lindsay Prior

Qualitative Research in Education

Interaction and Practice

Peter Freebody

SAGE Publications
London • Thousand Oaks • New Delhi

100312984 X

First published 2003

SAGE Publications Ltd
6 Bonhill Street
London EC2A 4PU

SAGE Publications Inc.
2455 Teller Road
Thousand Oaks, California 91320

SAGE Publications India Pvt Ltd
32, M-Block Market
Greater Kailash – I
New Delhi 110 048

British Library Cataloguing in Publication data

A catalogue record for this book is available from the British Library

ISBN 0 7619 6140 2
ISBN 0 7619 6141 0 (pbk)

Library of Congress Control Number 2002103332

Typeset by Keystroke, Jacaranda Lodge, Wolverhampton
Printed in India at Gopsons Paper Ltd, Noida

Contents

Preface

A book needs to locate itself in the story in which it aims to play a part. In the case of education and research, this story is long and complex. The spread of education through schooling and *as* schooling has perhaps been the singular achievement of the twentieth century. As in no other era, it became a hallmark of a contemporary society that its members believe in schooling as the embodiment of their aspirations for acculturating their young. As schooling broadened its purview, and expanded its moral, cultural and legal jurisdictions, so educational research grew apace. Researchers have both supported and contested aspects of mass schooling. Predictably enough, different modes of educational research have figured prominently at different moments and places in this growth.

The expansion of education through schooling was neither gradual nor linear. It shifted in its character, in the ways it claimed legitimation, and in how it aimed to respond to changing community, cultural and economic conditions. It intersected at various times and places with particular economic, cultural, political and ideological movements – indigenous and migrant 'assimilation' and post-colonial identity, urban industrialization, poverty alleviation, corporate management practices, citizenship training, the conservation and challenge of colonial, ethnic and national diasporas and heritage, and so on. Changing views of the role of research in education, and changing preferences for different ways of doing research relate to these shifts.

To paint in broad strokes, in the first part of the twentieth century Northern nations deployed schooling to maximize the capabilities of a workforce facing increasing demands for technical, literate and numerate competence. Schooling has been seen as an instrument of meritocracy. It has been seen as standing against the proposition, hanging over from previous centuries, that intellectual and cultural privileges are properly inherited. These nations invested more in schooling after 1950, in part because the enterprise of schooling became to be seen as a central platform for national and community development. At first these developments were built around a common public vocabulary: Keynesian accounts of economic growth and national accounts; state-sponsored collective bargaining in and about public institutions; sociological accounts of social inequalities; cultural investment; and the rhetoric of egalitarian and redistributive welfare systems. This is the period in which educational researchers began to draw in greater numbers on anthropologically-styled qualitative research accounts, as more of their readership and their trainees were exposed to ever-broader ranges of liberal arts studies as part of their preparation for teaching.

By the late 1970s, with the sharp decline in projections of economic growth and the beginnings of globalized capital and human movements, this common vocabulary seemed little more than a quaint minority creole in many debates about education and other public provisions. The prime functions of school had been revisited. The vocabulary of performance-measurement, competition-for-resources, and corporate, managerial accountability was increasingly applied to those institutions that were once more explicitly charged with meritocratic versions of equity and redistribution. Management through quantification provided, in many nations and education systems, the high-discourse of debate and research. Through these times schooling was installed as a lever for 'development' for those Southern nations coming out of European colonial administration. Many of these societies adapted the logics and regulatory practices developed in Northern nations to a variety of local imperatives.

This meant that, by the end of the 1900s, much of what people knew about and did by way of everyday educational activity was in danger of being written out of the considerations of educators. So self-sustaining did the managerial bases of schooling seem, so comprehensive and rarely challenged the separation of the social, intellectual, moral and ideological meanings and materials of schools from those of the everyday activities of the communities they purported to serve, that entire communities could, without irony, be described as 'failing at education' – as bizarre a notion as imaginable from a cultural perspective on education. As some put it, while the people can dismiss governments in the modern democracies, 'education' is the administrative retaliation: through schooling, governments can now dismiss the people. Some qualitative researchers reacted 'anthropologically' to that, exploring these out-of-school everyday activities, and providing non-schooled ways of thinking about them. The examples in this book aim to reflect some of these interests.

The developments outlined above have all been contested in a variety of ways. Their hold has remained at best provisional, partly because of the diversity of the research that has been taken to inform schooling. Some of the more evident reasons for the recent reinvigoration of qualitative approaches to researching education include:

1. a dissatisfaction with limitations on the capacities of conventional, quantitative research to describe educational events;
2. a perception, not always warranted, that quantitative representations of educational activities are only the instruments of governmental administration, rather than valuable sources of knowledge for educators;
3. growing incursions, from the 1980s on, of sociology, linguistics and anthropology into educational research; and
4. the development over time of more precise and informative analytic methods associated with qualitative approaches.

Along with the many others with similar focus, this book inhabits its own particular time and place in this history in these developments. It reflects my continued interest in documenting observations in ways that are at the one time conceptually informative, professionally useful and ideologically productive.

Trained as an educational statistician, I have often used quantitative analytic methods to explore patterns of capabilities, expressions of beliefs, and the linguistic and cultural features of educational texts. But long ago circumstances 'led me on', as it were. My early contacts with educational research occurred at about the same time as my first teaching job, and continued when I found myself asked to give 'advice-based-on-research' to teachers and at times to educational administrators and policy makers. It was these experiences that led me to consider what kinds of research could enjoy some theoretical integrity as well as have an impact on how educators thought about and conducted their work. Initially, like many with my early training, I considered qualitative methods speculative, provisional, useful as back-ups, supplements and opportunities to give support to the 'real findings' (generally, the statistics) through more 'in-depth' reflections. Gradually I came to see that an understanding of the more sophisticated forms of qualitative analysis offers a distinctive way of knowing and theorizing about educational and social practices and structures, and thus can make distinctive contributions to educational knowledge and debate.

I came to these understandings not solely because of the intellectual satisfaction derived from engagement in the details of educational events – the pleasurable shock of the familiar – but also because of exposure to the considerable bodies of knowledge accumulated through qualitative inquiry. This knowledge, the result of systematic work by researchers across a range of fields bearing on education, is about methods of analysis, the general conduct of research, and the nature of educational and cultural activities. The status of this knowledge and of our understanding of the nature and outcomes of qualitative analyses mean that qualitative approaches to research in education are no longer, if they ever were, speculative or provisional, certainly no more so than other forms of social inquiry.

The centrepiece of this book is a set of qualitative analytic methods for studying educational events and accounts of those events. The most obvious problem in presenting these methods is to find coherent ways through the variety of professional, theoretical and ideological traditions that currently both shape and divide the field of educational research. Needless to say, it is not possible to find methods that have broad consensus across the disciplines and positions contesting the field. There is, therefore, much that many educational researchers will disagree with, or at least find to be short-changed in the approaches I have taken here. This diversity of analytic investment is simply what experienced and novice researchers alike must recognize.

But it takes four chapters to get to this centrepiece. This is because I found that the less obvious task for such a project is to frame analytic methods in terms of some version of the field that they hope to inform: What are the boundaries of the activities that will count as 'educational' for this book, here and now? Can this work be about schooling, and more than schooling? In addressing these questions, we find that any contribution to educational research needs to display some sense of the contested terrain in which it appears, those assumptions, understandings and debates that traverse educational work about the place of research. Among these are the categories that locate the methods at hand. In this case, I have put these methods forward as 'qualitative', a descriptor that derives its sense from a contrast with 'quantitative'. As I try to show later, this contrast may be a good place to start, but it does not prove to be particularly fruitful when we consider how we can actually work with educational data. There are more significant conceptual and practical polarities and dialectics at stake.

The danger with 'methods' books is that the methods are presented for application as stand-alone procedures, apparently independent of the conceptual and practical issues that arise from studying the actual sites of the events under study. Offsetting that danger is one of the important goals of the first few chapters: there I provide the 'take' on education, research and qualitative approaches in terms of which the subsequent chapters can be read. I expand on the view that what is central to productive research is an organic and explicitly understood relationship between conceptual interests, analytic methods and methodological design. Each of itself cannot secure the productivity of a research project; it is rather their interplay in practice that can generate refined theory and analysis, and more professionally fulfilling practice. That is to say, this book approaches qualitative methods in education by taking the time to stalk them, trying to track them down and corral them into a position in which they can be seen as more than procedural guidelines. For researchers, methods need to be generative of significant reflection, not just equipment for producing conclusions.

There are some conceptual, collegial and material debts to be acknowledged. The book can be seen as an extended set of variations of a few key themes. First is the proposition that the mundane, generally unnoticed interactions associated with educational practices are more than static accompaniments, and that, indeed, they constitute those practices and make them recognizably 'educational'. The idea that the apparent untidiness, disorderliness and disarray of ordinary everyday interaction not only can be, but should be studied systematically was articulated in the 1960s by Sacks (1992). He was one of the first social scientists to take seriously the usually unremarked but highly remarkable ways in which people conduct their everyday business through talk. In pursuing that interest, he developed 'the distinctive and utterly critical recognition . . . that the talk can be examined as an object in its own right, and not merely as a screen on which are projected other processes' (Schegloff, 1995: xviii).

A proposition that takes this idea further is also central to the chapters that follow. This concerns the heuristic and programmatic idea that everyday interaction weaves and re-weaves social order. Dimensions of that order, including the 'big' sociological categorizations we commonly use to describe social and cultural experience – socio-economic status, gender, ethnicity, race, religion and so on – are built by people's everyday concerted activities; they do not provide us with the determinants or ready-made explanations or of those activities. As Schegloff pointed out:

> The point is not that persons are somehow *not* male or female, upper or lower class, with or without power, professors and/or students. They may be, on some occasion, demonstrably members of one or another of those categories. Nor is the issue that those aspects of the society do not matter, or did not matter on that occasion. We may share a lively sense that indeed they do matter, and that they mattered on that occasion, and mattered for just that aspect of some interaction on which we are focusing. There is still the problem of *showing from the details of the talk or other conduct in the materials* that we are analyzing that those aspects of the scene are what the parties are oriented to. *For that is to show how the parties are embodying for one another the relevancies of the interaction and are thereby producing the social structure.* (Schegloff, 1991: 51, emphases in original)

In Dorothy E. Smith's terms, we need to be clear what we mean when we say that we study education as a category of social activity: we mean that we are focusing on 'the ongoing concerting and coordinating of individuals' activities . . . people's ever-to-be-renewed coordinating of their activities' (1999: 6).

These two propositions taken together – that social activity can be studied in principled ways, and that this study can show how people accomplish the 'social facts' by which they give order and consequentiality to their experiences – are central ideas that motivate this book. I hope to show that the analytic and interpretive discipline that these ideas call for is at the same time a way out of some of the more bland, circular and unproductive ways of talking about education that are commonplace in the research community.

An additional idea central to this book is that educational research is a site of contestation over:

- the activities that count normatively as 'educational';
- the language by which educational problems and solutions are represented;
- the nature of the social relations that are embodied in educational practice, including the organizational practices by which institutionalized education is administered;
- the community practices by which educational activities are given public credibility; and
- the research practices through which education can be and should be studied.

As each of these contests is acted out and re-displayed in project after project, a particular configuration of positions is re-installed, re-legitimated and again made available for the reader. These positions affect what we can know and how we can think and talk about the context, goals and consequences of education, the cultural and political orders of social life, the nature and consequences of research texts, and the continued conduct and purposes of educational research.

Acknowledgements

The approaches I outline in this book have been influenced to differing degrees and in different settings by the work of James Heap, John Heritage, the late Harvey Sacks, Emmanuel Schegloff and Dorothy E. Smith. More immediately, Carolyn Baker and Brian Street have provided me with genial apprenticeships in understanding how talk and cultural practices can be described. But when it comes to learning about the conduct of qualitative research and clarifying ways of talking about it, there is nothing more engaging and educative than working with graduate research students. Many of these students have become valued colleagues, foremost among them Helena Austin, Ann Czislowski-McKenna, Bronwyn Dwyer and Jill Freiberg. As they came to master these methods themselves, these people taught me a lot about how to apply them, and kept showing me why they matter.

Three people deserve special thanks for material support they gave to the development of this book: Geraldine Castleton provided valuable help on the chapter concerning methodologies; Robert Campbell skilfully first-drafted most of the exercises provided at the end of each chapter and pursued wayward references; and most importantly David Silverman suggested this book in the first place while I was quietly minding my own business. David provided patient and friendly encouragement at key stages, and I thank him for the time he devoted to this project and for allowing me to draw on his conspicuous expertise.

I appreciate the efforts of my editor at Sage, Michael Carmichael, and his staff, who showed all the encouragement and patience that comes with being good at their work.

Simon, Kelly, Georgia and Virginia, for the most part unbeknownst to them, make the work possible, and even make it seem like fun. For this they deserve another indelible thank-you note.

1

Education as Social and Cultural Practice

Educational research is a more intellectually and professionally challenging field than most. The challenges for the researcher arise from at least four aspects of education: first, the importance of education is rarely denied. The last century, whatever else it may have been, was certainly the century of schooling. In the West, governments and communities have invested more and more faith in education to solve ever larger and more entrenched social problems. In developing nations, education is often regarded as a privilege and a prize, and many studies show that the simple number of years a young person spends in formal educational settings is a powerful predictor of, among other things, how long they and their children will live (Summers, 1994). So education matters.

Second, educational activities are inherently complex and dynamic, both in the local settings in which they occur and, beyond those sites, as part of a society's publicly co-ordinated activities. With changes in the socio-cultural make-up of the participants within the boundaries of an educational site (say, a family, school or state), we observe changes in the qualities of educational goals, outcomes and processes. So the practices that we term 'educational' are always debatable, always changing and thus always objects of contestation. Research has played a significant part in those contests.

Third, education matured comparatively late as an institutionalized academic research area and thus has spent some decades drawing its conceptual and methodological sustenance from neighbouring social disciplines, in particular Sociology, Psychology, Anthropology, History, Economics and Philosophy. The methods evident in contemporary educational research display features of work in these disciplines, often in combinations, as do the reasoning practices those methods support.

Fourth, while many equate 'education' with 'institutionalized education', most obviously with 'schooling', it is nonetheless the case that just as much education goes on informally, outside the school, college or university grounds as inside. Further, when we consider the ways people learn and are taught, it becomes clear that the forms of knowledge and inquiry that people encounter across the range of their family, community and institutional experiences impact on one another in important ways.

Partly as a result of the combination of these factors, educational research is probably a more multi-faceted and almost certainly a more contested and fractious field than most comparable research domains. In this book I introduce a collection of qualitative methods that are in use in contemporary educational research. This collection is not random, nor is it a 'best of' selection of the most popular methods. Rather, it represents ways of putting to productive work a selection of techniques bound loosely by a shared appreciation of educational practice as fundamentally social and cultural in nature. It represents as well a programme for viewing competing ways of theorizing about education, research and the nature of evidence.

Put bluntly, the book has a position on education and research: in many countries, an individual's education in school is legally mandated. The sentence is usually ten to twelve years; so there is no sense in pretending that studying education allows values, norms or ideological positions to be set aside, however temporarily. How individuals emerge from their formal acculturation into particular ways of knowing and behaving is not something that most societies leave to chance. The first known law making schooling compulsory, passed in 1647, was called the Olde Deluder Satan Law. In that law the Puritan communities of North America required every town of 50 or more families to hire a reading and writing teacher, to 'outwit' the ways of the Evil One by education. Since then, virtually every Education Act has justified itself through the rhetoric of moral, economic and social well-being. So for the researcher, being principled and disciplined is not the same as being neutral on matters of education. At the same time, matters of value are as much the objects of inquiry as are the practices they inform.

In this chapter I open the discussion by exploring the nature of educational practice and the distinctive part that qualitative research has played and can play in educational work. But first, some scene-setting.

Preview scenes

Before beginning to define education and proceeding to discuss how it is that research has had and can have impact on its conduct, we first consider a number of everyday scenes. We begin here because it is through everyday participation in ordinary activities that members of the society encounter this practical activity called 'education'.

Scene 1.1 A mother has been sitting for a few minutes reading a Roald Dahl book with her seven-year old child. Nearby is a younger brother starting to set up for a drawing activity on the carpet.

M   Well, that's the title up here is HOW TO BE LITTLE RAY OF SUNSHINE AND MAKE EVERYONE ELSE IN THE HOUSE FEEL LIKE VOMITING. That is ((raised voice)) <u>would you please take that pen out . . . you're not to write in here. And</u> ((brother leaves, very loud voice)) <u>you can go and look for your socks. I told you they are on the bed, in your room somewhere, on the bed or</u> ((extremely loud voice)) <u>on the floor. I put some socks in your room last night. Blue ones.</u>

C   ((reading)) FOR HOURS BEFORE THE DOCTOR COMES EVEN THROUGH//

M   //Did you read this title?

C   No, because I can't read it

M   Okay. HOW TO BE AN that word is OBNOXIOUS INVALID. Do you know what that means? Do you know what 'obnoxious' means? Totally horrible. What's an invalid?

C   I don't know.

M   A sick person. So when you're sick, how to be totally horrible

C   ( ) FOR HOURS BEFORE THE DOCTOR COMES EVEN ( ) KNOWS VERY WELL YOU DON'T HAVE TO HAVE AN INJECTION ((noise [sock-searching?] is building up dramatically in the background))

M   ((mock threatening)) Do you know what blood is?

C   No::o ((sing-song))

M   ((telephone rings)) I think we'll have to stop now

A scene such as a mother helping a young child with reading is highly familiar to us. In spite of the brevity and familiarity of the scene, however, we can note a number of features. For example, we can see the satirical and iconoclastic contents of the reading materials as a statement about the kinds of things that children find enjoyable and possibly a little 'naughty'. Our everyday theories about children (see Jenks, 1982, 1989) come to the fore here when we consider the fact that authors such as Dahl have achieved widespread popularity among children, in spite of the first-glance unpalatable nature of the contents of these stories, and thus their ambiguous status as reading materials 'for children'.

As well, we can see in this excerpt the ways in which Mother attempted to help the child learn to read, and how she responded when she found that the child did not know words on the page. Again, here, the unremarkability of these activities attests to its common-sensical availability in our culture as a way of teaching reading. We may also consider that the mother's valiant attempts to engage in the reading activity with the child during a heavy-traffic time of day attests to the significance given to literacy capabilities and their development in young children. If we look more closely, we can see how it is that this little event, however long or successful it was, was jointly produced by two individuals co-ordinating their activities. In this case, this co-ordination is visible right down to the child's mock-naïve assertion that, along with two previous 'don't know' answers to questions, he says 'no' to the question about blood. This allows Mother to have her quiet joke about the rowdy and persistent sibling, and to signal the impending termination (perhaps mercifully for both) of the reading event.

Scene 1.2 A parent is having a discussion with an interviewer from a university about her son Tom's apparently unsatisfactory progress in reading at school.

R   Do you talk with Tom's teacher?
M   Yeh. I first went to, I was called in for an interview and I had teacher parent interview on how, parent interview, on 'how your child is progressing' ((pseudo-formal voice)) and I found that before, like, when Tom started school at the beginning of the year, I found that the way he was learning how to read was a real problem with me. I mean, when I was going to school it was, like, repetition of 'a' is for 'apple', and you always knew what 'a' was. Whereas they didn't do the same, and when I went over there to see them about it, like, when we had the parent-and-teacher sort of thing, her and I actually had a really big talk, well it actually turned out to be a bit of debate about this, the way they're being taught, but then I sort of stayed right out of it, because I had my own views and I can't see the way they're being taught now is helping them in any way. So I've tried to stay away from the teaching, because my views are either old or they don't want to hear about it, and I can't help him at home.

This mother did not just speak as the biological parent of Tom, but also, perhaps more so in this setting, as a parent with responsibilities to supplement the work done in the formal setting of the school. When she indicated that the ways in which current reading lessons were being conducted became a 'problem' for her, she spoke as a parent who wished to help with Tom's reading at home, as we find out at the end of the statement. Her comments, therefore, were not mainly about Tom, but about her own role as a 'parent-educator' and the ways in which she felt that her actions in that role had been subordinated to the practices that Tom encountered in school. We can see the nomination of herself as the less-expert adjunct to the school's activity in her closing remarks in this statement, but we can also see indications in two small corrections that she made at the opening of her statement: 'I first went to, I was called in for . . .'; 'I had a teacher parent interview on how, parent interview, on 'how . . .'. In both of these corrections she realigned herself as a parent-from-the-school's-perspective, right down to naming the interview as a 'parent interview', even though she herself, as speaker, was the parent.

But the main point of interest for this speaker was her view that her own understanding of how she could help as an educator in the home with Tom's reading had been disqualified in the course of the 'debate' that she had with the teacher. Clearly, the mother expressed strong disagreement with the way in which Tom was being taught. But why did this lead her to 'stay away from the teaching' and to the conclusion that 'I can't help him at home'? In terms of Tom's education as a reader, this parent's statements make visible her understanding of the relative proprietal rights of the home and the school, at least on the matter of reading instruction.

Scene 1.3 A page from a book produced for use in beginning reading classes for young students, with the facing picture showing a coloured line drawing of children and a dog frolicking around a male adult who is hosing a car in the sunshine.

> 'Please will you hose me?' said Mark.
> Father hosed Helen and Mark.
> 'Please will you hose me?' barked Boxer.
> Father hosed Boxer too.
>
> (from Baker and Freebody, 1989)

Beginning reading books are written partly to help students learn to read. To do that, they usually try to interest and amuse students as well. We can consider how the writer of this text inserts a version of the reader into the social world, and how the child-reader (or 'beginning reader' – sometimes these texts have been used to teach adults to read) needs to know about and go along with that version. Children know that, apart from in books written for them, pets can neither talk nor 'bark' in words. The teacher using the book knows that too. So the assumption of the writer is *not* that this text will deceive children into believing that they do: if the writer thought children *did* believe that pets talk, then the story would lose its playful value. But further, the child-reader who finds the text amusing does so *not* by believing that pets can talk, or by believing that the writer believes they can. The amusement must arise from the child's appreciation that the writer is *playing with an idea that adults have about children, and is using that idea to motivate the learning.* So the text is not only for children, or even about children, but rather about children-not-being-altogether-like-adults, children-being-students, and children knowing what adults think about that. The child plays Child for the Adult in and by the act of appropriately reading, and maybe being amused by this text.

Our common sense and most of our formal scientific descriptions of how to educate children do not usually recognize the understandings they need to employ to bring off apparently simple dealings with adults – in the case above, understandings about little stories about talking dogs. The child-reader may learn a number of things about becoming educated when a teacher uses a text like the one above, but among those things is participating in adults' definitions about children.

Scene 1.4 Pa's speech from *The Adventures Of Huckleberry Finn* by Mark Twain.

> Looky here – you drop that school, you hear? I'll learn people to bring up a boy to put on airs over his own father and let on to be better'n what he is. You lemme catch you fooling around that school again, you hear? Your mother couldn't read, and she couldn't write, nuther, before she died. None of the family couldn't, before they died. I can't; and here you're a-swelling yourself up like this. I ain't the man to stand it – you hear?

Here is an educated man, the author, portraying the outrage of an uneducated man in the face of his son's involvement in school. This character is portrayed as equating his son's schooling with the putting on of 'airs' and 'a-swelling' himself up. He is shown as resisting his son's education on the grounds that none of the family could read and, furthermore, that schooling would not only lead to the putting on of airs but, more critically, to the putting on of airs 'over his own father'.

While most of the rhetoric surrounding education is couched in the positive terms of human development and the acquisition of skills, there is no doubt that education, as it is practised in most countries, is partly about the explicit production of a generation that is different from the previous generation in its knowledge, skills and attitudes. In contrast to the 'private-tutor' models employed in the past in some aristocratic and ruling classes, and in contrast to the 'enculturation-by-increasing-participation' models in many traditional societies, modern schooling gauges its success in terms of the difference it can create between the generations. This is not lost for a moment on the children and families from traditional indigenous, migrant or other subcultures who attend modern, state-regulated schools.

But the character of the father, as Twain presents him here, is an object of fun, perhaps sympathetic fun, but fun nonetheless. He presents the hard choice that the central character of the story faces; but, to the educated reader for whom the book was written, he is simply an unquestionably risible expression of the undesirable past of the uneducated classes, a past from which schooling can rescue them – a secular version of the sentiment expressed in the Olde Deluder Satan Law.

Scene 1.5 From the *Communist Manifesto* by Karl Marx and Freidrich Engels.

> The bourgeois claptrap about the family and education, about the hallowed relationship of parent and child, becomes all the more disgusting, the more, by the action of modern industry, all family ties among the proletarians are torn asunder and their children transformed into simple articles of commerce and instruments of labour.

Here we see a representation of Huck's father's complaint, certainly not risible this time, that places education firmly in the political arena. The disgust expressed by Marks and Engels is to do with the differential effects of education on the different social classes. According to this account, the families of the proletariat suffer from education in two distinct ways: first the cultural continuity among family members is disrupted; second, the experiences of their children are reduced to suit and perpetuate their place in capitalist economy, as consumers and workers.

Viewed from this angle, an effect of education is the production of objects of a particular economic formation; put another way, education, by this account, is implicated not only in the intellectual and moral development of people into the social and cultural ways of the society, but also in the formation of political and economic consciousness and practice. Thus all educational practices can be discussed and analysed within the terms of political economy, no matter how innocent they appear, and no matter how explicitly or how thoroughly the participants themselves may construe that relationship.

Scene 1.6 From *United Nations Convention on the Rights of the Child* (1989, http://www1.umn.edu/humanrts/instree/k2crc.htm), a document enumerating principles adopted by the United Nations and formally ratified by every member nation (except for the United States and Somalia):

Article 28

1. States Parties recognize the right of the child to education, and with a view to achieving this right progressively and on the basis of equal opportunity, they shall, in particular:

(a) Make primary education compulsory and available free to all; . . . [and] . . . make higher education accessible to all on the basis of capacity by every appropriate means;

2. States Parties shall take all appropriate measures to ensure that school discipline is administered in a manner consistent with the child's human dignity and in conformity with the present Convention.

3. States Parties shall promote and encourage international cooperation in matters relating to education, in particular with a view to contributing to the elimination of ignorance and illiteracy throughout the world and facilitating access to scientific and technical knowledge and modern teaching methods. In this regard, particular account shall be taken of the needs of developing countries.

Here the especially significant relationship of the concepts 'education' and 'childhood' is declared. In Article 28(1) we find that education is named as a 'right of the child', where 'the child' is taken to signify all children. Education is seen as a service, rather than a compulsion, and a unitary concept that we can all talk and know about, enough at least for the purposes at hand. Further, education is taken to be necessarily and a priori a good thing, a positive service to which some children do not have adequate or perhaps any access. We see as well the implication that there may be pre-existing limitations on the access of some children to this service, and that these unequal opportunities should be overcome. The point under (a) shows the categorization of education into 'primary', the free status of which as a service is asserted, and some other forms of education. We find then that, in contrast to 'primary' education, 'higher' education should be on the basis of capacity, but whether that capacity refers to the state's capacity or to the capacity of individual children is not stated. In Article 28(2) we find a critical move whereby education has become 'school', and that schools have 'discipline', again an issue that is not explicated and that we are taken to know about and to understand already. It is clear from the implications of Article 28(2) that this 'discipline' has the potential to violate 'the child's human dignity', and that, again, this should be avoided.

Article 28(3) tells us what education is fundamentally about: it is about the elimination of 'ignorance and illiteracy' and about the facilitation of access to certain forms of knowledge, here singled out as a scientific and technical knowledge. Interestingly, we also find that teaching methods may not be 'modern'. That is, there are some ways of teaching children, presumably, but not necessarily, in school, as they are understood and conducted in some states – those that are 'modern'. That means that others, elsewhere, are out of date. This must mean that the understandings some have of the processes of education, or, perhaps, schooling, have advanced in productive ways, but that this advance has not been universal, such that all nations can be bound to seek out and implement only 'modern' ways of educating their children. 'Developing countries' is presented as a category of states to which particular attention needs to be directed on the matter of the modernity of their teaching methods.

From the mother reading to the child at home to world leaders framing potentially binding international principles about children, we have seen, even in this small potpourri of scenes, people acting on and acting out ideas about education in their speaking and writing. In fact, they are speaking and writing these ideas 'into life', reflecting, adapting and regenerating familiar ways of reasoning and talking about education. The ideas themselves come from common-sense experience with children, with schooling and with educational practice, as well as from official sources such as curriculum theories, psychology, sociology and human development. They come as well from everyday knowledge of society – its cultural, economic and moral continuities, and its needs for change. We also can see how the enactment of these ideas, in these instances, is always embedded in particular social relationships, whether between family members, social groups, or nations, and that these are renewed and adapted as they turn their attention to everyday educational purposes.

Even though these scene-setters emanate from different vantage points in their gaze onto education, in and out of school, they draw our attention to the variety of activities we consider educational, and to the life and work of this concept in significant cultural, economic, political and moral discourses. So, more specifically, what can we say about these practices about which we use the term 'education'?

Education: effort, change and value

'Education' is the prime example of a term that weaves this way and that, shedding and assuming differing attributes and nuances. Those practices that we recognize as 'educational' stand at a meeting place of, on the one hand, one generation's vision *of* and *for* the future, and, on the other, the limits of that generation's imagination and ability to marshal the moral, intellectual and material resources to display that vision to the next. At the same time, institutionalized educational and training practices, more so than any other publicly deployed activities, constitute a central mechanism in the re-production and mutual reinforcement of particular forms of moral, cultural and economic order. Thus they are the main experiences through which the political dispositions and aspirations of one generation are enacted with, for and on novices – young people or 'pre-experts'. In these respects, educational practices stand at the meeting place of a society's contesting instincts for stasis and change.

Educational practices are nothing-but social and cultural: as the socio-cultural make-up of the clients and participants within the boundaries of an educational authority changes, so necessarily do the qualities of educational goals and outcomes. Similarly, as the economic features, or the cultural values, the material resources, or the projected futures of the community change, so do the qualities of educational practice. Teaching mathematics, for example, to a group of teen-aged students, who have the school's medium language as their first language, who have access to computing facilities, and who can project a high probability of subsequent employment is different from teaching a group of same-aged students who have none of these other attributes. This is so regardless of the fact that the same curriculum may be in place, along with comparable parental motivations, and similar professional backgrounds among the teachers. The experiences of all of the participants differ, making the educational efforts, their consequences and the public understanding and appreciation of those consequences, fundamentally, not incidentally, different. While some of these differences can be made visible through forms of quantification – test scores, for example – the differences, as they are experienced, are fundamentally differences of quality.

The forms of educational practice seen in institutional settings such as schools, colleges, universities and industrial training sites, are most visible to us. It is important to remind ourselves often that much of the less obvious (possibly unseen and often unpaid) work done by caregivers, workers in the media and in other professional sectors such as health, religion, social work and so on, is educational work. It is also important to recognize that it is not just children or adolescents who are the recipient-participants in educational practices. In fact, whenever we see a conscious effort by an individual or group accorded the status of 'educator', however transiently or locally, and whether through their age or expertise, aimed at changing 'for the better' the practices of others, then that work is educational.

The term 'work' is used to denote two of the criterial attributes of educational practice – its consciousness and effortfulness. The other criterial attribute for a practice to be educational is that it is 'for-the-better'; its processes (including the work put in by all participants) and the outcomes it projects, whether or not it achieves them, are publicly valued. None of this is to say that all members of a society or within the educational professions agree on all of these valued practices. While it is not, conversely, a criterial attribute of educational practices that they be fought about, contestation certainly is a perennial characteristic of communities and authorities that care about their educational efforts.

With these loose criteria for educational practice in place, a vast range of everyday activities can be said to be relevant to education. The domains of inquiry in the field of education are thus comparably varied and spread broadly across public and domestic sites such as homes, clinics, workplaces, neighbourhoods, churches, courtrooms and so on, just as surely as schools and colleges. So, we can recognize, simply common-sensically, an initial distinction between institutionalized and non-institutionalized forms of conscious, change-productive work we count as 'educational'. But it is important to note that in practice, particularly contemporary practice, these categories are often blurred: we have the phenomena of home-schooling, the use of the Internet in 'flexibly delivered' educational programmes, local learning communities, the development of open-access resource centres and so on. All of these traverse the border between institutional and non-institutional educational efforts. The categories do not permit a hard empirical distinction, but one that is useful in beginning a more detailed discussion of the nature of educational work in current societies.

We turn first to the matter of institutionalized educational practices, and within that category, to the most commonly recognized expression of education – schools. Many debates about schooling boil down to the premise that schools have or at least should have a single major function in society and in the lives of students. This is not true, nor has it been true for almost the entire history of the institutions we recognize as 'schools'. Hunter (1993), for example, has argued that schools have had, since their development and spread, many intersecting functions. These functions are in competition with one another, and the ebb and flow of these contests relate to the contemporary economic, cultural and social conditions in play at any given time. How much economic, cultural or military competition the society is under from external sources; how much internal competition formerly dominant categories of people are under from other cultural, gender, ethnic or class categories; and how children and adults are differentially positioned as members of a society. Issues such as these ensure that education, its very definition as well as the details of policy and practice, is a terrain traversed by much contest, a feature that ensures its continuous dynamism.

Some of the major functions of schooling, following Hunter (1993), have been:

- a *pastoral* function, that children are given caring and humane environments in school in which to grow and develop;
- a *skilling* function, that schools have a significant role in the production of a skilled and competent workforce;
- a *regulative* function, that schools transmit forms of orderliness and control to an otherwise disorderly populace;
- a *human-capital* function, that the investment of effort and money in schools directly enhances economic productivity;
- a function of *individual expression*, that schooling is properly the context in which individuals can learn to explore, develop and express their personal goals and aspirations;
- a *cultural-heritage* function, that people, especially young people, are introduced to the ways of thinking and acting that have been valued over time – cherished art works, and disciplines of scientific inquiry;
- a *political* function, that schools produce a citizenry dedicated to the preferred political principles of the society.

For centuries, these and other functions have competed for dominance in debates about schooling and in the practices found in educational institutions and their attendant authorities. Societies have perennially called upon schools for various combinations of these functions, depending upon the political, economic and cultural imperatives of the time.

We can recognize all of these discourses in public and professional debates about education and schooling. They appear in the vocabularies of self-expression, performance standards, moral education, supportive school environments, inquiry-based learning, multi-cultural education, education for democracy, citizenship education, critical education, vocational education, transitional education, and so on. These vocabularies have persistently traversed and contested educational debate, curriculum development and policy. Each, as well, has implications for what constitutes the specialist knowledge and practices of 'the teacher', projecting differing and potentially competing sets of knowledges and values for the teacher, as well as for the 'student', and, ultimately, for the 'educated society'. Each has distinctive implications for research.

Clearly, not all of the functions enumerated by Hunter operate separately from one another. It has become common among educators to cluster these functions under the headings of four competing philosophical positions that are routinely drawn upon to describe the essential functions of schooling and education. These are often termed traditionalism, progressivism, transformationalism and corporatism. Traditionalism takes the functions of schooling to be primarily related to the transmission of the culture's heritage – that education is about cultural conservation. This heritage again is variously considered intellectual, scientific, moral and or aesthetic. While such a position is often characterized as a conservative force within education, its proponents regard its motivations as radically transformative of contemporary cultures through the reinvigoration of values and practices found in 'the best from the past'. In its socio-political expressions, this position emphasizes the cultural value arising from training in public democratic practices in which individuals are treated comparably. This is taken to permit ready movement among a variety of public institutions and settings, and to acculturate beliefs and expectations about the comparable treatment of all individuals regardless of their backgrounds or individual attributes.

Progressivism proposes that non-institutionalized, humanistic values should be evident in the experience of the schooling and training, such as free expression, autonomous conduct, and materials that are drawn from and that enhance the experiences of the local community – education is about growth. Progressivism has had significant impact, particularly in English-speaking countries, on educational practice and policy since the late 1960s. Its supporters have pointed to the benefits of focusing on growth and 'natural' acquisition over instruction, on the liberation of schools' work from decontextualized and repetitive drills, and on genuine engagement with the personal meanings and significances of the curriculum.

Transformationalist approaches to education view educational experiences as arenas through which to challenge the entropy of the cultural, economic and political formations that education, unless it is explicitly aimed at transformation, will inevitably support. Such approaches come out of a range of critical perspectives including Neo-Marxism, anti-masculinism, -racism, -classism and -ageism. A premise typically shared by transformationalists is that the current bureaucratic and formalized manifestations of education necessarily make it difficult for the outcomes of education to result in challenges to the moral, economic and political organization of society. They also take it that education is, at the same time, the primary potential site for the productive change of social life.

As we saw in the United Nations' Articles, communities in the late twentieth century take governmental bureaucracies to be responsible for managing educational provision. In many countries over the course of the twentieth century, these bureaucracies have been centralized in capital or regional cities, and have pursued the role of informing decision-makers in government on policy-related information matters, such as the needs, expectations, aspirations, local support systems and so on, in the larger community 'outside'. In these ways bureaucracies, educational bureaucracies prominent among them, took control of the regional, rural and state activities to do with the rationale and equity of provision, combined, as best they could, with sensitivities to local needs. Both central management and regional responsiveness were necessary to secure a society's support for policies dealing with educational provision. Given the centralized nature of these offices, the pressure on the centre to secure valid information about the periphery increased directly with increased central responsibility and with the increasing breadth of that responsibility over curriculum, the training of professionals and para-professionals, the implementation of programmes, funding, assessment and accountability to other domains of government.

In assuming responsibility for mass and extensive schooling through their attendant centralized bureaucracies, governments drew educational practices into various moral, economic, political and procedural operating principles compatible with their own managerial logics and ways of doing business. Centralizing and formalizing curriculum amounts to setting an idealized scope and sequence of knowledge acquisition for the whole of each generation. In the bureaucracy's and thus in the schools' considerations, decreasing prominence comes to be given to the knowledges and dispositions that grow indigenously in the home cultures and communities from which the clients of education come. It is this decreasing space that provides for one of the particular contributions of qualitative research to educational knowledge and that gives such research its political and cultural significance.

In the case of education, this burgeoning of the state social–management apparatus was manifest in the spread of schooling and teacher education in the first half of this century. It also brought with it a need for a particular kind of 'research'. That research needed to entail certain principles for it to be usable by centralized bureaucracies: importantly, it needed to be both representative in its scope and compact in its reportage. That is, it needed to be broadly based in its representation of the clientele to be served so that conclusions could be considered valid and applicable to, if not all, then the bulk of the stakeholders in education. It also needed to be built on assumptions of comparability and the standardization of inputs to, and outcomes from educational practices. The forms of quantification and evaluation that developed in research areas such as agriculture, physics and survey-based forms of sociology and epidemiology were well-suited to these bureaucratic imperatives. They brought with them, as well, ways of talking about educational practice that redefined everyday activities as the interaction of abstracted 'variables', and that thus redefined inquiry into educational practices as the assessment and documentation of abstracted features of those practices.

As an early example of this process, Alfred Binet, founder and Director of the Société Libre pour l'Etude Psychologique de l'Enfant' was commissioned by the Paris Schools Authority to develop assessment instruments that would enable the Authority to distinguish those children who could benefit from public schooling from those who needed special remediation. Binet and his associates developed the 'Methodes Nouvelles pour le Diagnostic du Niveau Intellectuel des Anormaux' – new methods for diagnosing the intellectual level of abnormal people – the precursor of what we now recognize as intelligence tests. As an informative footnote to this example, it is also worth recalling that Binet's tests, although spawning many offspring around the world, were never actually used in France. They were also put to purposes different from those initially intended by Binet, and purposes that Binet, in all probability, would oppose (Pollack, 1995). In particular, Binet's position was that 'the best way to predict success in school was to measure success in school' (Rogers, 1995: 653) in ways strongly grounded in the contours of everyday school life. As the tests were applied more broadly across a more diverse range of cultural settings, the concept of Intelligence developed a functional autonomy, gradually assuming a position in theoretical, professional and policy discourses that hovers, as a 'variable', above everyday activity.

From this example, it is important for us to see the connection between four developments:

1. the institutional, policy-driven imperative of using funds for public schooling in apparently productive ways;
2. the production of an assessable variable (in this case, Intelligence);
3. the re-theorization of a child's various practices into stable, assessable, individual attributes such that the new 'social fact' of Intelligence could provide a criterion that would serve policy; and
4. the important ways in which the unintended consequences of research can have lasting effects on both the nature of research and the conduct of educational practice and debate.

A final lesson from this example is that educational research is, at the one time, a political activity, a moral responsibility, and an intrusion into the social and cultural spaces in the community and institutional lives of people. This applies to readers as well as writers of educational research. Participants in educational research, whether readers or writers, act in a world in which there is much at stake for individuals, communities and societies.

DISCUSSION TOPICS, QUESTIONS AND EXERCISES

1. Describe the characteristics (everyday procedures, activities, physical dimensions etc.) of a number of institutional and non-institutional educational settings (e.g. an ESL classroom, a family counsellors office, a taxation information 'hotline'). Discuss any similarities and differences and then answer the following questions:

   (a) What kinds of specialist knowledges and practices would you expect the 'teacher-professional' to display in these settings?
   (b) What kinds of expectations, life experiences, problems etc. might each 'learner' bring to the setting?

2. Choose one setting from above and discuss the following:

   (a) Who are the stakeholders in the setting (e.g. individuals, professional and/or community organizations, government bodies etc.)?
   (b) What claims might each stakeholder make about their involvement in the setting (e.g. how is government involvement/funding justified)?

3. Using the above setting, identify any assumptions and/or 'social facts' (about the characteristics of learners/teachers, models of human development, families etc.) that inform or make sense of the everyday procedures, activities and relationships in the setting.

4. Select an educational or issue that is currently being debated in the news. Find two to three different media texts (newspaper, television, radio) about the issue and then answer the following questions:

   (a) Why do you consider the issue to be educationally relevant?
   (b) Who are the stakeholders in the issue? How are they positioned in debates surrounding the issue? What do they have 'invested' in the issue (e.g. knowledges, identities etc.)?
   (c) What kinds of vocabularies (words, descriptions, 'proverbs' etc.) do stakeholders use to articulate concerns, opinions, facts etc. about the issue?
   (d) Using these vocabularies, can you identify the philosophies of education and/or functions of schooling informing debates surrounding the issue?

2

Research in Education: Problems with Practical Activity

If a society knows what it wants from its educational activities, and if it has the experience and resources to bring about what it wants, then why is there educational research? Where does the motivation for educational research come from? What is it about educational practices as they are currently undertaken around the world, in and out of formal educational institutions, that has seeded the evolution of research as integral to, rather than added to, the 'core business'? Is research best seen as a description or legitimation of common-sense business-as-usual, or as an interruption or an irritation? Or as simply background accompaniment?

These are the questions for this chapter. Here I outline the place of research in the overall educational efforts of a society, and briefly explore some aspects of the history, motivations and interests of research as a set of public practices. Specifically, these questions are addressed:

1. Where did educational research come from as a public activity?
2. Why and how did it assume significance?
3. Why do educators typically do research?
4. How do the kinds of things researchers do arise from, relate to, or inform theories about society and education?

The chapter establishes some of the jobs that various research traditions in education have evolved to perform. A key proposition to carry over from the previous chapter is that educational practices are fundamentally social and cultural practices. This has implications for how we can describe, relate and navigate our way through the various forms of inquiry we find informing education, and how we can appreciate the theoretical perspectives that relate to these forms of inquiry. Understanding the fundamentally social and cultural nature of educational practice also helps us connect the shifting nature of educational practice (the changing cultural formations it supports and helps to develop, changing students, developing pedagogical methods, and so on) with the equally variegated environment of educational research.

The rise of research in education

Educational research as we now observe it did not evolve independently from other cultural, political and economic developments. The interests and procedures of educational researchers have a history. In the twentieth century, across many domains of public life, a particular idea about knowledge was brought to its most forceful expression: that a category of activities termed 'research' is an especially privileged form of public discourse. The claims of research became firmly set against those of folk wisdom, custom, insight, intuition and dogma. Two converging developments attended and accelerated this elevation of research as a special way of knowing: the first is to do with developments in the philosophy of knowledge, particularly debates relating to the kinds of activities that may lay claim to the status of research; the second concerns the victory, however temporary, of interventionist over *laissez-faire* governmental administration. These developments taken together provide us with an account of why and how the special status of research has been put to such extensive public use in the conduct of education.

Along with other fields of social, technological and intellectual enterprise, educational research expanded its scope and importance along with a growing belief in the importance of research as a basis for public action. According to some commentators (e.g., Heap, 1995), the last two hundred years or so have seen reasoning based on speculation and dogma give ground to 'empirical inquiry' as the basis of individual understanding and public practice and policy. It was evidence that became the hallmark of modern inquiry, putting pressure on societies to undertake new forms of knowledge production, forms we have come to call research.

Both the Natural and the Human Sciences had grown rapidly and become more diversified by the end of the nineteenth century. Then, the Natural and Human Sciences were not generally as strictly differentiated as they later became. Darwinism, as an example, had a clear and, at the time, apparently unproblematic 'social' extension, and the political science of Marx and the sociology of Durkheim were theories about the ontology, the material, factual, thing-like nature of societies. The founders of these lines of inquiry often alluded, and not just analogously, to the directly comparable essence of the social and individual organisms and the material world. Durkheim's first 'rule for sociological method' is 'consider social facts as things' and he made it clear often that this consideration was to be more than by analogy:

> It is quite evident that, since [society] infinitely surpasses the individual in time as well as in space, it is in a position to impose upon him ways of acting and thinking which it has consecrated. (Durkheim, 1901/1938: 102)

As well, the nature of knowledge was under philosophical debate. The principal positions in Western European cultures at the beginning of the twentieth century can be delineated broadly as Cartesian versus Kantian: on the one hand the 'certainty and self-evidence' of mathematics stood as the model of reasoned theory and philosophy; on the other, the 'critique' of this offered by Kant (1781/1955), and developed later into many variants, argued that scientific and practical forms of reason should be seen as distinct lines of inquiry. In this latter view, individuals were assumed to reorganize and reinterpret sensory information coming from the outside by mental processes. Thus, social research was placed, even by the turn of the century, in a publicly contested space, fretted through with a dichotomy that still serves to organize much debate about its nature and purposes (see, e.g., Krimerman, 1969, Section III: Is Social Science methodologically distinct from Natural Science?, and Cohen and Manion, 1997, Chapter 1, for reiterations of this debate).

Around the beginning of the twentieth century, the nature and purposes of governance were also undergoing debate. In many countries, governments had been forced to consider the significance of the administration of large and diverse societies. After the French Revolution, these issues became matters of urgent debate. The efficacy of public administration, including educational practice, was now clearly tied to the stability and even the survival of a society's political organization.

The resolution for many countries was the emerging expectation of active, interventionist governance, as opposed to the *laissez-faire*, elitist administrations that had held sway before (Clegg, 1989). Again, observers of contemporary political movements in English-speaking countries will not find this polarity unfamiliar, but for our purposes it is important to see that an interest in social, including educational, research did not arise out of curiosity or out of developments in the philosophy of knowledge alone. Indeed, these philosophical debates themselves, and their accompanying reasoning practices, attended the growing expectation that governments should engineer social policies for the mass good and for community progress. As the example of Binet given in the previous chapter suggests, this led remarkably rapidly to the formation of a purpose-trained welfare professional class, probably the largest of which were and remain educators and health workers.

More significantly, this development, which intensified and broadened its scope as the century progressed, placed research firmly into the logic of responsible and responsive governance and administration. The logic goes like this:

1. from research can be developed general, normative statements about what people and communities are like and what they need and want;
2. such statements can result in the development of policies that can be defended in terms of their relevance, efficacy, comprehensiveness and fairness; and
3. these policies, with these evident qualities, can put in place or at least enable practices that are effective and acceptable.

These converging developments in the bases of both knowledge production and governance provided the platform for the expansion of apparently informed and thereby apparently defensible government-driven administration. They simultaneously established the public expectation that legitimate administrations would call upon this set of practices called *research* as a way of both finding out and acting effectively, fairly and defensibly in the management of social provisions such as education. Similarly, in the first half of the twentieth century, modes of parenting and other forms of educative care were gradually brought under the gaze, guidance and scrutiny of public administrations, all with the support offered by research.

But what were these 'statements' that research produced? How could such statements play such a significant part in the prosecution and maintenance of rational governance and thus rational institutional practice? These questions, which provide the context for books such as this one, were hotly contested, just as surely as now, in the last decades of the nineteenth century: compulsory education was becoming legally mandated in many countries. The technological and economic advances delivered to industrialized nations and their (gradually ex-) colonies were taken to be in part the outcomes of the workings of Science and its central logic, the Scientific Method, as developed within the Natural Sciences. The technological and economic prominence of such countries was taken as evidence of the power of this method and its ability to describe and master the material world. As a way of finding out and knowing, the applicability of the Scientific Method was often taken to be universal. This understanding itself was taken to be a hallmark of the modern society, one that had successfully moved through the theological and the metaphysical to arrive at the positivist, a reliance on scientifically established material and social facts (Comte, 1842/1970).

The development of research on human activities, then, appeared to involve a shift only of topic rather than of methods for finding out. Thus, for much of the twentieth century, especially in English-speaking countries, methods of conducting and communicating social research, and thus of producing official ways of thinking about social phenomena, were dominated by the conventions and dispositions of Natural Science. But not without contestation: critiques of the straightforward transfer of Natural Science methods to human issues appeared, and alternative methods came to be on offer. Moreover, in education, qualitative research of various kinds had already enjoyed an extensive tradition, long pre-dating quantitative methodologies.

Why turn events into research? Phenomena and inquiry

Research has come to serve several purposes in education. At the most general level, a major purpose is to provide principled bases for 'knowing' to guide practice and policy. Educational research is used to assess the efficacy of targeted initiatives in publicly defensible ways, in terms of both their intended and un-intended consequences. Because of pervasive change, and because of education's prominent place in a society's dynamism, trading as it does in the vital space between conservative and progressive forces, these changes are always at least potentially contentious.

Educational researchers employ empirical inquiry to test out theoretical ideas that inform practice. For example, over the course of the twentieth century, much inquiry was devoted to how children learn, grow and develop in ways that curriculums have been taken to, and are 'supposed to', reflect, and how these changes can be assessed and compared from site to site. In that respect, the curriculum provided a yardstick against which children's 'growth' and 'devel-opment' could be assessed. The curriculum, whatever it looks like, moves at a certain pace and has a certain scope of knowledge. In that respect, quantitative techniques can be used to 'measure' the relative position of an individual child or of a collection of children against the curriculum's expectations: 'this much by this time'.

Educational research has been used to inform, advance, or obstruct policy and practice in education. It is difficult to overstate the degree of direct and indirect support given to educational research by educational administrations of various kinds. In education, research conducted in or by educational institutions is most common. The sponsorship of educational researchers by policy-making bodies is one of the crucial ecological factors in the evolution of different theoretical positions and research approaches. Some theories, analytic strategies and reporting formats thrive partly because they provide rationales and 'findings' in forms that reflect or supplement the preferred ways of the funding and policy-making bodies. Other theoretical, analytic and reporting approaches may, by comparison, languish in conditions where funding bodies are either the same as or closely aligned to policy-making bodies in education. Which is to say that, unsurprisingly, educational research is no less political a pursuit than any other form of social inquiry. Having said that, the particular force of research and the basis of its credibility is that it strives and claims to be based on evidence. Directly because of that, researchers and the 'objects' of their efforts can be both 'objective' (make objects for discussion) and, to some, perhaps even the funding authorities, be 'objectionable' (make trouble for discussion).

Research is also conducted to advance methodology and analysis. The community of researchers needs to review and refine its ways of doing business. Often this entails not just the application of particular methods to a phe-nomenon of interest, but also the direct comparison of a number of analytic methods, in which this comparison is the prime purpose of the research itself.

This we may think of as 'meta-research' or 'second-order' research, an aim that seems undervalued in many graduate training programmes.

Educational researchers aim to solve or avoid practical problems, for example, by trialing curriculum materials, teaching strategies, assessment procedures, or other educational practices in various cultural sites. As in other aspects of life, many of these don't work, some work better than what was in place before, and some seem to work but in fact work to effect unwanted or unanticipated outcomes.

This includes documenting the special needs of certain groups of clients. The people who generally manage educational institutions and activities are themselves usually successful products of education systems. Thus they have been acculturated into standardized forms of knowing and finding out. In turn, curriculums, teaching and assessment techniques, and the theorizations that inform and legitimate them, relate in close-fitting, organic ways to some generationally 'pre-educated' sectors of a society, and less so to others. It is rare to find groups that are under-represented in circuits of economic or cultural authority that are at the same time influential in decisions about the structure, contents and organization of educational practice.

A final and related goal of educational research concerns the traditional concern of educators for social justice. Many studies that we would now recognize as forerunners of large-scale social research were aimed specifically at bringing to public awareness the extent of poverty and hardship. Significantly, many of these projects entailed the employment of qualitative methods. In the latter part of the nineteenth and the early twentieth centuries, examples of such studies were undertaken in Europe and North America: observational studies of working class families in France (Zimmerman and Frampton, 1935); life histories, anecdotal reports and interview studies of London's poor (described in Fried and Elman, 1968); and longitudinal interview and observational studies of urban blacks in the United States (Du Bois, 1899/1967). Clearly such studies were motivated by social justice. They called, often dramatically, for systematic public action, especially in terms of education, health and welfare provision.

Having said these good things, there is also an underbelly to the functions that educational research has performed, such as: to legitimate current attitudes or practices; to create 'intellectual management elites' who regulate the practices of their 'charges' through the privileged instrument of research; and to refine the operation of marketing-to-consumers (e.g., head teachers and central bureaux who buy educational products in the marketplace) regardless of the demonstrable quality of the 'product'. So the motivations for educational research are not always unquestionably 'educative' in their nature. Critical questions about its cultural, political, economic and commercial purposes are just as important as questions about its methods and educational goals.

In the remainder of this chapter I explore what I take to be key questions, concerns and cautions that come along with an engagement in educational research. To do this, I begin with an example of a qualitative research study.

I give a description of the study, a snippet of data, and an account of what the researcher was trying to do – theoretically and practically – with and through the conduct and reporting of the project. One reason for doing this is that it is easier to introduce key issues in a concrete rather than an abstract way, with recourse to a straightforward, but nonetheless sufficiently rich illustration. A second reason is that I wish to convey the significance and relevance of even a small-scale study, set not in a school or a college but in a family home, involving not students and professional educators but children with parents.

An example to set the scene

In this section, I present a summary of a study to exemplify some observations about educational research in general and qualitative forms of research in particular. I aim to highlight:

* some significant features of the design of a research project;
* some of the decisions that researchers have to make; and
* some of the opportunities and drawbacks that these decisions can entail.

The study in question was conducted by Wootton (1997) who reported on a longitudinal case study of a female child, his own, between the ages of 12 and 38 months. The interest was on the child's changing use of the knowledge made available to her in her immediate social situations in building her inter-actions with those around her. The methodological emphasis for Wootton was on rigorous analysis of a small number of events. 'Rigour' for Wootton entailed 'identifying the details within these exchanges which documented the under-standings of the participants involved' (ix). He noted that, over the long term, his studies had been aimed at providing an understanding of how it is that interactions are organized for and by the child, and of the consequences of these forms of developing speech acts for the development of the child's inter-actions and learning. Part of what motivated Wootton's report, therefore, was the question of 'how these [i.e., his] findings meshed in with the large amount of other knowledge about young children's behaviour which had been generated by alternative and more conventional modes of research' (ix). In that regard, his study is methodologically self-conscious, and part of his aim was to locate a 'minority methodology' in the larger field of child study in order to explore its particular contribution.

Wootton summed up one of the distinctions between his qualitative, (demographically) small-scale, detailed studies of the child's growth and other more conventional modes of research:

> Much of this other research was heavily quantitative, and thus generated through the application of various kinds of pre-specified taxonomy to the flow of what took place in children's interaction. These taxonomies usually came with some evidence of high

reliability, in the technical sense, but there was little compelling basis for selecting one taxonomy rather than another. And, more importantly, . . . there was little systematic attention paid to finding ways of figuring out the significance which these different forms of speech act had for the children themselves. (ix)

These more conventional methods of doing research, Wootton noted, mesh with certain established ways of thinking about cultural life, children, acculturation, learning and education. Many such reasoning practices are derived from tra-ditional sociology and psychology, and centre around the establishment of social facts, and, in turn, a reliance on those facts *as explanatory* of social practice. Such social facts amount, in some accounts, to elements of collective conscience and consciousness, and posit a particularly externalized view of education, seeing it as 'a continuous effort to impose on the child ways of seeing, feeling and acting at which he would not have arrived spontaneously' (Durkheim, 1901/1938: 6). As Wootton explained, this means that the traditional sociological view is that children are shaped by the norms of society, and that these norms are expressed in formal institutions such as schools (and families, religions and so on). Wootton started from a different position: that education and acculturation are not essentially processes of 'imposition', but rather are highly interactive and mutual achievements of children and those around them, and that the mind-in-society is constructed precisely through these resolutely cultural and social processes.

Wootton foregrounded his concerns in terms of large theoretical questions that social scientists and developmentalists have long pondered. In considering the implications of his work for a number of issues in developmental research, Wootton identified the specific questions that motivated the work:

1. How did the child first access knowledge of the contexts in which she was acting?
2. How was her knowledge of context built into the ways in which she organized her conduct?
3. How did she come to have knowledge of the internal states of other people?
4. How did this 'knowledge of other minds' first emerge into her everyday conduct?
5. What were the relative roles of agreement and disagreement between herself and those around her in the development of her cultural understandings?

Wootton observed that the answers to these questions have implications for the traditional separation of child development studies into cognitive, linguistic, affective and moral development, and, in particular, for the separation of thought from emotion in human conduct. We can see that this project arises out of his primary interest in providing principled ways of knowing about children and how they become members of a culture, ways that can supplement more discipline-bound, methodologically traditional research. But Wootton also noted, in less specific terms, an array of potential implications of this work. These, which we may consider his secondary interests, are about social interactions with children in homes, schools, hospitals or other settings in which talking with children is consequential.

Wootton gave a clear account of his research methods. He described how the tape recordings were obtained, how much actual time they represented over what period in the child's life, how they were transcribed, and what his general analytic approach was. Wootton was concerned not to trade off the rich, variable and fluid nature of human interaction in exchange for formalisms derived from some forms of linguistics or psychology. To this end, he put to work Conversation Analysis, a form of micro-sociology developed over the last 40 years (these points, along with a general introduction to Conversation Analysis are revisited in Chapter 5 of this book). He provided an explicit account of the bases of his selection of analytic method in these terms:

> The achievement of conversation analysis has been to demonstrate that, by proceeding in an imaginative and careful manner, taking especially into account all the relevant behavioural details of each occasion, it is possible to come to terms with the (epistemological and interpretive) insecurities in ways which permit the analyst to identify procedures that people appear to employ in their joint interaction. (18)

That is, Wootton saw in Conversation Analysis a way of guiding his close attention to the details of a corpus of data that he was well, perhaps uniquely placed both to obtain and interpret. This method he does not present as solving problems ('insecurities') of identification and interpretation. Rather his view is that it offers a principled and articulable way of 'coming to terms' with these problems – a way through questions about identifying the units of analysis and estimating their significance that can be made explicit to the reader.

What about generalizability? On the matter of representativeness of data gained with one child in this extended case study approach, Wootton made the following points. First, he asserted that the advantage of the study lies in the extensiveness of the data and his high level of familiarity with both the child and the setting:

> We can be reasonably sure that they [the data recordings] contain a representative range of the communicative skills which were then available to the child. And the fact that the recordings contain such a large number of instances of the key request behaviour which is under investigation adds a robustness to those generalizations which appear to hold across these various instances. (22–3)

So the point here is representativeness across the various experiences of the individual in question: How common, for each of these speakers whose words we have drawn on, are the themes, issues, dispositions, views and so on, that we find? This places a particular pressure on studies such as Wootton's precisely because they are concerned with capabilities that children or novices develop over time, an important aspect of most educational research projects.

On the matter of generalizing across children from such data, Wootton remarked that an obvious disadvantage of a single case study is that we may remain unsure, first of whether what we find applies to anyone else, and second of the degree of detail and specificity that such applications may contain: How *generic* is the generalizable process or procedure? These challenges are made more difficult when there is a lack of comparable research on the topic at hand. Wootton (23) attempted to overcome these drawbacks in a number of ways:

1. by indicating, wherever possible, other evidence that supports or fails to support a finding;
2. by exploring ways in which the findings are compatible or at least comparable with findings from other types of studies of children's requests in interaction; and
3. by identifying ways in which the findings are compatible with research traditions that have inquired into other aspects of child behaviour, for example, research into the emotional, cognitive, moral development of children.

The point of this type of generalization, therefore, is not to argue from a position whereby the participants are taken to stand for, in this case, all children and all parents. Wootton's emphasis was on the representativeness of the practices that were recorded and analysed as they stand for *others of these people's practices* (i.e., those that were not represented in the data corpus), and articulating the study with *other studies and traditions* of study in the general area.

Part of Wootton's aim in documenting his findings, therefore, was to work in the spaces created by two relationships: the relationship between what he could substantiate in his corpus and his knowledge of the setting and the other people (his wife and daughter); and the relationship between what he found, studying one child and using a combination of case study and conversation analysis methods, and what others have found using this and other approaches.

The significant point here is that the questions and issues arising from an awareness of these relationships and the pressures they put on the researcher will not go away. They are not amenable to simple methodological remediation by, say, changing design aspects of the study, such as collecting comparable data from another 20 children in 20 different homes, or by changing analytic methods, such as coding and counting linguistic formations. These modifications would present a different set of issues in these two relationships, but they would not make the problematic nature of these relationships disappear. Nor should they: the 'problem' is a productive pressure in a project, which opens interesting and necessary domains of interpretation and discussion, rather than embarrassing the study, and certainly rather than being conveniently ignored.

What did he find? Wootton proceeded to detail the ways in which his daughter requested, demanded and commanded, in sequences of talk over the period of the study's duration. He drew on related studies to offer interpretive support to the data at hand (which we may term as 'intensive' discussions), as well as on studies from nearby areas in order to make connections with other domains of inquiry into childhood, as a way of offering reinterpretations of those studies ('extensive' discussion). By presenting many examples of transcripts analysed in detail, Wootton kept a consistent focus on requests and imperatives as key features of acculturation through interaction for a child of this age. Here I present one of these excerpts, along with a summary of Wootton's discussion.

The following transcript is located under the heading 'shall we . . . ?' questions as they are used to handle offences. This is preceded by discussion of ways in which the child uses 'shall we . . . ?' questions to specify and further motivate courses of action to which the parent has already agreed. Wootton discussed the place of 'shall we . . . ?' questions in request and imperative sequences, and in considerable detail, the two forms of 'shall we . . . ?' questions already discussed. The context now is that the child (Amy = A), now 37 months, and the father (= F) are standing by the kitchen sink, having finished the washing-up. Two photographs are presented in the report immediately below the transcript, along with markers in the transcript (deleted here) showing the moment at which the photographs were taken. At the beginning of the transcript, Amy had her right hand on the water tap, out of which water was coming to wash the remaining suds away. The transcript is set out exactly as in Wootton (1997: 163):

```
 1  F:  Oka:y you watch it while the soap goes ((then F picks up a
 2         towel to dry his hands))
 3                             (3.3)
 4  F:  And I'll put thee: uh: ((A then leans forward and turns on a
 5         tap with her left hand; it jets loudly))
 6  F:  Ooh not too ha:r-d
 7  A:                     [Jus- jus- shall we (turn) it down  [ a bit
 8         ((during this turn A turns the tap down))                    |
 9  F:                                                         [Ye:s
10         ((smiley voice, then laughs))
11  A:  That's too (     ) isn't it, ((smiling and brief turn to F and
12         away again in the middle of the turn))
13  F:  It's too ha::rd, ((probably a correction of the untranscribed
14         word in A's prior turn))
```

As an initial and obvious observation, we can see that this does not look like ordinary written text. It does not even look like a script for a play. When we examine the transcript conventions supplied, we find that serious notice has been given to: pauses, as in (3.3) in line 3; overlapping speech, as in the [marks in lines 7, 8 and 9; particular sounds of words, as in the extended vowel 'ha::rd' in line 13; missed sounds, or sounds the transcriber could not pick up as words, as shown in the empty parentheses in line 11, all along with a collection of commentary notes from the observer, shown in double parentheses. So the speech has not been 'cleaned up', and, what's more, the researcher actually seems interested in these generally neglected instances of the clutter and apparent disorder of everyday speech – not much seems to be taken as irrelevant.

But even in spite of this thorough re-presentation of the event, it is clear that certain of its features are not shown. The combination of detailed transcript and photographs offers much to the analyst, but it is in no sense a comprehensive replication of the scene, the talk or the actions that together constituted the event and that, together, gave it 'sense' to the participants. In choosing this methodology, Wootton has, therefore, already made decisions about what will be central to the analysis and what will be left out.

Turning to the substance of the transcripts, Wootton made two central points about this transcript and those similar transcripts that surround it in the report: First, he noted that, even though the child uses the by-now well-established 'shall we . . . ?' formation, in this case it is *she* who performed the action she had suggested (lines 7 and 8); second, and this is a new procedure for the child in this corpus, she began the action *while* she was posing the 'shall we . . . ?' question. That is, while the move in line 7 above is recognizable as a grammatical question, she does not wait for any answer from the accompanying adult. Similarly, although the 'we' in line 7 implicates both participants (and the adult is the one who signalled the potential problem in line 6), she took it that it was actually only herself who was implicated. This formation Wootton took to show that the child demonstrated her understanding that 'that which might be a problem for someone else is, by virtue of this, also a problem for her' (166). Wootton took the child to be taking the warrant to act from the demonstration of the shared nature of the problem.

The contrast that these analyses make available to Wootton is that between the work done by the 'shall we . . . ?' formations and other forms of request and imperative. The important inference is that the child is demonstrated as understanding that there is a key differentiation in social life based on who has the problem and who can, should, and might act on that problem. Wootton concluded that, at about 30 months of age, there was a demonstrable shift in Amy's capacity to build into her talk understandings that differentiate the nature of her co-participant's involvement in the action at hand:

> Children can now encode new forms of sequential understanding, ones in which both parties to the interaction are taken to have a joint stake in any particular course of action. (171)

Wootton argued, in the light of the accumulation of contrastive evidence produced in his and other researchers' reports, that the child is showing the co-ordination of a range of understandings (e.g., that others have and will expresses preferences, that the preferences of others can be productively oriented to in the activity) in the child's pursuit of her own interests. The important distinction here is between 'who benefits from the action' and 'who owns (is responsible for and thus has a stake in) the action'. Wootton claimed that a demonstrated understanding of the significance of this distinction is critical in the development of further understandings of social life. It is in this sense that Wootton overviews his research with these comments:

> It is a statement about how one child enters the world of culture, and the central processes involved here turn out to be those through which her conduct comes to be connected to publicly established understandings which have emerged in interaction. I argue that it is these understandings which play a pivotal role both as regards her grasp of the culture which surrounds her and as regards the ways in which she employs the language which is at her disposal. (x)

We now return to a discussion of the processes by which researchers turn events into analyzable data, by which the complex conduct of social life, connected-at-all-points as it seems, can be reconfigured such that it is able to be rendered into the stuff of research – such that 'livings' becomes 'findings'. Following that discussion, we home in on the question of what constitutes qualitative research, drawing on the account above of Wootton's research report to give illustration to the points that are made.

How to turn events into research? Method *as* and *in* social theory

It is important to appreciate that the research process entails a series of practical activities in the world: observation, analysis and reporting. Because of that, all human research entails certain moments at which the phenomena, as they are experienced and observed by the researcher, are distilled, that is, reduced and distorted. The question is always: Is there in these reductive and distorting processes enough to unmoor the findings from the original question and thus enough to make the conclusions insecure? Whatever the consequences of this process of distillation, it necessarily involves the researcher deciding which artefacts are most and least important: some features of the phenomenon are given more importance than others; some are either omitted or simply not seen; some phenomena become 'findings' and not others.

Events can be turned into 'research' when:

1. the procedures of distillation (i.e., the analyses and the bridge they form between the event and the conclusions drawn from its study) are publicly accessible and thus can be evaluated as publicly 'knowable' and 'trustable'; and
2. the findings are disseminated in some way to other stakeholders in education, for information, for scrutiny and for challenge, and they are disseminated *in ways that afford* scrutiny and challenge.

These processes make the research report at the one time less and more than the event. The event has been recast into a set of observable procedures whose observability in turn makes their conclusions warrantable in defining 'findings'.

Doing that results in the positive outcome that these findings can be re-interpreted into new settings with the additional result that the theories, practices, and policies associated with the original event can be qualified, limited or expanded. The research thereby affords an open-textured scene in which the original event is placed into an interpretive arena that necessarily takes some features out of their original surroundings. This sets the event alongside the other events deemed to be comparable by the researcher. Its new neighbours are such that some of its features are brought to attention and others are not, potentially in ways that are radically different from those features that the participants themselves might recognize.

Here we arrive at a problematic point that constantly presents itself to the qualitative educational researcher: events occur in complex, local settings; the contours of events are given both outline and importance by complex factors at work locally. Therefore the issue is: Do researchers aim to re-present a particular event in terms of its particularities, in ways that may make it difficult to draw out comparabilities with other events? Or do researchers attempt to re-present only those features that can be placed against those of other events, on the premise that the essential, predetermined features of these events are directly comparable? That is, we can foreground the particularities of an event, its resolute 'localness', as a way of enhancing the internal validity of the work. But in doing this we make the addition of interpretations from this to other apparently, supposedly, or potentially comparable events more tenuous.

No simple set of rules for solving these ongoing tensions of intensive versus extensive design features can be put in place. Resorting to 'a random stratified sample' of teachers, or students, or schools or families (or three-year-olds and their parents, in Wootton's case), to ensure generalizability may or may not lead to the researcher's ability to document the phenomenon of interest in its indigenous habitat. Test materials (such as developmental, age-normed language checklists in Wootton's case) may or may not be the principal outcomes of interest of educational inquiries and interventions. Establishing a control group in a field experiment in schools, whereby the settings or the interventions of interest are contrasted with some version of standard operating procedures, may or may not lead to a clear view of the particular effects of the intervention under examination. These moves do not offer the researcher any protection against the escape of the phenomenon of interest. Therefore, they do not offer any guaranteed increase in the usefulness of the research to those who wish to learn from it.

In much research, the particular local-ness of the event, while noted, is merely the accompaniment to the themes that allow comparison across events, allowing and perhaps enforcing generalizations about 'these kinds' of events. In this case, the ordinary ways in which the participants may have described, categorized and explained the original event may be marginalized or omitted if they are not in tune, or at least in harmony, with the researchers' perception of what mattered as the event occurred.

Wootton's discussion of data incorporated other research findings and, more commonly, angled different theoretical perspectives onto the data. Importantly, a great deal of transcript data was presented in close detail, with accompanying activities and props, so it is hard to see how Wootton could have provided the readers with more opportunity to disagree within the logistic confines of the printed word. What we do not get in Wootton, which some sociologists would regard as embarrassing the validity of the project, is a traditional demographic description of 'the Woottons' – the socio-economic and ethnic profile of their neighbourhood and themselves, their own parents, and the rest. This is not accidental: the theoretical machinery that Wootton puts to work explicitly sets aside such macro-concerns as explanatory devices.

These issues relate to the tension, never finally resolved, between the demands of internal and external validity: Is the report valid in its own terms, true to its own logic and to the features of the events upon which it draws to produce findings? Is the report generalizable across settings, using either common-sensical or technical procedures for determining the degree of such generalization? The degrees of richness of the data recording and reporting will inform this tension, but they will not resolve it, because the recording and reporting of data are necessarily selective processes. Keeping Wootton's project in mind, we can see at least three ways in which these are selective:

1. Not all of the potentially relevant experiential features of the original event can be recorded. Even with multiple video cameras, microphones or observers, there will be aspects of the scenery (things that are see-able, hear-able, touch-able and so on) and aspects of the action that will remain unattended by the data recording source, even though they are potentially experienced by the participants, and thus potentially relevant to them. This is the problem of *spatial* selectivity.
2. Even if every possible feature of the scenery and the action could be recorded, the significance of each of these features (e.g., seating arrangements, pictures on the wall, certain ways of talking to students) may not be known by the researchers unless they have lived through the history that led to this event in that place and at that time. This is the problem of *temporal* selectivity.
3. Even if every possible feature of the scenery and the action, along with the significance of each of these, could somehow be reliably recorded, the relative importance of these and of their various relationships within the conduct of the event cannot be comprehensively or definitively conveyed through the researchers' records. This is precisely because the researcher is acting *as a researcher* in the event, just as Wootton acted as a father, husband and researcher simultaneously in the events re-presented in his report. However unobtrusive that activity, a researcher will experience an event and its representations *as a researchable event*, regardless of whatever else it may be or could have been to anyone else involved. This issue is not about intrusive methods of recording data that might make the participants behave 'differently' (better, more self-

consciously, more publicly or whatever). It is rather about the fact that researchers' seeing and understanding of features of the scenery and action are fashioned selectively by their history of participation in this event, and other events that they, as researchers, have learned to regard as comparable. A parent who records and analyses interactions with his or her child, for example, sees and understands the features of the scenery and the action of these interactions through the history of his or her own participation in such events, as that history is re-rendered for recording and analysis. This is the problem of *interpretive* selectivity.

While these tensions cannot be resolved finally, they can be acknowledged and managed within the practical purposes at hand in the research project. The provision of high levels of detail in descriptions of the scenery, the action and the researchers' roles in the event are all necessary, but they are not sufficient in this management. More important are the self-consciousness of the recording and analytic processes, and the explication for the reader of this self-consciousness on the matter of how *relevance* will be determined – this time, in this project, for these particular practical purposes. What is relevant to the research project can be derived from a number of sources. What is relevant comes from:

- the theories about culture, society, education, learning, communication and so on, held and operated on by the researchers;
- the researchers' understandings of other empirical work conducted apparently on this topic and in this setting;
- the researchers' understandings of what the various readerships of the eventual report (students, teachers, parents, school administrators, policy makers, other researchers and so on) might take to be relevant;
- what the researchers understand of what participants in the event might or could take to be relevant; and
- what the participants in the event showed to one another (and thus to the over-hearing researcher) to be relevant in and for the conduct of that event, at that time and in that place.

It is the researchers' self-conscious decision on how these potentially diverse relevances will be hierarchically arranged, or at least on how the interplay among them will be managed and reported, that forms a critical element of how the researchers construct their relationship with the participants and the imagined readership. In a sense, all debates about research methods come down to how these relevances should be dealt with.

DISCUSSION TOPICS, QUESTIONS AND EXERCISES

1. Find an article that reports research findings in an educational research journal. Review the article and then identify the following:

   (a) General purpose of the research.
   (b) Primary interest(s) of the researcher(s).
   (c) Possible implications of the findings of the study towards educational research, policy and practice.
   (d) Any theories about culture, society, education, learning, communication etc. informing the research.

2. Think of a research topic that interests you and then answer the following questions:

   (a) Why are you interested in this topic?
   (b) Who else might be interested in the research and why?
   (c) Will the research be a single case study or involve multiple settings? How many participants will be involved? Explain your decisions.
   (d) Will the participants be interested in the research findings? Why?
   (e) Where would you expect to publish the findings of the research? Why?

3. You are about to undertake an observational study in (a particular setting). Think about issues, problems etc. that might be of interest to you and/or others and then consider the following:

   (a) Describe the different kinds of information you could collect from the setting that would generate or support possible research findings. When, where and how would you collect the information?
   (b) Describe how you could disseminate the information that you collect from the setting along with your analyses and research findings in 'ways that allow for scrutiny and potential challenge'.

   and/or

   (c) Suppose that, as part of the study, you intend to analyse transcripts of audiotaped events from the setting. What kinds of information or events will you be able to document using an audio tape recorder? What kinds of information will audiotaping fail to document? What other ways are there to document events in a setting? Choose a particular issue and decide which method would be most suitable for documenting relevant events and information. Explain your decision.
   (d) In order to publish your research you will need to provide detailed transcripts of the audiotaped events from the setting so that others can see (read) the information and analyses that your findings are based upon. Again, focus on a particular issue and decide how you will transcribe the audiotaped events. What kinds of information will you include in your transcription (e.g. sounds, silences, voices, words, intonation, accent, foreground/background noise etc.) and what will you leave out? How will you represent these sounds on paper?

(e) Finally, consider any of your ideas, beliefs, opinions etc. about the issue that you have chosen and about the findings an observational study such as this could possibly generate. Identify any personal or professional experiences and/or theoretical perspectives that are informing these ideas, beliefs, and opinions.

3

Exploring the Neighbourhood in Search of the 'Qualitative'

What does it mean to describe a piece or a field of research as 'qualitative'? What are the criterial features and the associations or connotations of 'qualitative' inquiry? We now explore how researchers have characterized qualitative research and located it among its methodological neighbours. We also address the question of whether or not qualitative research can and should be intermixed with quantitative methods, and what the gains and losses arising from such intermixing might be.

It is important to note at this point that every piece of educational research is predicated upon a set of propositions concerning what can properly count as 'an educated person' – for that study, and in a particular society at a particular moment in its history. The attributes comprising such a characterization are *qualities*. These qualities may end up being talked about as scales or continuums, and they may be tested, scored and measured; they may be correlated among themselves or with other qualities. But regardless of all that, these quantitative manoeuvres do not circumvent the qualitative work that needed to have been undertaken in order to identify, demarcate and name those attributes in the first place, that is, in advance of any counting. So all educational research is necessarily founded on qualitative analysis, a set of decisions, theorized and explicit or otherwise, about the basic moving parts that the project will take to be the objects of its study. While there are common-sensical ideas about what it takes to be 'literate', 'numerate', 'informed' or more broadly 'educated', inquiry into these issues is not a matter just for philosophers. Researchers in all domains of education act on and act out some notion of these qualities. When an educational research programme or project takes the matter of these fundamental qualities *not* to require inquiry and explication, then all that means is that qualitative reasoning and decisions have already been undertaken and committed to, however deliberately and with whatever degree of reflection and explication.

Here we encounter distinctions among the various forms of scientific inquiry, and the various conventions for representing knowledge that each has developed. In one view, social phenomena are taken to exist, and to exist in some quality, independently of their methods, sites or conditions of measurement; so the issues here are the reliability, validity and utility of their representations. On the other hand, we find those who emphasize the local, variable, contingent and multiple nature of cultural, social and institutional practices. The view here is that the very existence of a social phenomenon is partly a matter of the conventions that have developed in the work of identifying, naming and assessing it, and thus it remains a matter of variation and debate. As Desrosieres put it:

> The student, research worker, or statistical data-user receives compact concepts, encapsulated into concise and economical formulas – even though these tools are the result of a historical gestation punctuated by hesitations, retranslations, and conflicting interpretations. (1998: 2)

This observation reflects an appreciation of the two simultaneous interpretations of Durkheim's rule. The first and most foremost rule is: consider social facts as things. This can be read as: 'because they are things'? and/or 'as if they were things'. These two readings form the basis of, respectively, realist *versus* interpretive accounts of social experience, a distinction that will be explored in this and later chapters.

Like 'education', 'qualitative' is a slippery term, put to a variety of uses, and carrying a variety of conceptual associations. Qualitative research methods grew in popularity, into what Gitlin (1994: 1) termed 'a tremendous flood', out of a particular concern with the ways in which quantitative research methods, and their attendant techniques evident in experimental and survey research in the Social Sciences, were being applied to the study of education. To put it bluntly, many educational researchers came to feel that research activities structured through the logics of quantification leave out lots of interesting and potentially consequential things about the phenomenon – interesting and consequential not just in terms of the concerns and understandings of educators, but also in terms of the richness of the accounts of educators' experiences. By comparison, many have felt that quantitative research projects made available relatively stripped-down portrayals that seriously limit the potential for application to professional practice.

In addition, the proposition was often put that qualitative research could suggest and generate hypotheses, while only quantitative approaches could test hypotheses and thereby offer us secure knowledge. For some educators, this choice was too restrictive. They wanted long-standing wisdoms or bureaucratic practices to be actively challenged by research, and the theoretical premises held deeply and unquestionably by educational authorities and practitioners to be brought into the open for re-examination and scrutiny. They did not see, in quantitative approaches, any compelling means to conduct or even begin this kind of work.

To explore the nature of educational research that is 'qualitative', therefore, we need to consider the ways it has been used to distinguish one set of research practices from other sets – the contrastive games in which it has played. If we scan the field of educational research, we find a number of polarities relating to the quantitative–qualitative distinction. A variety of aims, procedures and outcomes of research methods and dispositions have become attached to the term 'qualitative', as have, often indirectly, a variety of theories and ideologies about the individual, society and education.

If we survey a range of methodology texts in use in educational studies, we see this process of attachment at work in the different designators that 'qualitative' has been set alongside, to which it has been contrasted:

- experimental (with 'qualitative' as interpretive);
- positivist (with 'qualitative' as constructivist/interpretive, anti- or non- or post-positivist);
- empiricist (with 'qualitative' as naturalistic, humanistic);
- hard (with 'qualitative' as soft);
- nomothetic, aiming for 'general' laws, applicable 'generally' (with 'qualitative' as idiographic, aiming for descriptions of the orderliness of individuals' systems);
- mechanistic (with 'qualitative' as non-mechanistic or organic; see Howe, 1988);
- mind-independent (with 'qualitative' as mind-dependent; see Smith and Heshesius, 1986);
- objective (with 'qualitative' as subjective);
- concerned with the consequences of independent variables (with 'qualitative' concerned with the organic wholeness and subtleties of meaning; see Eisner, 1979; Mertens, 1998);
- explanatory (with 'qualitative' as non-explanatory or generative, see Taylor and Bogdan, 1984);
- a concern with the products of education (with 'qualitative' concerned with the processes; see Gage, 1988); and
- a focus on the quantification of the characteristics of situations (with 'qualitative' focusing on their meanings (see Wainwright, 1997).

We also find these contrasting attributes defined in terms of a variety of propositions. For example, positivism has been said to be based on the notion that social phenomena can be viewed and treated as 'things', whereas phenomenological approaches take the nature of social phenomena to be available only from the actors' point of view, through the documentation of the 'internal ideas, feelings, and motives' of individuals (Douglas, 1970). But, on a moment's reflection, we find that such characterizations, stated in these ways, are not mutually exclusive: These internal ideas, feelings, and motives can themselves be treated as 'things' or as documentations of fixed entities in the world that can cause other things to happen, and that can act with the same empirical distinctiveness and autonomy as, say, rain, a banana, or an atom.

Sometimes, as in Taylor and Bogdan's (1984: 5) influential account, we find that, 'qualitative methodology' is taken to refer most generally to research that produces descriptive data about people's words and their observable behaviour. In this sense, these authors aligned the descriptor 'qualitative' with a domain of data, a set of interests, rather than, primarily, with a philosophy of knowledge or theories of the individual, society or ideology, or even a set of analytic procedures or techniques. Taylor and Bogdan (and see Bogdan and Biklen, 1992) listed the following central characteristics. Qualitative research, they claimed:

1. is inductive and holistic (e.g., develops from such positions as 'grounded theory' (Glaser and Strauss, 1967) as opposed to operating by deduction from set premises, and by attention to the atomistic components of cultural practice);
2. is sensitive to researcher effects (as opposed to insensitive);
3. draws on 'natural settings' as the source of data (as opposed to, say, laboratories) and the researcher is the key instrument of data collection (as opposed to assessment 'instruments' such as surveys);
4. is interested in the subject's point of view (as opposed to uninterested or disinterested);
5. is descriptive (rather than neglectful) of the taken-for-granted experience of members;
6. reports all valuable perspectives available (as opposed to omitting some 'valuable' perspectives, or deciding in advance that some are insufficiently 'valuable' to warrant inclusion);
7. is humanistic (as opposed to depersonalized, one-dimensional or anti-subjective; see Atkinson, 1990: 8, 21);
8. is interested in 'the inner life of the person' (as opposed to the observable 'outer life' of the person or the group's 'averaged' life); and
9. has an emphasis on validity, regards all settings and people as worthy of study, and regards research as a craft (as opposed to emphasizing reliability, selective sampling of settings and people, and a regard for itself as a science, an art, a trade, or perhaps a business).

In those instances where qualitative research approaches have been aligned with a notion of subjectivity, they are sometimes offered as means of recognizing or 'capturing' the unpredictabilities, idiosyncrasies and quirkiness built into the experiential 'life-world' of human beings. In this sense, the claim is that they can convey an 'alternative' view of 'truth' – one 'bound to human caprices' (Burns, 1994: 12). Again, the alignment of these agenda with the rubric 'qualitative' is not useful. First, much qualitative research is aimed at documenting our mundane, thoroughly recognizable but unremarked daily practices. It is a heightened appreciation of these and precisely the ways in which they are thoroughly recognizable but unremarked that many qualitative approaches take to be a prime analytic interest. Second, asserting validity on the basis of qualitative analyses is in no sense a more 'subjective' assertion on the part of a researcher than one based on other forms of analysis. Recall the point made above concerning the necessarily prior analysis of qualities entailed in all forms of research, and the fact that such qualities remain unexplicated in much quantitative forms of analysis. Such research usually asks readers to take much for granted and, further, to take for granted that which the researchers themselves originally took for granted as they designed the study in the first place. In that sense, such research entails the mutual exchange of considerably more 'subjectivity' than a carefully explicated qualitative project. Finally, as Gubrium and Holstein (1997: 198) noted, claims about capturing or relying on 'subjectivity' in the production and interpretation of research are essentially claims that need to be verified within recognizable, public forms of representation, for the most part, representation in language. The questions for the analyst and for those who wish to understand, appreciate and trust the analyst's work are: By what publicly available cultural criteria did the analyst recognize that which was 'subjective' (capricious, emotional, unpredictable, idiosyncratic and quirky)? And by what means can that recognition be credibly reported?

Approaches such as these often take the looming complexity of cultural life to be the prime motivation for the use of qualitative research in education. As an example of the consequences of this approach, Burns went on to suggest that qualitative research has made educators realize 'that reality should never be taken for granted, given that attention must be paid to the multiple realities and socially constructed meanings that exist within in every social context' (1994: 12). Similarly, Gubrium and Holstein (1997) viewed the development of qualitative techniques for understanding social life as a response to the descriptive challenges posed by an unrelentingly multi-faceted empirical world. This says that the facts of the world press the researcher into the use of conceptual and analytic techniques that can capture its multiplicities as fundamental, not incidental, to its organization and to the ways it is experienced and interpreted. The argument is that, whatever a particular research approach may technically denote by way of content, its force is to connote a *way of knowing*. In that sense, the significance of qualitative research is that it points to a paradigm – a coherent collection of propositions about the world, their relative importance, and particular ways of finding out and knowing about them – rather than just to a collection of techniques.

Any survey of the representations of the features of 'qualitative research' in education, however, also reveals the dubious status it is sometimes accorded. Many influential texts depict its uses as essentially 'exploratory', the status of its findings as useful only in that they may stimulate more systematic, rigorous or 'hard' research, and its audiences as beginning researchers, not even researchers at all, or even non-researchers who are additionally lacking in 'sophistication'. This from Burns (1994: 14): 'Ordinary teachers, who may not have knowledge of sophisticated measurement techniques, could turn to qualitative reports.' The implication here, of course, is that 'qualitative' reports do not typically entail domains of specialized knowledge, but are more readily accessible to 'ordinary teachers'.

Again, this is a matter that will be taken up over the course of this book, but it is worth noting that the extent to which a research report employs technicality in the analysis or interpretation of findings is not of itself a distinguishing feature of any one mode of analysis. As we will see, careful and principled qualitative research in education may often involve reporting techniques that are specialized, and *must*, at the least, rely on complex theorizations about the nature of educational practice and the ways in which research can reflect and enhance that practice.

As a final and influential example, Silverman (1993) outlined four central features of qualitative research. First, he argued, such research should be driven by theoretical interests rather than by technical or procedural preferences. That is, each project embodies a particular relationship between theory and practice, and that relationship is the key interest. Second, Silverman argued that a critical distinction between social inquiry, qualitative social inquiry in particular, and other forms of inquiry is that the 'objects' under study, that is the ordinary members of a society, themselves already have and work on theories of social action and social order. This, Silverman pointed out, should encourage researchers to examine social practices as procedural issues, asking 'how' questions about routine and apparently unremarkable social activities.

Researchers routinely construct, recognize and assess variables, which they imbue with 'explanatory rights'. Silverman argued thirdly that field research should attempt to make problematic these common-sense reasoning practices used by other researchers. The qualitative researcher aims to explore what it is that has been conducted in order to arrive at a reasoning procedure or practice – the distinctive forms of 'rationality' – that has allowed such variables to find their way into research accounts. Finally, Silverman argued that the qualitative researcher should approach data that is not found in a naturally occurring context with scepticism and with an interest in how it is that the artificial context itself has been defined and acted on. That is to say, in the case of, say, a laboratory, the qualitative researcher would be interested in how it is that the participants in the laboratory experiment construed and acted in the social situation, there and then, of the laboratory experiment.

What to make of this array of polarities into which 'qualitative' research in education has been placed? And of the array of attributes that have become attached to it? We can start with a reconsideration of the array of cultural practices we treat as educational. Recall that I argued in the first chapter that 'education' is a term referring to cultural activities that are taken by the participants to be effortfully and consciously aimed at enhancing the capabilities, and their attendant attitudes and habits, of young people and novices. Central to this characterization is the participants' notions of what is going on – do the participants take themselves to be engaged in some activity the *quality* of which is 'educational'? The participants' understandings of their actions are fundamental to the characterization of those actions as 'educational'. Do they take this event to entail work that projects in some way into their future cultural practice?

To distil the discussion so far and to reattach it directly to education as cultural practice, we can see that qualitative researchers, from our brief survey above, tend to:

1. place the notions of the participants – as they show one another what they take to be going on – at the forefront of the analytic problem;
2. take the variety of sites in which education can take place as relevant and as shaping a variety of interactive activities that bear on one another in an individual's developing capabilities, attitudes and habits;
3. view activities characterizable as educational as necessarily and comprehensively mutual, that is, as being 'brought off' interactively by both the experts and novices on that site; and
4. suspend judgements about the quality of educational activities until a full documentation of the qualities of the activity has been explicated, and, even then, until a full account of the qualities entailed in 'good' practice has been made.

We should note here that the educational activities we see people engaged in every day often involve numbers: people reason with numbers; the frequency of an event is often taken to be an indication of its importance; researchers and the people they study take statistical information into account in certain ways as they plan and act out their plans. For the qualitative researcher, issues of quantity are not irrelevant, precisely because they are not irrelevant to the people whose activities are under study. A qualitative orientation, however, makes people's work with numbers (including researchers' work) an object of study and explication, rather than taking that work as analytic explication in and of itself. Does quantification fit in a more significant way into 'qualitative' research? Should these approaches be kept apart, allowed to be on speaking terms, or allowed to cohabit? And does it matter?

The selectivity necessarily involved in 'introducing' qualitative methods in educational research entails taking a stand on what is the particular genius of qualitative approaches to educational research as science, informed by a view of the particular gains that such research offers those interested in understanding and enhancing education. The four key choices suggested in this chapter relate to researchers'

1. foregrounding the propositions that participants used to organize the event under study;

2. taking as relevant the relationship between the local contours of the sites in which educational activities are being conducted and the ways in which the activities themselves are structured;

3. focusing on the jointly produced nature of educational events, not just on the activities of one category of participants; and

4. developing descriptions and explications of educational events before applying evaluations of those events.

We can summarize a number of characteristics that tend to come along with this qualitative territory, as attendant interests, perhaps rather than defining attributes, or as correlates that have attached to qualitative research in education throughout its history: First, qualitative research approaches are interested in *unintended as well as intended consequences*. This does not amount to a neglect or a dismissal of cause-and-effect based research in education, but rather to an insistence on the inevitability of the unintended consequences of interventions into a shifting environment, and, moreover, of the unforeseeable nature of some of those consequences.

Second, qualitative research approaches have a particular attitude to the issue of statistical '*normality*'. This is a professional and cultural attitude, but it is also an important theoretical issue. It has two aspects: first, it is in examining anomalous or borderline cases that we can see how theories need to be refined and how certain assumptions about contextual factors may be holding the original theoretical idea in place. These contextual factors can show how some accounts apply only to the special cases, the so-called mainstream or statistically normal category. A second aspect to this issue is that qualitative researchers have, as opportunity and responsibility, the task of examining all of their data to explore and document the quality of diversity they encounter there. Unlike quantitative analysts, the qualitative analyst does not relegate some of the data to 'error variance' in the pursuit of the aggregate picture. This is a specific point picked up in later chapters when we examine particular analytic techniques, but it can be noted here that findings that are in the minority in a corpus of, say, field notes or interviews are in no meaningful sense 'error variance' for qualitative inquiries. Such cases may indeed (as may be the case in statistical studies as well) prove more illuminating or more significant for theory, practice or policy than the more prevalent or anticipated findings.

Third, there is an axiomatic understanding that *the phenomenon of interest can escape* when it is decontextualized or when it is mistaken for a pre-theorized variable. This escape has typically been discussed in two senses. The first sense is derived from social science's perennial concern with the ethnographic history of a practice, and the relevance of this history to what the practice is and how it is recognizable. In this sense, we can consider educational practices as having material, interactional, institutional and ideological histories – histories of things (the materials and props of educational activities, such as books, blackboards, websites); histories of ways of talking, reading and writing (e.g., between teachers and students); histories of institutional practices (the ways of organizing the learning experiences of students of different kinds in different settings); and histories of assumptions that may serve the interests of some cultural groups more fully that others. One commitment within a qualitative approach is to ensure that the phenomenon as it is observed is not artificially disentangled from these life-giving histories.

A second sense in which phenomena can be seen to escape the researcher's attention relates to the use of certain methods of collecting data that lead to simulations or idealizations of everyday activity. These techniques include pre-coded schedules for recording or scoring talk, the use of experimental manipulations to re-create events, the use of invented data based on the researcher's intuitions, and the recollection of events by the researcher. With these and similar approaches, the specific details of naturally occurring social behaviour are 'irretrievably lost and replaced by idealizations about how interaction works' (Heritage, 1984: 236).

Research is a systematic attempt to re-see the everyday, partly by stripping away from our observations the typifications made available by our culture, and, in turn, by treating those typifications as crucial aspects of everyday experience itself – available for analysis. In this sense, research can help us re-see the everyday as shared events, understood in comparable and shared ways, which are possible precisely because the understandings are shared. The opposing tendency is for researchers to re-enamel the everyday with reminders of other commonplaces, in frameworks of analysis and language whose effects are directed, mainly and often in the first instance, to reminding us of points of commonality, points that are pre-known and pre-evaluated. One of the most consequential pre-emptive moves that researchers can make about the lived experiences of the members of a culture is that it is only or even mainly these points of commonality that are interesting and important.

Fourthly, qualitative researchers show determination to *identify the phenomenon in situ* and to understand that its location is separated from it only at the peril of rendering conclusions thoroughly invalid. That is, the qualitative researcher understands that research can be immobilized by a lack of interest in the very issues that render an event a valid instance of a particular educational practice – its sense in the precise location in which it occurred.

Finally, qualitative research is characterized by an understanding that *contextual considerations should not be assumed to operate as distinctive 'variables' consistently or independently* across a range of sites, somehow in isolation from one another. Resorting to the use of sociological variables such as ethnicity, social economic status or gender, does not solve explanatory problems for the qualitative researcher. This is precisely because the question of relevance ('whose rele-vance?', 'relevance from where?') is always part of the analytic problem, rather than something that can be solved algorithmically from the previous literature or from a predeveloped theory. Rather, the relevance of celebrity variables such as gender, age and so on, is something the analyses may or may not demonstrate in the course of the project.

So when quantitative and qualitative research approaches are enacted in educational research, they are taken to signify more than simply a focus on the countable features of an event versus the distinctive qualities of the event. For some, the relationship of quantitative and qualitative traditions in education is a contrast between approaches of competing philosophical approaches to cultural experience. Depending on how profoundly the contrast is taken to be between qualitative research approaches and their neighbours, researchers will or will not admit to the possibility (or, again, for some, the necessity) of projects and programmes that attempt to combine them.

Setting the scene

Let us again make more concrete and specific these abstract issues. As in the previous chapter, we can locate aspects of the debates swirling around the question of the compatibility of quantitative and qualitative research methods through the use of an illustration. The extensive longitudinal study of language change and development conducted by Wells and others (see Wells, 1981, 1985) provides us with a good example of a well-known and influential programme that used both quantitative and qualitative methods in pursuing educational research questions. I give a brief description of a research report by Wells, and interleave some commentary relating to the issues discussed so far. In the summary description I provide here, I use the terms used by Wells to account for the issues addressed in the study. Another researcher using another array of concepts or analytic tools might have used different key terms to describe the fundamental phenomena under scrutiny.

Wells's research programme aimed to compile a corpus of language data that would be useful in answering a range of developmental and educational questions. The portion I use here is drawn from Wells (1985), in which the question addressed is: Are variations in educational attainment related to differing linguistic patterns to which children are exposed in the home before the onset of schooling? This question did not come merely from curiosity. It came from a long tradition of inquiry, which reached often heated levels of debate about education, language, literacy and disadvantage from at least the mid-1960s onward (Wells, 1985 cited Bernstein, 1971, 1975), as providing the conceptual background for the programme). Further, debates on the above topics have long had significance for policy, especially on the matter of equity of educational provision.

Wells reported on data drawn from a sample of 128 British children, 32 of whom were selected for close study through recording, observation and interviews. The first phase of the programme employed analytic methods drawn from linguistics to chart some features of the course of language development. These features included the emergence of grammatical, lexical and pragmatic functions. The project explored relationships between these features and environmental conditions in which the children and their families lived and worked, in particular the socio-economic conditions and the educational levels of the parents. We can already see how it is that certain key terms in the overall question have been inflected or made operational as they find their ways into the workings of the sequence of activities that we call 'the project':

1. communicational patterns are operationalized as grammar, vocabulary, and so on;
2. the 'home' is operationalized as a set of features to do with parental levels of education, income and occupation; and
3. further, these are construed as 'levels' rather than, say, choices, so that they can be placed on a quantifiable continuum of, say, 'quality'.

Wells's (1985) paper reported on issues concerning the relationship of prior-to-school literacy practices such as reading stories, adult–child interaction in homes and schools, to educational attainment in the later school years. Wells found that the rate of children's language development was statistically correlated with their rate of participation in conversations, and with the number of utterances they received from others especially when those utterances were contingently related to their own utterances and to their understandings and activities. Correlation analysis further showed that the frequency of these features was not related to the socio-economic background of the children and their families.

It is important to note here that it is the *frequency* of occurrence of these features, as shown in the random segments of talk recorded from each child, that does or does not correlate. Variations in their quality have not yet been addressed. Other qualities of the homes and the people in them that may have caused these frequency variations have also not been addressed.

As soon as the children went to school, standardized tests showed that some children were more 'ready for school' than others, and were perceived by their teachers to be 'headed for more success' in their school years. Furthermore, and here is the apparent anomaly that motivated this research report, these judgements, the test scores and the teachers' perceptions, *were* related to the socio-economic background of the children and their families. Two years later, these assessments were shown to be accurate predictors of success, and the correlation with socio-economic status persisted.

How to explain these developments in the results? Wells and his colleagues were struck by a set of recurring features in the classroom data. They found that

> there were certain contexts – and they were ones that were found to occur with considerable frequency in the classroom – in which the less successful children did seem to have particular difficulty. These were sequences of interaction organized around question–answer exchanges in which the child was required to demonstrate his [*sic and ff*] knowledge of some piece of information or his understanding of some principle. Because the answers to such questions are already known by the questioner, we refer to them as *requests for display*. (1985: 230)

As an example, Wells (1985: 230–1) presented the following transcript of a brief incident from one of the recorded lessons. (Note that the transcript conventions shown in the transcript below are those used by Wells in his report of the findings. Slightly different and a more complete set of conventions will be presented and discussed in a later chapter.)

Scene: A small group of children are looking at slides in a viewer; the viewer has just been passed to student Rosie (R), to whom the teacher (T) begins to talk:

1. T They're Indian ladies and what else?
2. R [*Looks through viewer*] I can see something.
3. T What can you see?
4. R And they're going in the sand.
5. T [*Fails to understand*] Mm?
6. R You have a look.
7. T Well, you have a look and tell me. I've seen it already. I want to see if you can see. [*6-second pause*]
8. R [*Looks through viewer*] Oh, they're going in the sand. They're going in the sand. [*20-second pause; T doesn't hear as she is attending to other children*]
9. T What's behind the men? Can you see men in the red coats? [*2-second pause; R still looking*] Can you see the men in the red coats? What's behind those men? [*4-second pause*] Can you see?
10. R [*Nods*]
11. T What is it?
12. R They're walking in . . .
13. T Pardon?
14. R They're walking.
15. T They're walking, yes. But what's walking behind them? Something very big?
16. R A horse.
17. T It's much bigger than a horse. It's much bigger than a horse. It's big and grey and it's got a long nose that we call a trunk. [*Mimes a long trunk*]
18. R Trunk. [*Imitates*]
19. T Can you see what it is? What is it?
20. R [*Nods*]

And so on until teacher points directly to the elephant and asks 'what's that?' and Rosie answers 'an elephant', with the observer's comment 'as if knowing all the time'. Wells's commentary on this segment of talk is as follows:

Although perhaps not entirely typical, episodes of this unsatisfactory kind are all too frequent in the classrooms we have observed: teachers trying hard to elicit answers that are self-evident and straightforward from their own point of view, but succeeding only in securing responses that they judge to be wrong or irrelevant or, in some cases, failing to secure any response at all . . . even when the topic is not outside such children's experience, they may still be unable or unwilling to provide an answer that is acceptable. (231–2)

Wells mentioned two possible explanations for such 'problems' with requests for display and for their possible relationship to socio-economic status. One explanation that has been offered is that some children have little experience with request for display sequences. Wells dismissed this on the grounds that his own data showed that the display sequence itself was not uncommon among all children in the study. The difference, which Wells took to be the difference that mattered, related to the question of whether or not the request for display was about 'contexts of meaningful and purposeful activity' (232) for the child. In classrooms, Wells argued, requests for display are typically about topics that are 'in isolation from the particular experience in which they are rooted in the child's individual biography' (232).

Wells went on to implicate reading and writing activities in the home as an arch example of a training ground for such decontextualized interactive practice. To support this, he reported both statistical and qualitative evidence that opportunities to listen to stories in the preschool years (rather than, for example, just to look at books or draw and colour in), predicted oral and written school performance on tests administered two years later. The relationships traditionally reported, and reported by Wells and others, between socio-economic status and literacy achievement Wells accounted for in terms of the relationship between the educational levels of parents, their literacy practices and the role of these in training for certain ways of thinking (e.g., 'looking for explanations of particular events in general principles and of making such connections explicit'). Thus the argument is developed that levels of educational attainment are transmitted inter-generationally through the predominance of particular ways of talking about books in the preschool and early school years. Of interest here is the nature of the interplay between quantitative and qualitative data and the consequences of that interplay on the researcher's interpretations.

What can we learn from Wells's report of these findings? First, Wells takes the quantitative and qualitative domains of the research to be in a mutually inform- ing relationship – signposts for one another in a shuttle process of reporting and interpretation. For example, qualitative analysis of the corpus led to the location of an interactive routine that was distinctive enough to deserve its own name: display requests. The quantity of display requests led Wells and his colleagues to examine their quality, because their frequency/quantity made him believe they were important generally, and important conceptually for the specific question at hand in this part of the project. Both of these designations of 'importance' needed to come from somewhere, and it seems that they came from attention they had received from previous researchers and from Wells's theoretical premise that it would be linguistic domains of experience that would be important in mediating the relationship between school attainment and socio-economic factors. This sets the boundaries for the answers that the project can offer. The important observation, again, regardless of whether this is somehow independently 'right' or 'wrong', 'productive' or not, is that it represents a choice on the researchers' part.

Second, while there is much quantitative reporting in the piece, it seems to be the qualitative analyses that actually offer the theoretical account that clinches the answer to the question. The statistics establish that a coded form of activity labelled 'reading stories' accounts for a robust proportion of variation in later educational attainment. Further than that it does not go. In this study, the statistical analyses serve the purpose of alerting the researcher – 'look over here!' To establish both the quality that is captured in the term 'display request' and its significance for educational attainment more broadly, Wells presents 'satisfactory' and 'unsatisfactory' examples of the phenomenon in schools and in homes. It is in the presentation of these sites, for points of qualitative comparison, that the reported findings can be taken to have addressed the original question that the researcher promised would be answered: *Are variations in educational attainment related to differing linguistic patterns to which children are exposed in the home before the onset of schooling?*

Related to this is the third lesson, that the final accounting procedures – the core explanatory business – that Wells offers in this piece are couched almost entirely in qualitative terms: the notion of decontextualized interactive practice; the significance of parents' literacy practices and the role of these in training for certain ways of thinking (e.g., 'looking for explanations of particular events in general principles and of making such connections explicit', 1985: 236).

Considering the compatibility or otherwise of qualitative and quantitative approaches to research in education, as exemplified in the study by Wells, brings us to a significant distinction in contemporary social science, one that has profound implications for how research can be conducted and interpreted – written and read – with integrity. On the one hand, we (as members of a culture and/or as social scientists) can 'read' social activities as representations of 'larger' theoretical accounts of some sort (say, linguistic, sociological, psychological accounts) or as reflective of larger ideological dialectics, as instanced by Gitlin's comment above. We can see everyday activities, including the variations in the ways things are done and the people who accomplish them, as standing for, or as enactments of, official or folk theorizations (about, say, 'gender', or 'self-concept'). That is, we can see only those features that can be theorized in these ways, as the operation of 'variables' we have gleaned from these theorizations – we can see that 'this is the kind of event that can happen when this kind of event happens'. Doing this allows us to work with the notion of 'generalizability', a motivation drawn directly from Natural Science agenda.

On the other hand, we can focus our initial or even our complete attention on 'discovering' social order *in* the activities we study. This directly observed social order might but does not necessarily draw on the broad theorizations that are available to us from elsewhere. Rather, it is primarily a social order that informs and inheres in the particular activities themselves, as the participants accomplish them in orderly and practical ways.

These are distinctive answers to a fundamental theoretical question that has comprehensive implications for studying and reporting on everyday educational practices: How do we, as researchers of social life, and the people whose activities we study, 'read off' order from social experience? The two answers outlined above may be termed respectively the 'aggregated' and the 'distributed' approaches. An aggregated approach takes it that the order of society is both visible and understandable at an overall level, when all of a society's sectors and activities are taken into account. In that sense, the order is an abstraction, empirically visible only through its various imperfect and partial manifestations: the Order of Society is realized, and thus available, only from an aggregation of partial moments, partially glimpsed. In contrast, the distributed approach takes it that what is visible and interpretable is 'order at all points' (Sacks, 1992: 484). Schegloff commented on Sacks's discussion of the alternatives in these terms:

> An alternative to the possibility that order manifests itself at an aggregate level and is statistical in character is what [Sacks] termed the 'order at all points' view. . . . This view, rather like the 'holographic' model of information distribution, understands order not to be present only at aggregate levels and therefore subject to an overall differential distribution, but to be present in detail on a case by case, environment by environment basis. A culture is not then to be found only by aggregating all of its venues; it is substantially present in each of its venues. (1995: xlvi)

A fundamental difference in the worldview of researchers is highlighted here: on the one hand, social life is viewed as instancing primarily social-organizational features such as gender, class, ethnicity (the 'Holy Trinity' of sociological research, according to Kincheloe and MacLaren, 1994: 145), or more locally, as instancing such institutional orders such as 'classroom life', families and so on. On the other hand, social life is viewed as instancing primarily its own orderliness, that is, the organizational features of social practice built through the actions of people as they function in a variety of settings.

Types of science

To discover the 'qualitative' in qualitative research, we need to see how it has been distinguished from its neighbouring categories of research. When we examine that, we find that the qualitative–quantitative distinction has brought with it, and is thus conflated with, many other philosophical, social and ideological dichotomies. What is clear is that we need some principled way through the variety of angles that relate to this contrast, and to its possible relevance to the conduct of research projects in education. One such way is offered by Heap (1992), who described two large families of scientific inquiry that have been mentioned in passing already: the first of these he termed Natural Science, which has an interest in the causes of behaviour and in explaining and predicting behaviour. Instances of Natural Science in education include behavioural psychology, physiological psychology, cognitive science and educational economics. It is Natural Science approaches in the study of social life that are the most direct descendants of natural-scientific approaches to the study of the material world.

The second form of science Heap termed Human Science, which takes as its interest the conditions under which human beings behave and the ways in which these conditions influence that behaviour. Instances of these in educational inquiry include some forms of sociology, anthropology, history and philosophy. Heap further divided Human Sciences into Social and Cultural Sciences. Under the heading of Social, the principal interest is in documenting the normative grounds for human action, the learner's intentions and beliefs, the participants' compliance with certain conventions and expectations. In contrast, Heap characterized Cultural Science as fundamentally interested in how it is that particular activities come to be constituted normatively *as* aspects of culture. That is, the Cultural Science programme is about explicating human activities with respect to their recognizable content and their organization as part of social life. To Heap's taxonomy we add a growing domain of educational inquiry that self-identifies as 'critical'. This term applies to research that operates from a variety of theoretical perspectives drawn from critical sociology and anthropology (the latter sometimes referred to as 'critical ethnography', Carspecken, 1995), aiming to make visible the political motivations and consequences of educational practice, and, in some cases, what steps might be taken by educators or communities. These distinctions are summarized in Table 3.1.

We can see in Table 3.1 the significance of recasting the distinctions that matter in educational research into Natural, Social, Cultural and Critical Science. It becomes clear as we pursue the interplay between quantitative and qualitative elements of Wells's study, for example, that these apparently antagonistic approaches to managing and interpreting data in fact have no trouble being civil and helpful to one another; in fact, we see them cohabiting. To see why this is so, we can ask 'what kind of science is this?' Quantitative and qualitative approaches, in this instance, live so happily together because the project is an instance of Natural Science: the objects under study are taken to be naturally-occurring and directly observable (e.g., 'requests for display' – 'unsatisfactory' and otherwise – 'parental educational level'); and the interest is in establishing both the existence of these objects as 'variables' and the relationships among them. The two analytic approaches are put to work in the service of this form of science, and, while they do different parts of the project's work, they are co-ordinated seamlessly within the logic of Natural Science. Even the detailed examination of classroom talk derives its status as a move in the project from the representativeness of that talk, or at least from the generalizability of what are taken to be the key aspects of the transcript, as it shows *that kind* of talk.

TABLE 3.1 *Adaptation of Heap's (1992) distinctions among various programmes of research*

Natural Science

The 'Objects' of inquiry are:
* naturally occurring observable phenomena;
* phenomena whose boundaries are clear and self-evident;
* observable both as they seem and as they are.

The goals and interests of the inquiry are to document and prove:
* the existence of empirical variables – regularities, patterns and structures;
* the relations among them and other objects in the field;
* and the functions of these in the production of observable phenomena.

Social Science

The 'Objects' of inquiry are:
* observable social activities;
* the intentions motivating those activities;
* 'within' individuals, that is, with individuals, in context, but as the prime sources of activities.

The goals and interests of the inquiry are to document and give commentary on:
* the normativity of social activity;
* publicly knowable grounds for a person's actions, in terms of intentions;
* including statements of their personal beliefs; and
* their individual norms.

Cultural Science

The 'Objects' of inquiry are:
* a group's shared history of actions;
* and the shared, available interpretations of those actions.

The goals and interests of the inquiry are to document and explicate:
* the normative content and reasoned properties of observable, mutual actions;
* the particular reasonableness of the organization of actions and of the resources through which recognizable social activities are co-ordinated and jointly accomplished.

Critical Science

The 'Objects' of inquiry are:
* the structure of societies;
* the patterns of daily experience as they reflect these patterns;
* oppressed, marginalized and/or silenced groups or subcultures within a society.

The goals and interests of the inquiry are to highlight, document, critique and transform:
* awareness of the processes of oppression, marginalizing, and/or silencing, in our case, in educational practice (including policy);
* educational practice, especially among groups systematically ill-served or actively neglected in the course of educational practice.

Conclusions

All four categories of scientific practice outlined above have claimed special status as forms of knowing, and privileged ways of finding out. Traditionally, the special status of science, in contrast with other forms of knowing and finding out, has rested on two propositions about its goals and interests: that the goal of 'science' is the production of knowledge that can somehow stand apart from any specific instance of experience we have in the world; and as a consequence, that its methods are reproducible from place to place and time to time.

These propositions have guided explorations of the nature and operation of the non-social, physical, material world. When we consider these forms of scientific inquiry into the nature and operation of individual and collective human behaviour, in our case, into its educational practices, we see that these propositions are challenged by contrasting views of scientific inquiry into social life. Cultural and Critical Sciences, in particular, point most forcefully, in their understanding of the basic goal of their programme, to the impossibility of documenting the social world in the same terms and with the same research apparatus as used to document the physical world. At best, cultural and critical scientists see the goals and reasoning practices of Natural Science's approach to the material to be applicable to the study of social life only by distant analogy. What is more crucial is that Human Science's methods arose in large part as a critique of Natural Science applications to the study of human behaviour, and, in turn, the various forms of human sciences likewise arose as critical reactions to one another.

We need to consider that, just as surely as the object of its study – educational practice – educational research itself is purposeful action in the world. It gets certain types of work done, partly by standing as an instance of a particular privileged way of finding out and knowing, a way that stands against or at least 'beyond' anecdotal observation in many critical respects. A particular research project is itself a purposeful action in the world, and part of its credibility lies in its presentation of itself as a special kind of knowledge, which we may term 'scientific' knowledge.

Two considerations now arise. First, it needs to be pointed out that the distinction between quantitative and qualitative research activity is not of itself a distinction about the structure or purpose of inquiry. It is rather, in its technical, minimal sense, a distinction based on a way of conceiving the object of study and on analytic method. A second point concerns the matter of the compatibility or potential 'complementary' nature of quantitative and qualitative research. It is here that the distinction between research as project and research as science is pertinent. As a practical activity in the world, shot through at all times with matters of policy and decision-making, education attracts researchers who will, at least at times, want to influence both practice and policy, based on the ground that they, as a research team, may share on particular educational matters. As instances of scientific research activity, however, the compatibility issue is irrelevant: the theoretical and practical interests of particular projects may draw their bases and their credibility from the fact that they are participating in a certain form of either the Natural, Social, Cultural or Critical sciences. In that respect, there is no particular need for quantitative and qualitative methods to be considered either compatible or incompatible. They are purposeful within the terms of their own interests, and in terms of the histories of their development as ways of knowing about educational activities and, more broadly, about cultural practice.

We can restate the matter of the possible, productive relationships between quantitative and qualitative forms of research in the terms in which Heap has framed the issue: as a choice initially between forms of scientific activity – Natural, Social, Cultural and Critical Sciences. Heap's (1992) advice is useful in this regard as well. Both qualitative and quantitative analyses can be applied informatively to research projects that are located in any one of the Natural, Social, Cultural and Critical approaches. That is, both forms of research can inform a variety of influential readerships in a variety of ways. As they act on their various premises, however, they cannot, taken together, discover anything new about the phenomenon of interest. We need to be clear about this assertion: nothing new can emerge from the juxtaposing of thoroughly differing constructions and interpretations of a domain of educational practice, when the various languages the different sciences use to name and demarcate that practice differ in kind. What they may 'discover' is a variety of readers who can be informed, aligned and influenced by quantitative or qualitative language, or by the focused combination of these languages. In terms of changing educational practice for the better, such a mixture may bring off a broader consensus than would any single approach.

Second, our response to the issue of mixing Natural, Social, Cultural and/or Critical approaches depends on the practical goals and aims of educational research projects. In light of the differences between these approaches as summarized in Table 3.1, it is hard to see how anyone could imagine they could be compatible, or even on speaking terms: They construe the very phenomena they are observing differently; they consider things that can be legitimately said about those phenomena differently; they aim to produce accounts with thoroughly divergent consequences. Given the different interests of these forms of scientific inquiry, it is important to consider closely how, for what purpose, and with what effects – what gains and losses – particular kinds of approaches can be juxtaposed. If a major outcome of a project, and thus a major goal of the reporting of that project is, for example, to convince an educational authority of the need to spend more resources on a particular programme, and the researchers on the project have worked differently with different kinds of data, then the multiple re-presentation of the outcomes in different 'shapes' may serve their goal well.

Those charged with advancing scientific knowledge about the set of cultural practices called 'education', from within one of the particular forms of inquiry summarized above, have comparatively little to offer those working with the other forms of scientific inquiry on the matter of the advancement of their disciplined understanding. On the other hand, co-operation among scientists using different approaches has been productive in refining research questions and expanding the purview of particular projects when those projects are aimed at policy issues, including policies that are implemented in classrooms and assessment boards. Thus Heap (1982) endorsed a co-operation-in-discussion for the sake of policy.

Having said that, it needs to be re-emphasized that such 'co-operation' may entail dispute, and that, when differing *forms* of science are in dispute on the matter of the outcomes or the interpretation of outcomes, there are no principled criteria for reaching consensus. There is no Security Council of the United Nations of Educational Research that can arbitrate on conflicts using a set of resolution procedures that relate with equal force to each of those research forms. The belief that differing approaches will, should or can generally converge itself reflects a belief in a final cultural reality, viewed only imperfectly through different but merely differently-distorted lenses – that is, a presumption of an aggregated-order approach.

The important point emerges that the issue of relevance in analysis and reporting is both the special genius and the potential demon of thoughtful, careful and detailed qualitative research, compared with other forms of research in education. In general, qualitative researchers lay claim to acting on complexity at the potential expense of simplicity, on fidelity to observation at the potential expense of formalized techniques of design and analysis, and on the distinctiveness of experiences at the potential expense of their standardization across people and settings. To some researchers, these are serious losses; to others, they impose new rigours that can offer the promise of higher-impact research in education and a professionally honest relationship between the people doing the studying and the human objects of their study.

DISCUSSION TOPICS, QUESTIONS AND EXERCISES

1. Select a setting that you are familiar with and observe the activities and events that people are involved in. While you are watching or participating in the events in the setting imagine that you have four 'hats' in your possession each labelled separately as follows: Natural Scientist, Social Scientist, Cultural Scientist and Critical Scientist. In turn, try 'wearing' each hat, thus being 'transformed' into the corresponding identity of each hat's label, as you consider the following (based on Heap's distinctions):

(a) What or who are the 'objects' of your inquiry?

As the Natural Scientist you might begin by identifying and categorizing *observable phenomena (reportable events and activities)* as they occur in the setting. As the Social Scientist you may ask various members about their *motivations* for performing and participating in observable events and activities in the setting. As the Cultural Scientist you might focus on the ways members make sense of and display their understanding of the events and activities (as an 'event', an 'activity') to each other in the setting. And finally, as the Critical Scientist you may be looking to see whether the interplay between members' identities and the events and activities they perform reflect or present challenges to pre-existing social norms (e.g. gender, morality), systems (e.g. politics, education) and structures (e.g. families, class formations).

(b) What might be the goals and interests of your inquiry?

As the Natural Scientist you might be interested in identifying regularities or patterns of members' interaction in the setting. You might also be interested to see if these regularities or patterns hold across different settings of the same type. As the Social Scientist you might be interested in finding out what it is members are trying to achieve by their (inter)actions in the setting. As the Cultural Scientist you may wish to explicate how it is the members collaboratively produce and make sense of their interactions in the setting. And again finally, as the Critical Scientist you may be interested in highlighting discursive modes of oppression that systematically marginalize the interactional rights of particular groups (identifications/categories) of members in the setting.

2. Look for any marginal or exceptional events that occur in the setting. Can you formulate an explanation for their occurrence that 'fits' with the logic of the setting (are there any central features of the setting, members' interactions etc. that make these kinds of events, however exceptional, likely to occur, however infrequently)?

3. Points for discussion:

   (a) *For the Natural Scientist*: How did you decide if an event or activity was observable or reportable as such? How were reportable events and activities categorized (what procedures did you use to arrive at these categorizations)? How can you be certain that the events and activities you have observed, identified and categorized are adequate descriptions of what the members were actually doing?

   (b) *For the Social Scientist*: Were there any differences between what the members said they were trying to achieve in their interactions and what you observed them achieving in their interactions? If so, how do you account for this?

   (c) *For the Cultural Scientist*: What resources do members use to display their understanding of events and activities in the setting?

   (d) *For the Critical Scientist*: How can you be certain that the categories you have observed and used to identify members as belonging to a particular category of persons (women, children, middle classes, Aborigines etc.) are the same categories that members observe and use to organize the interactional order of events and activities in the setting. How, could you be sure that members' interactional rights are always (sometimes, or not at all) distributed according to, for example, gender and age and not, again for example, ethnicity and class (or a complex combination of all of these)?

4

Are the Insiders Really 'Family'? Categories of Qualitative Research

We see varieties of qualitative research practised in educational settings. In this chapter, I recruit the distinction within the Human Sciences outlined earlier and draw out some of the features of Social, Critical and Cultural Science to describe these varieties. In the following chapter we consider three general method-ologies for conducting qualitative research in education prior to exploring the analysis of educational data.

Educational practices are fundamentally about social relationships in two senses. Educational activities take place in social interactions (face-to-face, and/ or mediated by printed or electronic pictorial or auditory records). Also, the point of educational activity is taken to be to project the learner's future through the enhancement of both specific and general capabilities and dispositions, into new social relations and affiliations. These new relations comprise communities that trade in and with those capabilities and dispositions. In both of these senses of the social nature of educational practices, issues of normativity – the good, the proper, the normal – are necessarily implicated. Educational activities, then, however fleeting or extensive, formal or informal, public or domestic, are moral enterprises in terms of both their enactments and the 'goods' towards which they project learners. Both these enactments and projections alert us to the political nature of educational practices. Educational practices have histories that we can view as the story of their victories and defeats. In this sense, educational practices can be seen as the traces or records of the successes and failures of the interests, dispositions, capacities and cultural modes of operation of certain groups, who act out their particular cultural and economic interests through education. One result is that different kinds of learners are offered different kinds of practices, knowledges and trajectories.

We proceed now to examine variations that we find within the clan 'qualitative'. Are the clan members really 'family'? Do they squabble? Are they on speaking terms? Or, worse, do they ignore one another and do things just as diverse as if they were strangers who happen to share a common family name? I conclude this chapter with a summary of the position I adopt in this book on some foundational issues to do with qualitative educational research.

Varieties of qualitative research in education

There have been many ways in which research in the category 'qualitative' has been categorized. The categorization provided in the last chapter, comprising Natural Sciences and three branches of Human Sciences – Social, Cultural and Critical – is a loose, imperfect, but productive means of organizing the wide range of disciplines in education that have put varieties of qualitative analytic methods to work.

Each discipline approaches people's experiences with a particular goal and a preferred set of explanatory techniques. What is clear nonetheless is that they all have an interest in what people say and do, ordinarily, and in the course of mundane social activities. While researchers in all of these disciplines may use qualitative methods that have family resemblances, the issues to which these methods are applied nonetheless retain the particular preoccupations of their base disciplines.

Social Science and the naturalist attitude: 'once you get close to it . . .'

A *naturalist* attitude pervades much of the qualitative research work done by researchers working within a framework of Social Science. They are interested in understanding and documenting reality 'as it is, naturally'. Their genealogy includes anthropologists and some practitioners of sociology. They aim to deal with the people they are studying by documenting their various ways of life on their own terms and turf, by participating in these ways, and by discreetly observing people, events and interactions. They seek 'rich descriptions of people and interaction as they exist and unfold in their natural habitat' (Gubrium and Holstein, 1997: 6), looking to 'track down relationships' (Strauss and Corbin, 1990: 112).

This line of research takes it that a knowable social reality exists, and, further, that the 'textured and dynamic detail' of that reality (Gubrium and Holstein, 1997: 19) is knowable too. These patterns are taken to be knowable because they are taken to be 'there', that is, evident and amenable to discovery if the researcher is close enough and uses a set of data collection strategies that can do justice to the complexity and subtlety of social experience. As Goffman (1961: ix; cited in Gubrium and Holstein, 1997) put it, people 'develop a life of their own that becomes meaningful, reasonable, and normal once you get close to it'. It is the meaningfulness, reasonableness and normality of observed practices that Social Scientists take to be comprehensively, or at least adequately describable in their own terms.

Therefore the guidelines for the conduct and development of research in the Social Science tradition include:

- an appeal to *multi-disciplinary approaches and multiple data sources* to provide some 'triangulation' on the social realities of the setting and the people;
- an essentially *neutral disposition* on the part of the researcher, whereby presuppositions are minimized;
- *being with the participants* to the extent perhaps of being a 'participant-observer', immersed in the site; and
- *fidelity to the stories that the people* on the site have told in representing their activities.

It is important to be aware that even these basic guidelines are under debate in many circles, partly as a result of the critiques offered by researchers working in the other traditions that are outlined below. For instance, Denzin (1997), a long-established Social Scientist who has been instrumental in developing the area of ethnographic research, has recently questioned the attainability of these guidelines. Denzin's challenge comes from a perception of the rapid changes that have, he claimed, refashioned societies and all of their ways of doing business. Denzin pointed out that 'Culture has gone postmodern and multinational, so too has ethnography. The ethnographic project has changed because the world that ethnography confronts has changed' (1997: 11). That changing world, Denzin claimed, includes the world of ethnographic research itself. Researchers are grappling with the entanglements of a new and complex field. It is precisely this predicament that causes the researcher's own commitments to be brought to the fore through the realization that it is the 'narratives' that people tell and show one another, domestically and publicly, that constitute the new realities within which the ethnographer is committed to working.

For Denzin, the new social scientist needs to abandon the naturalist disposition to the people whose activities are under study and to focus, again naturalistically, on the new cultures that the production of research itself brings into being. In spite of these concerns, in the main stream of educational research we discern a continued commitment to the careful documentation of social activities, intentions and interpretations that has traditionally characterized Social Science more generally.

Critical Science and the political attitude: 'contradictions and constraints . . .'

Critical-analytic traditions have arisen as responses to advances in a variety of theorizing in sociology, politics, economics and education. As categories of research activities, they are united principally by their opposition to the application of Natural and Social Science methods to cultural life. These latter methods, usually summarized under the rubric of 'positivism' and including methodologies such as laboratory and field experiments, surveys and quantitative performance measurement, have been criticized as liberal analyses of an eerily dehistoricized and depoliticized version of social life. In the critical tradition, Natural Science's contributions to education have further been held to account for not having delivered equitable, effective and 'empowering' education, in spite of a century or so of methodological dominance in education and in spite of their perennial claims that they have found (actually or almost) 'the glorious educational answers' (Ladwig and Gore, 1994). Researchers in education who describe themselves as 'critical' are never content merely to advance knowledge in the field. Discovering new phenomena or ways of thinking about apparently familiar educational phenomena are goals that share equal status with ideological and political motivations.

To paint in broad strokes, critical analytic traditions can be considered under three headings: collaborative, standpoint and post-modern research. These traditions draw on one another, in particular at the level of the research project, but it is also important to note that, in recent times, the field of critical educational research has been characterized by persistent debate among the neighbouring traditions themselves, as much as with the customary, and often stereotyped 'positivistic' Natural Science.

By 'collaborative', I refer to the tradition in educational research that aims to use the context of the research process to help develop a productive 'community of change' (Gitlin and Russell, 1994: 200; and see Bottery and Wright, 1996; Fielding, 1997). This development is taken to be effected principally through the practical discovery, by researchers and educational practitioners in collaboration, of the material, theoretical and ideological conditions under which educational practice is taken to operate. A central question for researchers in this tradition concerns the issue of the legitimation of certain kinds of knowledge in and through organized educational practices, such as schooling, and in and through the research that describes and informs these practices: Who gets to tell official stories about education?

Research approaches that describe themselves as primarily collaborative in their processes and goals begin from an understanding of the differing material and institutional positions of the researcher and the researched, and the relative power-over-knowledge that each occupies. The argument is that these conditions offer the researcher and the researched substantially different opportunities to produce and disseminate new knowledge about education, and different reward structures for producing different kinds of knowledge. Gitlin and Russell (1994; and see Gitlin and others, 1992) outlined an approach, which they termed 'educative research', for the collaborative production of new knowledge about education. They offered a summary of educative research, which they describe as a domain of practice in which

> [a]ll participants are united by the quest to examine the topic at hand as well as to reveal contradictions and constraints within the educative process itself. The intent of this dialogue is not to discover absolutes, or 'the truth', but to scrutinize normative 'truths' that are embedded in a specific historical and cultural context. (Gitlin and Russell, 1994: 185)

The key concepts that Gitlin and Russell (1994: 185–9) suggested can deliver this intent relate to the following (note that these and related concerns are discussed further and exemplified in Chapter 5):

1. The provision for multiple 'voices' in the analysis and reporting of the findings, in particular the voices of those on the research site who have been silenced in and by certain educational practices, including traditional research methods.
2. An insistence on the inextricable connection of understanding to practice, largely through the assumption of responsibility of the practitioner, with the researcher acting as a resource in the research process.
3. The location of the research process within authentic accounts of the backgrounds and evolving personal views of both the researcher and the researched.
4. A redefinition of the claims made by 'reliability' and 'validity' in terms of these three precepts; that is, a redefinition of validity as involving the documentation and reporting of the ongoing attempts of the researchers and practitioners 'to come to a mutual understanding based on their own strongly articulated positions' (187); and a redefinition of reliability in terms of 'satisfy[ing] the underlying principle of voice and its relationship to a desired form of schooling' (188).
5. An emphasis on the process of the research activity rather than the products; that is, a re-ordering of the traditional relativities of the disseminable outcomes of the project (often, research reports) and the productive development of a community of change within the research site.

Under the second heading, *standpoint approaches* (sometimes referred to as 'partisan research'; see, e.g., Kincheloe and MacLaren, 1994), we can locate a range of research activities in which the researchers put into place a set of analytic and interpretive procedures that are pre-designed to highlight the particular ideological operations of cultural practices such as education. These ideological operations are taken to permit, give rise to, or necessitate those cultural discourses that are purpose-built to naturalize and perpetuate existing inequalities in a society. Such inequalities may be on the grounds of traditional ideology critique – race, gender, and social class – or they may be concerned with particular subcultures that are deemed to be marginalized or educationally disadvantaged by a combination of these categories, or by other processes, such as sexual preference, HIV status, disability and employment status. Some commentators (e.g., Olesen, 1994; the collection edited by Gitlin, 1994, in particular the chapters by Gitlin and Russell and Ladwig and Gore) have suggested that research about and by members of such marginalized groups has led to a loose consensus around a set of general approaches to research that include foregrounding the position ('voice', 'authentic experience' or experiential 'realities') of the disempowered and subordinated group by selecting research topics that permit such foregrounding, and by focusing the analysis of data on revealing the work of ideology in all facets of educational practice (including policy, see Apple, 1996).

Standpoint research begins with an understanding of the context of educational practices that is pre-tuned to an interest in a particular category of oppressive practice and presumption – often masculinism, classism or racism. These forms of organized, legitimated or naturalized oppression are often taken a priori to be relevant, that is, necessarily relevant, to the phenomena under study. This relevance comes from an understanding of social system as a set of aggregative patterns – beliefs and activities that we take to be prevalent in the society as a whole. This knowledge of the aggregation is then taken to be analytically relevant across all possible sites.

Post-modernism refers to a particular orientation to accounts of social truth, rather than to a particular collection of theoretical propositions, methods or methodological procedures. In that respect, it is difficult to summarize post-modernist approaches to methods of studying educational questions. Such as summary, however, has been attempted by Rosenau (1992). The account here draws heavily on Rosenau's distillation of the post-modernist orientation to a series of core propositions (and see Birch, 1989, chapter 1; Harvey, 1989; Kincheloe and McLaren, 1994: 142–54; Macherey, 1978):

1. any knowledge claim is debatable, even understandable, only within the interpretive community in and for which it has been produced;
2. therefore, the claims of traditional science to a privileged way of knowing amount to an act of imperialism on the making of meaning;
3. these privileged ways of knowing and the ways of knowing that give them coherence and legitimacy take the form of 'grand narratives';
4. for the researcher, therefore, these grand narratives, wherein meaning is presented as 'knowledge' by traditional science, need to be continually subverted; and

5. these observations apply to natural, social, cultural and critical forms of scientific inquiry.

Researchers working in the post-modernist tradition (as close to an oxymoron as it is possible to get in discussions such as this) can be divided, according to Rosenau, into two broad families: sceptics and affirmatives. As Rosenau characterized it, sceptics confront what they see as the uncertainty of social and cultural experience, claiming there are simply no adequate means for representing socio-cultural realities. In the place of such realities, sceptics point to the linguistic conventions that we use to exchange understanding. Scientific explanation, and indeed the conduct of activities traditionally recognizable as research, are impossible, from sceptics' point of view, on at least two counts. Socio-cultural experience presents as random; and each element of socio-cultural experience is so tightly intertwined with all of the other elements that order is no longer visible or documentable in any systematic way, or, more importantly, in any way that can do justice to the multiplicities that constitute contemporary societies.

The affirmative wing of post-modernism does not conduct its work from an established view of the impossibility of representing socio-cultural practice. Its interest in the conduct of research is not to establish causality, but rather to demonstrate the relationships among various forms of representation (partly through the documentation of intertextual relations). That is, affirmative post-modernists operate on the premise that socio-cultural experience is complex but fundamentally relational, and amenable to explication in terms of those relationships.

The aim of post-modern analyses, in most of its forms at least, is to offer, in Rosenau's words:

> indeterminacy rather than determinism, diversity rather than unity, difference rather than synthesis, complexity rather than simplification Post-Modern social science presumes methods that multiply paradox, inventing ever more elaborate repertoires of questions, each of which encourages an infinity of answers, rather than methods that settle on solutions. (1992: 117)

Post-modernists have critiqued the grand narratives of traditional science, including those evident in standpoint research, finding them overly constrained and ultimately offering only a trivialized representation of social experience. They have done this partly by explicating intertextuality, not only among their own accounts, but also among traditional scientific accounts and between these and the policy pursuits of the modern nation-state. To do this, post-modernists have drawn for their explicative possibilities on the interpretations and texts produced at the margins of the traditionally-conceived state – 'non-mainstream' experience, re-directing attention onto

> what has been taken for granted, what has been neglected, regions of resistance, the forgotten, the irrational, the insignificant, the repressed, the border-line, the classical, the sacred, the traditional, the eccentric, the sublimated, the subjugated, the rejected, the

non-essential, the marginal, the peripheral, the excluded, the tenuous, the silenced, the accidental, the dispersed, the disqualified, the deferred, the disjointed . . . (Rosenau, 1992: 8)

Rosenau offered a number of general guidelines for the conduct of research based on a Post-Modern orientation (drawing on Wellberg, 1985), with a particular focus on the deconstruction of communications (which include written documents but, as well, other forms of communication and display, all of which can be treated as 'texts'). Two of the more central of these guidelines are to:

1. find the contradictions and silences in the text and develop these to undermine the generalizations towards which the text is striving or that make the text possible in the first place; and
2. emphasize the ambiguity, incompleteness and indeterminacy of a text, the expanding multiplicity of its interpretations and the constant deferral of closure on the matter of its 'meaning'.

In important respects, post-modernist research in education is aimed at developing new knowledge at the same time as disrupting, interrupting or at least playing with, other more dominant modes of inquiry in education. It embodies a very specific challenge. What's more, it actually inquires, as it proceeds, into the nature of that challenge to current forms of research, to their claims to be able to determine 'findings', and to their innocence as political practices in themselves. In that sense, a piece of post-modernist research constitutes a piece of scientific street theatre, aimed at disruption in its topical focus as well as in its processes. These primary goals of interruption and disruption represent both a theoretical and methodological response to the 'contemporary condition' as it is named by post-modernists:

a contemporary era marked by the delegitimation of the grand narratives of Western civilization, a loss of faith in the power of reason, and a shattering of traditional religious orthodoxies. (Kincheloe and McLaren, 1994: 142)

In general, then, post-modernist research in education aims to conduct an ongoing attack on the grand narratives that have given theoretical and cultural shape to the practice of education; this attack itself, as shown in the quote above, is drawn from a grand-narrative account of the current intellectual, cultural, moral and economic conditions that face societies and those in them who conduct and support educational practice.

Cultural Science and the 'accomplished' attitude: culture is achieved, day to day

Educational researchers working in a Cultural Science framework do not operate on the premise that firm knowable realities about social structures are 'out there', either in the forms of explanatory ideological or cultural structures, or in the sense of explanatory states of minds. They do not consider that there is a 'there' to be 'out there' until it has been socially constructed. Thus, social realities are accomplished and re-accomplished everyday in all kinds of different settings; what appears socially and culturally natural is always in-the-making-and-re-making by the participants. Therefore, at a most general level, the central guidelines for the conduct of Cultural Science research are:

1. the 'bracketing' of social realities; that is, treating the realities of social life as interactively and purposefully built;
2. explication of the rebuilding, through explication in research, of what everyone knows from simply being a member of a culture; and
3. the use and display in research of instances of the data, the analyses provided, and the ways in which the events studied are analyzable.

The most developed and one of the most widely used forms of Cultural Science in educational studies derives from a branch of sociology known as Ethnomethodology (henceforth EM). Heap has given a broad definition of this approach:

> the study of formal structures of situated practices as these practices are used by members of a culture to organize their reasoning and actions and their interactions, as rational, recognizable, orderly, identifiable events in a social world. (1985a: 46)

EM has been developed over several decades as a form of micro-sociological analysis (see Goodwin and Heritage, 1990 for a comprehensive review of EM's first 30 years), and has been applied extensively in such areas as legal discourse (Atkinson, 1992; Drew, 1992), exchanges in health and industrial settings (Button, 1992; Maynard, 1991; ten Have, 1991, 1995), media studies (Greatbatch, 1988; Jalbert, 1999), and in education (Baker, 1991; Heap, 1980, 1985b, 1990; McHoul and Watson, 1978). One overall aim of the application of EM to educational research arises from the fact that educational practices, as I outlined at the beginning of this chapter, have particular formal structures – topical, temporal and social patterns – that people together put in place, and about which they behave as if they know. That is, it is the patterns of educational events of various sorts to which people 'orient'. These practices are also aimed at producing certain kinds of consequences or states of affairs, by their very definition as 'educational'. As Heap has pointed out:

> Applied Ethnomethodolgy aims to recover and formulate the functions served by some sets of practices, and to do so it formulates how those practices foster, facilitate and limit the formulated functions . . . [it is] work whose arguments and findings have hope of being consequential for decision making regarding the continuation or modification of some set of practices. (1986: 46–7)

Traditional accounts available from social scientists and the community generally may regard the nature of relationships and interactions as *effects* of social and institutional conventions, structures, and roles; ethnomethodologists, in contrast, turn the explanation the other way around, aiming to show how the orderliness of particular social activities is shown in 'the collaborative ways in which members manage their conduct and their circumstances to achieve the orderly features of their activities' (Zimmerman and Boden, 1991: 7).

It is clear then that everyday talk is given a prime place in ethnomethodological studies. The 'primordial site of social order' is taken to be the use, by members of a culture, of particular ways (or 'methods') to conduct their daily affairs, make sense of them, and see that sense as reasonable and accountable, as they conduct themselves in their local daily circumstances (Boden and Zimmerman, 1991: 6).

EM's aims are:

1. to document the details of daily social life as mutually constructed cultural events;
2. to analyse detailed features of the interactions through which people encounter and construct what counts as social order in domestic and institutional sites such as educational settings; and
3. to show the various ways in which certain understandings about social life come to be imparted, understood and co-ordinated.

EM aims to offer understandings of social experience, based on a set of core propositions, among them:

- That the understandings and practices of members of a culture are inherently and resolutely social – concerted and mutual (Jayyusi, 1984, 1991) – and accomplished by multiple parties, and by the fact that multiple parties are involved in and required for that accomplishment (Boden and Zimmerman, 1991; Drew and Heritage, 1992). We do society together.
- That actions are culturally reflexive; that is, that members of a culture perform certain social activities to accomplish events and at the same time, and through those very same behaviours, to provide one another with accounts (descriptions, explanations and warrants) of those events (Boden and Zimmerman, 1991; Button and Lee, 1987; Hester and Eglin, 1997). When we act socially, we show one another why and how.
- That the accounts of cultural practices that members provide one another, generally through their talk, by which social order is constructed at all points of daily practice (Schegloff, 1995), are contingent, that is, accountable primarily in the local terms of the practices themselves, and that these accounts may or may not explicitly be seen to be explicable in terms of accounts, including explanations and evaluations, coming from outside the local event (Schegloff, 1991). When we act socially, we look for the logic in the here-and-now.

- Therefore, that the orderliness of the properties of commonplace actions needs to be discovered 'from within' the actual settings, as ongoing accomplishments of those settings and the participants (McHoul, 1978);
- All of which is to say, it is not satisfactory to investigate (recognize, explicate or assess) features of organized cultural practices, such as classroom lessons or educational policy decision-making sessions, by invoking a rule or a research generalization, obtained from outside the setting within which the practices are recognized, used and accounted for, no matter how much that importation may at first make the activities appear more recognizable, coherent or planful (these last two points are derived form the 'research policy' in Garfinkel, 1967, and elaborated in Heritage, 1984).

EM's goal is to explore how people co-ordinate their everyday courses of action in and through the routines of their talk, without pre-empting what the structure of those routines might look like. It takes cultural practices, such as those we consider to be educational, to be embedded in and built by courses of everyday action, the argument being that this is how members of a culture encounter them, rather than as externally determined.

By way of illustration, in his detailed studies of brief segments of early reading activities in classrooms, Heap's problem, in a sense, was the huge array of research already done on early reading, leaving the area replete with, and theoretically governed by pre-theorized concepts about what reading is and what should be done about that, to the point where the actualities of practice were pre-fitted into these concepts or 'philosophies' of how to teach reading. Heap attempted to re-theorize the teaching and learning of reading using EM.

Heap showed (esp. Heap, 1982) that teachers engage in a range of activities that are not endorsed, or even recognized, by any of the currently popular theories of reading acquisition and pedagogy, including those variants explicitly named by the participating teachers as characterizing their practice. The warrant for these 'unclaimed' activities Heap showed to arise from the sequential interactive demands of the lesson. That is, these activities could be accounted for because they made available propositional and procedural knowledge that enhanced the probability of the students' participation in later classroom activities. It is this participation in sequences of reading lessons that educators take to be crucial to the efficacy of both teaching and learning early reading. This, again, is a consideration not provided for in most accounts of these topics.

What was needed, Heap contended, was to approach reading acquisition and teaching from a Cultural-Science perspective, treating the theorizations and assumptions that teachers and parents worked with as phenomena to be explained in their own rights, and beginning with the details of the actual activities, as sequences of socio-cultural practice, rather than as good, bad or indifferent representations of those theories and assumptions.

What is required here, Heap and others have argued, is a priori understanding of the cultural practices of teaching and learning to read, including detailed documentations of the progression of capabilities. This work could then locate propositions about the nature and course of teaching and learning in various actual circumstances, where these propositions come from, and how they are displayed in everyday cultural interactions associated with the contact between teachers and learners. According to a Cultural Science perspective, it is the communally recognized features of teaching and learning that dominant research models have systematically screened out of their considerations, conveying thereby the presumption that they are uninteresting, and asserting that they are inconsequential to both researchers and educators. EM in education represents a concerted attempt to reinstate the significance of these fundamental interactional features of teaching and learning events.

Lee (1991) provided four principles that characterize the way a Cultural Science approach directs researchers to particular ways of studying social life. First, he suggested that researchers suspend general questions such as relationships among gender, socio-economic status, ethnicity and the observed phenomena until those 'demographic' or 'background' attributes of people have been translated into ascriptions and their attendant courses of action that are observable and understandable by the participants in the culture. That is, we ought not take it that describing a person or group through the use of a socio-cultural label is somehow, of itself, explanatory of practice. Indeed, the force of the Cultural Science approach would be to treat that belief itself as something that required explanation.

Second, Lee reiterated the need to treat social interactions of any sort as jointly produced, observable events, rather than as products of say, cognitions or linguistic choices or the personality or cultural attributes of people. As observable, and observably understandable events, our topics of study present as both driven by and aimed at cultural understandings and accomplishments – accomplishments with other people, and accomplishments that are recognizably so because of their shared history in a culture.

Third, researchers should, according to Lee, explore how people co-ordinate their everyday courses of action in and through the ways in which they communicate and the locally responsive routines of that communication, without pre-empting what the structure of those routines might look like. Cultural Scientists consider cultural life to be flexibly co-ordinated action, rather than a list of customs or objects, and rather than an expression of individual intentions, aspirations or desires. Therefore, it is people's methods of co-ordinating social activity that makes up, at the one time, the fabric of the culture and the visible ways in which members of a culture explain that culture and their own behaviour within it, to one another.

Fourth, Lee insisted that researchers treat the orderliness of culture as something that is achieved day to day in ordinary activities by people, and that therefore that orderliness can be revealed in the details of courses of everyday action, rather than something that is given as a 'backdrop'. In that sense, we can think of culture as embedded in and built by courses of everyday action, because that is how members of our culture encounter it, rather than as something that is external.

A standpoint for this book

In the remainder of this book, the study of education is approached as a Cultural Science. In the three methods chapters that follow, which focus on interaction, interviews and textual materials, techniques drawn mainly from EM are applied. EM has developed two related analytic branches – conversation analysis and membership categorization analysis. These are explained briefly and put to work in the three following chapters. In this section, I draw together some of the central points and analytic attitudes on which much of the following rests.

Educational research is practical activity

A research project not only reflects what it finds – the observations – as they are filtered through a set of theoretical and analytic dispositions. As well, it asserts the validity of these dispositions as they are offered in the research question in the first place; it affirms the transparently appropriate nature of its 'take' on the research question and of the interpretive boundaries within which the answers are best offered.

These observations reflect in part a recognition that research is an intervention into ongoing activities in the world, not a passive portrait of them. Therefore, research is not an act of reflection on or description from within 'common sense', including the common sense that is based on accumulated professional wisdom. Researchers are necessarily, and therefore should self-consciously be, agents of social and educational change, however we perceive that role. These concerns lead us to reconsider the role of the qualitative researcher as, at the one time, a commentator, a collaborator and an educational activist. The necessarily interventionist role of the production of educational research is a direct reflection and consequence of the necessarily interventionist role of educational practices, no matter how formal, institutionalized or legally mandated.

A view of both education and educational research as cultural practices means a number of things, among them:

1. That significant ways of thinking about and doing education intersect at all possible points, and produce observable order-at-all-points; further, that this order is relevant and observable both to the participants and to the researcher.
2. That the educational practices we observe through our research activities are not natural; they have histories that could have gone along different lines, and that, at the moment of researchers' entry into a particular educational field until they leave it, that history is continuing.

3. That the traces of these histories are visible in institutional, cultural and social practices, and that the educational phenomenon of interest does not exist independently of its history of practice and belief.
4. And therefore, that an educational research project always comes *in media res*, halfway through the story. The order it discovers at all points is a 'built environment' – built materially, interactionally, institutionally and ideologically.

However well or however long the phenomenon of interest can be made to strike a motionless, life-drawing model's pose, the surroundings that give it meaning, the ecologies in and off which it 'lives', are changing in both pre-dictable and unpredictable ways – ways that are central, not peripheral, to the phenomenon's very definition and to the relief with which it can be made to emerge from among its setting in the first place. Another way of saying this is that the researcher's theoretical choices should be aimed at developing and applying a set of interpretive reasoning practices that give place, shape, contour and colour to what is relevant in the researchable field. These choices, in a sense, name the relevant categories of objects, people, the interactions among and between them, and the particular 'machinery' they offer for interpretation, within the context of their material, interactional, institutional and ideological histories. The method-in-action is then a 'machine', a procedural apparatus, for producing 'findings-that-count-as-evidence', in the here and now of this project.

Adequacy matters

The view I take here is that it is the clarity, comprehensibility and comprehensiveness of the researcher's description of methods – as they fit into the larger methodological framework of the project – that constitutes the report as 'research'. It is the defensibility of these methods as technologies for reasoning our way from the research questions to the conduct undertaken by the researcher and on to the production of findings that can count as answers to the original questions that defines the reliability, significance and value of the project. It is the ability of method to act as the bridge from questions to reasonable answers that distinguishes research from other ways, perhaps perfectly reasonable ways in other terms or settings, of asserting knowledge and opinion about education.

The seed of the productivity of a research programme or project in education lies in the nature of its publicly knowable and inspectable procedures. It is in the nature of the researcher's choices of procedures that the potential for the work to inform and influence theory, method, practice and policy is sown. In standardizing the interpretive procedures to enhance comparability across the sites of the project or across other educational research sites, the researcher may over-write or even omit the very features of a phenomenon that render the research valid and its outcomes novel. It is important to note that considerations of validity, in qualitative research perhaps more urgently than in other forms, call for an explicit and careful treatment of the relationship between the original events, the research process, and the nature, scope and warrantability of the conclusions.

For the qualitative researcher, the issue of warrantability comes from two central sources: first the meticulous collection of a variety of observations and recordings in the setting of the study; second, the reliance on comparability of interpretation among a variety of researchers on the team, or colleagues, or other project participants.

Similarly, the validity of the findings is of prime concern. Validity is fundamentally about the adequacy of the re-presentation of the social events and practices to which the research project refers. The basic issue here is to do with the potential for refutation, the provision of sufficient access to the data and the interpretations such that the reader or another observer can offer a principled disagreement. As Silverman (1993: 153) has pointed out, some qualitative researchers have attempted to avoid or at least minimize the impact of the question of validity by characterizing their work as 'generating' hypotheses rather than testing them. Similarly some have reverted to the presentation of anecdotes or a selective set of snippets of the data to give at least a 'suggestion' of the valid interpretations that are available or that are preferred by the researchers themselves. These strategies in fact detract from the credibility of the research project. Without grappling directly with the ways in which the validity of the findings and the interpretations can be assessed, researchers who claim to let the data or some subsets of the data 'speak for themselves' in fact give no grounds for the assessment of interpretation. This work is therefore always suspect, and vulnerable to the claim that the selection process itself and the primacy given to chosen anecdotes lead us to believe that there is only one inevitable interpretation.

I take a view here that is unfashionable among some qualitative educational researchers. I do not regard research of any kind as bricolage – to put it unkindly, as the innocent acquisitions of the disinterested curiosity collector, who encounters everyday cultural practices in the manner of a wide-eyed tourist in an airport craft emporium. Rather, I have taken the view that the doing of research is fundamentally the willing adoption of certain responsibilities, made evident as guiding disciplines or principles of method, which, in turn, accord the products of research a particular status as ways of knowing about cultural practice.

That is, unlike some commentators on methods and methodology in education, I do not regard the qualitative educational researcher as engaged in an activity somehow less 'objective', 'empirical', or 'rigorous' than any other researcher in any other discipline. Indeed, because of the diversity and fluidity of cultural practice, the onus on the qualitative educational researcher is to be, compared with other kinds of researchers:

- more *objective*, in the sense of understanding what constitutes a cultural 'object', what is the phenomenon of interest, in and as a part of the context it inhabits and helps to construct;
- more *empirical*, in the sense of attending meticulously to the anomalies and contradictions evident in the findings, as well as to the foreseen and unforeseen consistencies, rather than relegating some observed variations to the 'unexplained variance' or the 'error' bin; and
- through the use of transparent and consistently-applied techniques for analysis and interpretation, more *rigorous*, in the sense of resisting the 'escape of the phenomenon' into pre-emptive explanatory formulas, into the a priori commitments of the researchers or the participants, or into the themes extracted from other studies or other sites in the study at hand.

I spell these out partly because researchers employing other approaches have sometimes tried to monopolize these descriptors – objective, empirical and rigorous – in their own work. As we have seen for some decades, and still see in some methods texts, qualitative research has been characterized politely but almost apologetically as less disciplined and, in some often unspecified sense, less 'scientific' than quantitative approaches. In fact, the opposite case can be respectably made: qualitative approaches to the documentation of educational activities can explicitly make space for the unforeseen, the statistically non-normal, and the culturally non-mainstream. They insist on concerning themselves with the phenomenon of study as it is experienced and built by the participants in a naturally-occurring educational activity. As such, qualitative researchers need to be more respectful of and intrigued by the objects of their study, more preoccupied with the empirical details giving significance to those objects, and more reliant on the rigours of analysis and reporting, if they are to make their case as distinctively informative and powerful accounts of the features of educational experience.

Research works in and on the world

For a 'science', the first motive is advancing understanding through the disciplined consideration of valid knowledge. But in education, particular dispositions to knowledge, evidence, proof and significance are also 'at stake' with each new project. That is why we often find conclusions to research projects such as 'the usefulness of applying this theory/method/analysis/approach to this problem/question/hypothesis has been shown'. Projects operate in and on their contexts of production and consumption, rejuvenating the theoretical, methodological and interpretive inclinations of the project. Thus a research project, like any other set of co-ordinated cultural practices, is both context-reflective and context-renewing for production and consumption.

DISCUSSION TOPICS, QUESTIONS AND EXERCISES

1. Read the article below and then answer the questions that follow:

Survey shows many youngsters home alone after school

September 11, 2000

Web posted at: 7.33 a.m. EDT (1133 GMT)

WASHINGTON (AP) – Despite attempts to lower child-care costs and expand choices, many children are left alone after school ends and before their parents come home from work.

One in five children ages 6 to 12 are regularly left without adult supervision after school, according to a survey of working parents.

Older children are more likely to spend their after-school hours home alone rather than in day-care, activities at school or under the supervision of a relative or baby sitter, researchers at the nonpartisan Urban Institute reported Monday.

They also found that more affluent, nonminority workers reported leaving children home alone even if they worked 9-to-5 jobs. That surprised some analysts and parents who believed the main barrier to supervision was cost.

'Self-care among school-age children is clearly a fact of life for millions of working families,' said report co-author Gina Adams, an Urban Institute researcher.

The report, based on a telephone survey of more that 44,000 households in 1997, does not explain why parents make the choices they do.

'I'm sure they are anguishing and struggling and talking to their kids on the phone as frequently as they can, cobbling together from one day to the next,' said Lois Salisbury, director of Children Now, an Oakland, California-based group that deals with the affect on families of health care, media and tax policies.

Researchers, policy-makers and child advocates say the time any child spends unsupervised is filled with risks such as injury, drug use, falling behind in studies.

'Millions of children without care in the hours after school are in harm's way,' President Clinton said in a statement. He is seeking $1 billion for after-school programs for more than 2 million children.

Salisbury said parents face new challenges in caring for their youngsters.

'Working parents could once count on a neighborhood of caring, watchful adults to fill in the gap,' she said. 'Neighborhoods are now ghost towns during the day, and that is regardless of economic background.'

Parents surveyed tended to find care for the youngest of children, regardless of income level or work hours; 10 percent of 6- to 9-year-olds were in 'self-care,' compared with 35 percent of 10- to 12-year olds who cared for themselves until their working parents get home.

By contrast. 55 percent of children 9 and younger were sent regularly to supervised care or activities while parents worked; 35 percent of the older children in the study were usually supervised after school.

The survey was conducted by Westat Inc. of Rockville, Maryland.

Source: http://www.cnn.com/2000/US/09/11/homealone.ap/index.html

Questions:

(a) Who in this article gets to tell 'the official story' about the issue? Who else would you expect to have an opinion about the issue, but whose views are not included in the article?

(b) What general claims are they making about the issue (i.e. are they advocating or opposing after-school supervision for school-age children)? Why? What kinds of supervision are they advocating (the activities that count as legitimate after-school activities for children)? Who are 'the supervisors' (the people considered as legitimate supervisors)? Who are 'the supervised' (the people who need supervision)?

(c) How was the research conducted? What was its scope? What were its findings? The report of survey findings 'does not explain why parents make the choices they do'. Why did the research not attempt to answer this question? Can you think of other research approaches that could?

(d) What normative (good, proper, legitimate) versions of parents, school-age children, neighbourhood life, researchers, child advocates, politicians, policy-makers etc. are (re)presented in the article? Are there any contradictions between these versions that undermine arguments and generalizations made in the article (consider Lois Salisbury's statement 'Working parents could once count on a neighborhood of caring, watchful adults to fill the gap. . . . Neighborhoods are now ghost towns during the day, and that is regardless of economic background')?

(e) '[President Clinton] is seeking $1 billion for after-school programs for more than 2 million children.' After reading the article, why is this action not likely to address the issue of working parents leaving their children home alone after school?

2. Read the transcript and then consider the questions that follow:

A So we have a concentration
   (0.2)
A of commercial activities
   (0.2)
A n the heart of the city
   (0.2)
A then of course we must have smaller regional
   (0.4)
A er shopping centres or shops
   (0.4)

A e::r satisfying customers
   (0.2)
A on the outskirts of town
   (0.3)
A Right well that finishes our discussion for Portsville eighdeen eighdy to eighdeen ninedy
   (0.3)
A Now I did ask you f' homework to read Portsville eighdeen eighdy to ninedeen hund'red
   (1.2)

Source: McHoul (1978).

Questions:
  (a) What kind of (institutional) event is this? How do you know?
  (b) Who is speaking? Does this person's talk display features that reveal a particular biographical and/or institutional identity? List the features.
  (c) Who else is present in the setting? Again, list the features displayed by the person(s) that reveal their particular biographical and/or institutional identities? How do you know they are present without being present yourself i.e. list the features that mark the talk as being produced for 'a hearer'.
  (d) Where would this event take place? Do you need to know where the event takes place to make sense of what is going on in the transcript? Would your recognition and understanding of the event (as a particular kind of event produced by particular kinds of people) change if it was later revealed to you that it had occurred in any of the following settings: community hall, hospital ward, family living room etc.? Why?
  (e) What features of the talk give a sense that the event is being jointly produced or coordinated by the participants in the setting? Think about the features of an ordinary conversation between two adults i.e. members taking equal turns at speaking and listening, interrupting, avoiding long silences etc. Now compare your knowledge of ordinary conversations with the transcript. Who does all of the speaking? Who is this person speaking to? Why doesn't the hearer interrupt the speaker i.e. ask a question, change topic etc. given these events frequently occur in ordinary conversations.
  (f) What kind of orderliness (order at all points) is revealed through and by members' courses of action in the setting? Consider here the courses of action shown to be available to the members of this particular setting on this particular occasion, for example, the right to speak, set topics etc., and the obligation to remain silent for extended turns at talk.

5

Methods and Methodologies: Ethnography, Case Study and Action Research

---

Action is a mode of purification

Oscar Wilde, *The Picture of Dorian Gray*, 1891

Along with forms of scientific inquiry, we consider the methodologies used in educational research. The term *methodologies* indicates frameworks for the conduct of projects. Observation, running notes, talk, interviews and texts generally form the bases, in a variety of mixtures, of the data that most educational methodologies bring together. This chapter examines Ethnographic, Case Study and Action Research methodologies, partly because of their prevalence in educational research, and partly because of the convenience these categories offer for organizing discussion about research activities. There are clear family resemblances among these three sets of methodologies, and the methodological categories used to organize this chapter are not hard and fast. My aim in each of the three major sections below, dealing in turn with Ethnographic, Case

Study and Action Research, is to introduce and exemplify their distinctive characteristics – their overall purposes, their standard procedural sequences and the distinctive ways each collates data of different kinds to make its contribution to educational knowledge, practice and policy. Each section opens with a 'starter' to give a flavour, and a brief set of further readings is provided for each methodology at the end of the chapter.

Ethnography and Education

Starter: When play becomes Play?

What is the significance of children's 'play'? How are children's interpersonal processes socially constructed, and how do they change throughout childhood? Evaldsson and Corsaro (1998) examined play and games as part of a process of interpretive reproduction in children's lives. The researchers relied on two data sources: a study of 5- to 6-year-old Italian children in a *scuola materna*, a local government administered preschool programme, in Moderna, Italy; and observations in two Swedish after-school programmes attended by children aged 6–10 years. Observations were of several kinds: audio- and videotapes of events, transcriptions, fieldnotes and participant observations. Drawing out common patterns from their observations, the researchers found that preschool children prefer improvisational play, a finding they interpreted as indicating that the overt rules of games are overly demanding of young children's cognitive skills. In contrast, the pre-adolescents in the study displayed a preference for games, because, the researchers argued, the overt rules, due to their hypothetical, 'as-if' nature, protected participants from potential embarrassment. Evaldsson and Corsaro concluded that play and games are appropriated to fit with the values and concerns of both preschool and adolescent children and that they can be seen as setting the foundations for later developments and activities in the children's peer worlds. The convergence of observations across the culturally and geographically different sites was taken to add to the generalizability of the findings.

What is ethnographic research?

Ethnography developed as a form of Social Science aimed at describing and analysing the practices and beliefs of cultures and communities. It is important to note that the Natural, Social and Cultural Sciences have all, in their own ways, come to lay claim to the generic descriptor 'ethnographic', or at least have had it applied to them.

The origins of ethnographic research can be traced back to the fifteenth and sixteenth centuries, arising from the interests of Westerners in the new cultures they came across as the European empires expanded (Vidich and Lyman, 1994). Ethnography thus initially expressed, pre-anthropology, a motivation for exploring other, different cultures. Most contemporary definitions of Ethnography are compatible with Denzin's notion that Ethnography is 'that form of inquiry and writing that produces descriptions and accounts about the ways of life of the writer and those written about' (1997: xi). Thus, Ethnography is, by definition, a hybrid approach, characterized by two demands on researchers: one as observing a setting and gathering data, and the other as directly involved in the setting under study, including the researchers, as themselves objects of inquiry (Silverman, 1997: 10).

Ethnography is traditionally associated with the fields of sociology and anthropology. Via these fields, it has been taken up by educational researchers to explore ways of describing and interpreting what is happening in formal and informal educational settings. Ethnographic research, with its emphasis on context and 'thick descriptions', has been seen as offering a range of procedures that give it applicability and flexibility in educational settings.

Green et al. have put the focal interests of ethnographers in these terms:

> Ethnographic observations involve an approach that focuses on understanding what members need to know, do, predict and interpret in order to participate in the construction of ongoing events of life within a social group, through which cultural knowledge is developed . . . ethnographers seek understandings of the cultural patterns and practices of everyday life of the group under study from an emic or insiders perspective . . . the exploration will not stop with the analysis of the individual event. Rather, the information obtained from this analysis will be used as the basis for the exploration of other aspects of the culture or phenomenon. In this way, a 'piece of culture' can be examined in depth to identify larger cultural issues and elements. (in press: 6, 22 and 36)

Green and others argued (and see Putney et al., 1999 for an extended example) that the key logic of inquiry for an ethnographer lies in the interplay between the exploration of the site and the questions guiding the researcher's activities. Thus, as an ethnographer explores a site over time, new questions arise, new analytic opportunities are presented, and new approaches to the analysis of data are indicated.

Green and Bloome (1997) have asked the question 'what counts as Ethnography?' making a useful distinction between Ethnography *of* education and Ethnography *in* education. They claimed that the ethnographer of education (usually a sociologist or anthropologist) seeks to understand what counts as education for members of a particular group, while the ethnographer in education (usually an education 'insider', often a teacher) is concerned with the social and cultural dynamics of a school or classroom – respectively, the sociological and anthropological interests of educators. Ethnographic studies of learning and knowledge in education ask the question 'what counts as knowledge and learning in classrooms to teachers and students?' Green and Bloome concluded that

> ethnographic practices – like any set of social and cultural practices – are ways that people in a site act and react to each other in the pursuit of an agenda: including research agenda, educational agenda, and social, cultural and institutional change agenda. (1997: 199)

Debates around the reliability and validity of ethnographic research in education involve the researcher's familiarity with the site, the people and/or the activities (Delamont et al., 2000), the question of presentation and re-presentation in the ethnographic text, the authorship of the interpretations and the text, and the authority claimed by the writers (Knupfer, 1996). One way of approaching these issues is to draw on Goetz and LeCompte's (1984) two types of reliability in ethnographic research – external and internal. External reliability involves the extent to which independent researchers working in the same or similar context would obtain consistent results. Internal reliability involves the extent to which researchers concerned with the same data and constructs would be consistent in matching them. Because it is conducted in naturalistic settings and often focuses on processes, ethnographic research is susceptible to problems of replication. However, these problems have been addressed and procedures have been suggested for averting them (from Wiersma, 1995: 273ff).

The fundamental ways to enhance reliability and validity are the same for ethnographic research as they are for any other kind – through ensuring the clarity and accuracy of the representations of: the context of the research; the statement of the problem to be investigated; the ways in which the researcher gained access to the data; the assumptions of the participants; and understandings on the site about the researcher's role as a researcher.

A significant outcome of taking field notes, the textual re-production of sites and the participants in them, is the way in which the events and the categories of actors may be more definitely drawn, clearly bounded, and unambiguous in the written textual formation of the field notes. Such events and categories may well be more fluid, ambiguous and open-textured for the participants themselves – a process sometimes referred to as 'monographic totalization'. This draws our attention to the issues raised in the previous chapter about the drive to produce 'one-voice, one-story' accounts of events and people when we are presented with the task of producing written accounts.

Ethnographers consider that internal reliability is enhanced through the use of multiple data-collection procedures and 'triangulation', defined by Wiersma as 'a search for convergence of the information on a common finding or concept' (1995: 264). Common procedures include observation, interviews, site documents and other supporting sources, and ethnographers aim for sufficient quantity to instil confidence in their interpretations and conclusions (Mertens, 1998: 165).

Disconfirming or anomalous evidence is important, and its analysis and explanation are important indices of reliability and validity for the reader. Repeated viewing/listening through video- and audiotaping, cross checking between two or more observers and among individuals involved in the research process, for instance, are strategies used to improve the clarity and consistency of the explanatory concepts, so that they can be installed more confidently in the research account. Equally important in ethnographic research, and a provision for which the research design should explicitly allow, is the continual revision by the participants of the hypotheses and interpretations that are central to the project, as part of the learning experience of the research (Goetz and LeCompte, 1984: 217).

How does Ethnography proceed?

As with all research, there are critical decisions to be made concerning the selection of participants whose educational practices or accounts are to be studied. There are a number of approaches to the selection of participants. Each of these approaches follows a particular rationale:

- *Expedient selection*　These people are available and appropriate to the inquiry, perhaps because they are interested, are engaged in relevant activities, show characteristics of interest to the study, or perceive problems relevant to the terms of the study.
- *Purposeful selection*　These people are selected because they are taken to represent instances of best cases or worst cases (e.g., according to some external criterion such as test scores), clusters of cases (e.g., teachers in small, remote communities), variations commonly encountered (e.g., adult classes with a spread of clients who do or do not have the language of teaching medium as their first language), typical cases (e.g., beginning teachers with 'average' university grades) or special interest (e.g., experienced teachers of severely intellectually impaired students).
- *Probability selection*　People selected on the basis of knowledge of the larger population to which the researchers wish to generalize the findings. This may involve random selection, or stratified-random selection in which random choice occurs through a proportional selection from within predetermined groupings, in proportions that directly reflect the prevalence of those groupings within the larger population relevant to the study.

Ethnographic studies, along with case studies and Action Research programmes can vary in their structures. They may be: single site, 'single shot' studies, where one site is studied; multi-site, single 'shot'; longitudinal (single or multiple); or cumulative, sequentially building on one another over time, with the questions and methods increasingly refined. Indeed, one of the strengths of ethnographic research to which its practitioners often refer is the flexibility of its conduct. In traditional Natural Science approaches to studying social phenomena, we typically find the development of the hypothesis, the selection of an appropriate sample of people, the prior development of assessment or codable instruments or materials, the collection of data, and the drawing of inferences concerning the findings. Ethnographers use many of these steps, but draw attention to the fact that, as a researcher becomes more immersed in the research site, the use of particular materials, the pursuit of hypotheses developed prior to entering the site, and the nature of what may be inferred from the findings will all have a highly interactive effect on one another.

Key points on Educational Ethnography

Ethnographic research is an open-textured notion. It covers a range of dispositions, procedures and designs with family resemblances. Educational researchers
working with post-modernist approaches have argued variously for a
reconceptualization of Ethnography, with a strong focus on the texts that are its
products. Some have suggested that these be regarded as narratives (Packwood
and Sikes, 1996), theatre scripts (Adams et al., 1998), 'confessional tales' of oral
and life histories (Knupfer, 1996). Overall, the attempt is to articulate more
'authentic' representations of the complexity and richness of people's lives than
do traditional research accounts. As text is produced, however, as we will see in
Chapter 8, the notion of 'authenticity' becomes more of a problem. So the field
of Ethnography is traversed by considerable debate.

Challenges to ethnographers have emerged largely around issues of representation and legitimation. The first is whether or not ethnographers can actually
capture lived experience, because, it is argued, such experience is brought into
being partly through the texts written by the researcher. The second assumption
that is critiqued is the criteria employed for evaluating and interpreting qualitative
research. This critique calls for a rethinking of terms such as *validity*, *generalizability*
and *reliability* (Atkinson, 1990; Denzin and Lincoln, 1994; Denzin, 1997). In the
practical realities of contemporary qualitative research, these issues become
blurred, with researchers taking on the requirement to legitimate any representation in terms of some specific set of criteria that permits the researcher (and
reader) to make links between the text and the world that is being written about.

Ethnographers put effort into 'bracketing' their own cultural knowledge and
values, focusing on how the members under observation show their knowledge
in the patterns of their practice. They seek to write a 'cultural grammar' that
makes visible the logic that connects members' actions with their knowledge
and values.

Co-ordinated cultural actions are not neutral: along with getting the business
of the day done, they inscribe values and beliefs about who it is that has a
particular set of rights and responsibilities in a setting, what counts as relevant
and appropriate action, and who has and can have access to the material, social
and symbolic resources relevant to conduct on that site.

Four key planks for Educational Ethnography have been identified (following
Green et al.; and see Heath, 1982).

* *The instinct to compare*: the critical comparison of theories currently informing
  the phenomenon under study, the available data, and how the coordinated
  actions over time of the people under study do or fail to match up to these
  perspectives.
* *The instinct to contrast*: the use of a variety of contrasting analytic approaches
  to document what the people under study take to be relevant and
  consequential to their conduct in the site.

- *The instinct to look to the history*: the exploration of the ways in which things have been done in this site in the past, including the texts that have informed and governed conduct, the folk memories of the participants, and the archive of knowledge and values available to current participants.
- *The instinct to move from part to whole*: documenting how the participants relate the details of their behaviour to broader cultural expectations and values, and how the researcher accounts for these details (names, interprets and evaluates them) in terms of broader theoretical perspectives and policy formations.

Case Study

Starter: Can a whole nation be a case?

As part of the International Mathematics and Science Study commissioned by the US Department of Education, the National Institute on Student Achievement, Curriculum, and Assessment (1999) conducted a Case Study of the entire Japanese school system with particular reference to the teaching and learning of Mathematics and Science. In a sense, the entire system was 'the case', and its success relative to other systems was the motivation for the study. The point of inquiry concerned the traditional view of Mathematics and Science education in Japan as drill-based and reliant on memorization and repetition along with the established finding that Japanese students performed well on a range of conceptually demanding activities.

The case was documented largely through interviews, observations, and the study of school and national achievement records. In broad terms, the finding was that aspects of the Japanese school system were successful in motivating students through a 'well-rounded curriculum, using whole-class instruction, encouraging school-related after-school activities, and supporting collegial teacher and student interactions' (Abstract).

In Japanese whole-class instruction, students of all ability levels deal with one subject at the same pace, interactively in whole-classroom groupings. For example, instead of strictly lecturing, mathematics teachers ask individual students to present publicly solutions to the whole group, and ask other students to evaluate solutions. Japanese whole-class instruction was interpreted as offering greater motivational support than streaming and drilling by: emphasizing effort over ability; engaging students through social activities around tasks; and building strong and academically-focused classroom relationships.

Along with these strengths, the study concluded that some students might not succeed well in Mathematics and Science in Japan's system because of: a loss of interest in school; school-refusal syndrome; and school violence. While some Japanese students still have problems, the researchers concluded that Japanese educators recognize that remedies lie in expanding on motivation-building activities and organizational guidelines.

What is Case Study methodology?

Unlike most ethnographies, case studies focus on one particular instance of educational experience and attempt to gain theoretical and professional insights from a full documentation of that instance. Researchers in a variety of professional and practical domains use case studies as a way of conducting and disseminating research to impact upon practice, and to refine the ways in which practice is theorized. In law, medicine, social work, engineering and public administration, for example, we find that it is often the 'case' – the particular story of an experience, the context of its production, its development in particular circumstances, its consequences and its professional significance – that serves the purpose of bridging the work and exchanges of researchers and practitioners.

In education, Case Study has enjoyed considerable prominence as a research methodology for some decades. One reason for this is researchers' frustration at the apparent lack of impact of more traditional forms of research on daily educational practice, and, conversely, educators' frustration at the apparent 'non-translatability' of many research findings:

> Too much of teacher education is unbearably generic, offering vague and general principles and maxims that purport to apply broadly to a vast range of situations. (Shulman, 1996: 198)

In contrast to what might emerge from laboratory-based studies of human behaviour, people's practices and experiences in particular educational contexts have been described as displaying uncertain, complex, messy and fleeting properties, which together call for distinctive research approaches to description, understanding and explanation (e.g., Boaler, 1997). Case Study methodologists stress that teachers are always teaching some subject matter, with some particular learners, in particular places and under conditions that significantly shape and temper teaching and learning practices. These conditions are not taken to be 'background' variables, but rather lived dimensions that are indigenous to each teaching–learning event. In that important respect, case studies show a strong sense of time and place; they represent a commitment to the overwhelming significance of localized experience.

The goal of a Case Study, in its most general form, is to put in place an inquiry in which both researchers and educators can reflect upon particular instances of educational practice. One central premise is that it is only through regular and structured interactions between explanatory principles and particular cases that both educational practitioners and researchers can avoid the restrictive applications that come from, on the one hand, theorizing 'in a vacuum', or, on the other, appreciating the complexity and uniqueness of practice without presenting inspectable procedures for interrogation and explication.

We can consider a variety of purposes for the Case Study:

- In *exploratory* case studies, fieldwork and data collection may be undertaken prior to any specification of the research questions, even though the generic framework of the study needs to be created ahead of time. Such studies may be seen as preludes to some other form of educational research.
- *Explanatory* cases are aimed fundamentally at causality. In complex, multivariate cases, analyses can search to document patterns of practices and accounts as a way of testing competing theories of the issue.
- *Descriptive* cases require that the investigator begin with a descriptive theory, or face the possibility that problems will occur during the project. What is implied in this type of study is the formation of hypotheses of cause–effect relationships. Hence the descriptive theory must cover the depth and scope of the case under study.

So what is a 'case'? There is considerable latitude in most accounts of Case Study methodology on the question of what it is that constitutes a 'case'. Researchers and educators have reflected on a particular student, a particular exchange, a lesson, a school, a district, an educational programme, a nation's educational policies and provisions and so on. Conceptually, a fundamental question to be considered is 'what is this a case of?' What is critical here is a clear statement of the object of reflection, a readiness to describe unforeseen consequences of educational practices (e.g., not just the students' test scores or survey responses as the outcomes of an intervention), and, as Stake (1995) put it, a commitment to interpretation, a focus on issues, on the value and utility of stories, verifiable and otherwise, on the need for validation through multiple accounts of a phenomenon, and with the aim of making principled but naturalistic generalizations.

Shulman (1996: 207–8) outlined four central attributes of an educational 'case'. A 'case' for study is available when there is:

1. *Intention*: a plan, itinerary or purpose, however explicit or formal.
2. *Chance*: an intention that is interrupted by a surprise, a glitch, something unexpected.
3. *Judgement*: the exercise of judgement, when no simple answer is available in the face of the glitch.
4. *Reflection*: examination of the consequences of action taken in the light of the judgement in a way that produces the basis for a new intention.

Case studies are empirically omnivorous: as with Ethnography, the data that make up a Case Study can entail observations, interviews, transcripts, notes, documents (policy, syllabus, assessment records) and so on. The distinctive feature of a Case Study is not so much the source of its data, or pre-set procedures for its collection, but rather its focus on attempting to document the story of a naturalistic-experiment-in-action, the routine moves educators and learners make in a clearly known and readily defined discursive, conceptual and professional space (the 'case'), and the consequences of those people's actions, foreseen and otherwise, for learning and for the ongoing conduct of the research project.

How does Case Study methodology proceed?

Define – clarifying the research question

As with any research project, it is important to develop some understanding of the focal domain of the research inquiry as a way of entering the field, and beginning with a set of initial procedures to which the researchers can refer as the project proceeds (Stake, 1995). This preparatory and definitional stage may also entail some initial examinations of the political, historical, cultural and personal factors that have given shape to the setting and to the case in question.

Design – planning data gathering

Case Study researchers determine in advance whether to study cases that are distinctive or those that are considered somehow 'typical', that is, those thought to be representative on a set dimension, such as geographic region, cultural composition, socio-economic level and so on. A central design feature concerns the level of analysis attempted. For instance, a Case Study can include more than one unit of embedded analysis, involving study of a single school district and a school in that district, a particular teacher within a faculty, or a parent within a community. Such studies involve multiple levels of analysis, with each level constituting a case, one nested within the other.

In the field – collecting and storing data

One of the things any qualitative researcher can attest to is the ways in which fragments of memory are triggered at certain times during interpretation of data, even though that aspect of the data may not have seemed so significant at the time. Retrieving such fragments accurately and efficiently calls for a systematic storage and retrieval system.

Analysing data

Case Study methodology uses multiple data collection and analytic procedures. These are aimed at providing researchers with opportunities to:

1. compare and contrast interpretations;
2. expand on the relevance of the project by developing unforeseen findings and interpretations; and
3. explore findings that are anomalous to or disconfirming of original hypotheses and impressions.

Some specific techniques commonly used include information arrays, matrices of categories, tabulating the frequency of events, flow charts and the use of quantitative data that has been collected to corroborate or challenge interpretations from the qualitative data. As well, some case studies have used multiple investigators to provide a variety of perspectives from which to explore patterns in the findings.

Reporting

Reports of case studies aim to explore a complex, embedded phenomenon in a way that conveys a coherent experience to the reader reviewed by the participants in the study.

Key points on Case Study methodology

Case Study methodology rests on an important assumption concerning the ways in which teachers represent their professional knowledge to themselves and to one another: that this knowledge assumes a 'narrative' format, and that, therefore, research that privileges that format has more chance of impacting on practice among both beginning and experienced teachers (Shkedi, 1998). Similarly, Stake (1995) stressed the benefits of qualitative Case Study methodology arising from its emphasis on the uniqueness of each case, and the educator's subjective experience of that case.

To offset this localization and apparent subjectivity, Stake pointed to various kinds of triangulation (e.g., multiple case comparison) as ways of enhancing the validity of the researcher's conclusions. Yin (1984, 1989, 1993, 1994) pointed out that generalization of results, from either single or multiple designs, is made to theory and not to populations. Multiple cases can add weight to the results by replicating the pattern-matching, thus increasing confidence in the robustness of the theory.

But the issue of the 'singularity' of the theoretical accounts of the findings remains a point of contention. Hamel, Dufour and Fortin (1993), for example, have characterized the singularity of the Case as representing a concentration of global processes in local sites, whereby the site is taken principally to be a reflection of larger educationally 'singular' forces or relationships among variables. Others (e.g., Yin, 1989) have argued that the issue of general applicability relates more strictly to the specifiable set of methodological qualities applied to the case, and the rigour with which the case is constructed and documented.

Action Research

Starter: Knowledge and 'development'

Karnieli (1998) was interested in the professional development of teacher educators. To pursue this she engaged in an Action Research project that entailed community-based interventions in a number of schools in two communities in Israel: one a Bedouin village and the other a development town. The teacher educators themselves acted as school co-ordinators, with an independent evaluator overseeing the process and adding critical commentary. One of the tasks that team members set themselves was to develop a strong analysis of each of these communities and to provide each community with a common language for the discussion of educational issues, problems and improvement. The longitudinal data collected consisted of observations, interviews and document analyses.

Karnieli found that both communities were seen to have large and complex community and administrative systems, strong compartmentalization within each section of each community, little investment in collaborative or co-operative work patterns, and little reliance on long-term planning with systematically stated goals and outcomes.

Over the course of this project the teacher educators themselves became significant resources within the school communities, as well as developing their own understandings of these communities and the diversity of educational needs that their own college students would be expected to meet. These gains on the part of teacher educators arose from a number of aspects of their involvement with the communities and the schools:

1. they imparted theoretical and practical information and teaching strategies;
2. they studied and organized new curricular materials;
3. they participated in the ongoing re-examination of the role of the teacher and, indirectly, of the teacher educator;
4. they managed leadership and pedagogical teams; and
5. they evaluated and monitored the overall process of the project.

Effectively, Karnieli argued that the major impact on teacher educators came from their understanding of the need for community analysis, and for a redefinition of educational practice as entailing community capacity building, alerting them to

> the need to integrate college departments with the educational field, both to develop the field and at the same time to train students for that field as it really is. Since culturally different pupils' needs change constantly, making continuous evaluation imperative . . . teacher educators and teachers can acquire the means they need to meet and evaluate them continuously. (1998: 408)

What is Action Research?

Action Research usually incorporates selected ethnographic and Case Study techniques to document and explore purposeful changes in educational practice. It has been defined by Johnson as

> deliberate, solution-oriented investigation that is group or personally owned and conducted. It is characterized by spiraling cycles of problem identification, systematic data

collection, reflection, analysis, data-driven action taken, and, finally, problem redefinition. The linking of the terms 'action' and 'research' highlights the essential features of this method: trying out ideas in practice as a means of increasing knowledge about and/or improving curriculum, teaching and learning. (1993: 1)

A number of features of this definition show that Action Research aims to advance on ethnographic and Case Study methodologies:

1. It is a 'deliberate' rather than a purely exploratory entry into a naturally-occurring educational setting. That is, it is planned and self-consciously focused examination of changing practice.
2. It is 'solution-oriented investigation', aimed explicitly at solving particular problems rather than simply documenting their instances, character or consequences.
3. It is 'group or personally owned and conducted'. This is a reference to the politics of knowledge ownership, which is discussed further below, and which emphasizes the importance of the educational practitioners' role as determinants of the description of the problem, what counts as solutions, and what forms the reporting of the project will take.
4. It takes the form of a series of iterations on and around the problem, its documentation and theorization, and the analyses that are used to display how it has been redefined and solved. These iterations are referred to here as 'spirals' but are more commonly known as the Action Research cycle, which is explained below. This 'cyclic' feature of Action Research is taken to be central to its core emphasis on the documented improvement of practice.
5. The 'trying out of ideas' is not undertaken solely for the purposes of re-theorizing educational practice or adding to knowledge, but is also aimed at improving educational practice, then and there. In that respect, Action Research is concerned as much with outcomes on the original research site as it is with generalization to other sites or leading to theoretical refinement.

Action Research covers a range of activities that share the idea that teachers' research questions come not only from either theoretical or practical concerns but also from their reflection on the intersection of these two traditionally distinct domains (Cochran-Smith and Lytle, 1990; and see Goodson, 1993). Action Research was first designed by Corey (1953) to restructure the conduct of educational research by studying and solving practical problems in schools rather than the 'theoretical problems' defined by researchers working within the terms and restraints of a, generally university-based, discipline of knowledge.

How does Action Research proceed?

Typically, Action Research involves the following phases (adapted from Kemmis, 1993):

1. selecting the focus of the inquiry and studying the available literature;
2. collecting the data from a variety of sources, using forms of ethnographic and Case Study techniques;
3. analysing, documenting and reviewing the immediate, cumulative, and longer-term effects of teachers' and students' actions;
4. developing and implementing interpretive analytic categories;
5. organizing the data and its interpretations by grouping instances, events and artefacts into systematic, interconnected displays;
6. taking action, on the basis of redeveloped short- and long-term plans; and
7. repeating the cycle.

Key points on Action Research

It can be said that the core of Action Research is professional self-improvement through focused collaboration. Its proponents aim to allow teachers to be both more deliberate and more accountable in their efforts to change educational practice. As Grundy (1994: 28–9) has pointed out, Action Research aims to challenge traditional educational practice and research in a number of key ways:

- Action Research challenges the separation of research from action.
- Action Research challenges the separation of the researcher and the researched, emphasizing the reform of educational practices over the whole school as a community, and thus offering the potential to break down the ideology of individualism in education.
- Action Research challenges assumptions about the control of knowledge.
- Action Research challenges assumptions about the nature of educational reform.

The proponents of Action Research (see the Action Research International website) have also typically been involved in concerns about social justice, including as these relate to the conduct and ownership of knowledge generated from educational research. There have traditionally been three ways in which educators (see e.g., Kemmis, 1990, 1993) have theorized the relationship between research and social and educational change:

- As a technical and instrumental issue, where the concern is to improve the observable outcomes of education, conventionally defined in curricular terms.
- As an issue of practical reasoning, in which embodied action builds and refines theoretical understandings.
- As an issue of the joint production of critical social science, expressed by Kemmis as the 'concrete and practical expression of the aspiration to change the social (or educational) world for the better through improving shared social practices, our shared understandings of these social practices, and the shared situations in which these practices are carried out' (1990: 3).

In this light, Kemmis (1990: 4; and see Carr and Kemmis, 1986, and papers in Zuber-Skerritt, 1996) has characterized Action Research as self-conscious about the place of research as a social activity, with a history. It is also regarded as a set of practices unavoidably embedded in, and necessarily informed by other social practices such as bureaucratic administration, academic disciplinary work, and social-activist movements. A question for all research, argued Kemmis, was 'on whose behalf?' One aspect of the contribution of Action Research is that it makes that question prominent, and offers researchers a distinctive answer.

Some Action Researchers view the conduct and products of research as commodities, whereby the knowledge emanating from them is for-profit, raising the inevitable questions: Who controls the 'surplus advantages' from research? Who decides their movement? What are the relative gains to researchers and others involved in the production process? Where the surplus advantage goes is taken to depend in part on the nature of the product itself. Its benefit to the teachers involved, for instance, is related to the centrality given to their representations of the problem, the ways it is addressed, and the forms of accounting, including recommending changed practices, that it makes available.

Conclusions: methodologies and methods

Ethnography, Case Study and Action Research are three methodological families commonly found in the study of education. As with human families, there are variations within each and clear relationships among them. One thing that they have in common is that they are empirically omnivorous. Their proponents advocate the collection of all manner of potentially relevant artefacts and events, including quantitative data. But it is clear, even from the brief examples cited above, that many reports of projects within these three methodological families are analytically light. They foreground, usually specify, and sometimes mandate the frame for the conduct of the research process, and for the construction of relationships between the researcher and the researched. But what is often striking is the contrast between the strict guidelines provided on these matters, and the comparative disregard for the analytic methods that are to be applied to the data collected. Within each of these methodologies, these data include observations, interviews and documents, analytic methods for which, as the following chapters show, are comparatively well-developed. Often reports of the findings from Ethnographies, Case Studies and Action Research projects, including those examples summarized above, consist of little more than collages of fragments of observations, interviews and documents, with commentaries that link each fragment into the ongoing narrative worked up by the researchers.

A principal point to be made here, then, is that methodological frameworks such as these cannot act as substitutes for the provision of accessible analytic methods. That is, the deployment of an Ethnography, Case Study or Action Research methodology does not obviate the need for analytic methods that can stand as the means for producing public knowledge of a kind that can be acted upon by educational practitioners and policy makers. The transparency and theoretical adequacy of the means by which the argument moves from findings to conclusions – the analytic methods – remains the key to the informativeness of a project, and to its conceptual and professional consequences beyond the time and place of its conduct. This is not so much a criticism of the method-ologies themselves, or a demurral from their ideological aims and professional claims, but rather a criticism of how they are often enacted and how reports of their conduct are presented.

DISCUSSION TOPICS, QUESTIONS AND EXERCISES

1. *Starting an Ethnography:* You have been asked, as a social scientist, to conduct an ethnographic study of youth suicide prevention organizations and strategies in your local area. Discuss any assumptions you may have about the causes and prevention of youth suicide and then answer the following:

   (a) Where and how would you find subjects for the study?
   (b) Who are the people that you consider as most relevant to the inquiry? Why?
   (c) Where would you find these people?
   (d) How would you approach them?
   (e) What artefacts or events do you consider are potentially relevant to the study? Again, why?
   (f) How would you gain access to these artefacts and events?

2. *Selecting a case*: Choose one 'aspect' (i.e., person, place, event etc.) from the above as a case for focused study and analysis. First, consider briefly the question 'what is this a case of?' and then answer the following:

   (a) What purpose(s) would focused study and analysis of the case serve?
   (b) What methods would you use to collect, organize and analyse data?
   (c) What procedures would you use to enhance the validity of your findings?
   (d) How might the findings from a Case Study such as this be applied to the field of youth suicide prevention in general?
   (e) To whom and by what means would you communicate your findings?

3. *Becoming part of the action*: Consider youth suicide prevention as an issue and it's relevance to you as an education professional. What role, as an education professional, might you play in the prevention of youth suicide? If you are uncertain, consider how you might find an answer to this question? Otherwise, consider how you might go about designing and conducting a course of inquiry aimed at enhancing your role in the prevention of youth suicide. Do you think this is an appropriate course of action for you to take? Discuss your answer

6

Studying Educational Interactions

> Social interaction is the primordial means through which the business of the
> social world is transacted, the identities of the participants are affirmed or
> denied, and its cultures are transmitted, renewed, and modified.
>
> Goodwin and Heritage, 1990: 283

Why interaction?

The burden of educational work is carried by the spoken word, by its representational forms in writing, and by its attendant communicational forms such
as images, diagrams, gestures, and other print and electronic symbols, mediating
novices and texts – acted, spoken, printed or electronic. Education is both made
up of interactions, and aimed at the enhancement and spread of certain kinds
of interactions.

These representations embody the curricular content of educational practice,
whether that content be formal or informal in its design, scope, and sequence.
Communication is also significant in that it forms the framework in which such
materials are brought to life and given their preferred interpretations as the bases

for practice and for later learning. Finally, it is through communication that the social order in which educational activities take place is itself displayed, and thereby given structure and significance. The normativities of teaching and learning – what is normal, proper and appropriate in this educational setting, here and now – are made available to teachers and learners in talk, and in the varieties of other communicational forms they use. Students learn not only about curricular content, and not only about the communication patterns that characterize acceptable educational practice around that content, but also about the structure of society, the place and function of schooling, their place as students, and the nature, significance and consequences of their learning. They learn these things through their participation. That participation is both the means and the outcome of learning.

Adapting Heap's (1985a) analysis, we can think of these three domains of educational activities as *propositional* (the contents of the knowledge), *procedural* (the ways of dealing with, talking about, re-presenting these propositions), and *cultural* (the ways in which these propositions and procedures form part of broader cultural norms, arrangements and dispositions). Novices are acculturated into these domains through talk and through other symbolic artefacts. As well, novices navigate their way and use these artefacts on the basis of their encounters with the 'expert navigators', in and out of classrooms. All of these domains of learning are embedded in interaction, moment to moment, in educational events. That is, education, like other cultural activities, is 'done'; it is accomplished, brought off, every day, and the culturally-based knowledges, dispositions and attitudes that are both the means and the outcomes of these accomplishments are visible in the activities that give shape to educational practices (Hester and Eglin, 1997: 153).

This chapter is about analysing talk, specifically, the talk that goes on in educational interactions. Saying that people know commonsensically what education is also says that they are members of a culture, which in turn means that they have learned to have at their collective disposal a particular set of understandings about the interconnectedness of their communications and their actions – about what others will take their actions to mean. There is a reflexive process at work here: it is the orderliness of a culture that gives sense to these interconnections at the same time that the orderliness of a culture is reproduced and made visible and sensible – given sense, 'understand-ability', 'explain-ability', 'justifiability' – by what the members see, unremarkably, as the interconnectedness of communication and action, as they conduct educational activities.

All of which is to say that to do educational research is to study how education is 'done', brought off collectively, collaboratively and recognizably by the members of a culture, with a view to understanding and changing practices. It is the interactions in which people are engaged educationally – modelling, watching, chatting, lecturing, listening, accessing, reading and writing textbooks, websites and all the rest – that make up our prime sense of what education is, and thus that comprise our objects of study.

Talk-in-interaction happens on the fly. Unless it is recorded in some way, it is effectively gone once it occurs, apart from the memories of those involved or of those observing. So a first task for researchers is to develop some kind of record of the interactions that have occurred. This needs to be a record that we can re-examine and mull over at a later time, with a view to considering at length its structure and the ways in which the people variously co-ordinate their actions through interaction. It also allows us to juxtapose what we find when we study other comparable or distinct events. While there can be no perfect record or transcript of any event, having a reasonably accurate record of some sort is a crucial beginning step. There are three reasons why transcripts of tapes need to be made:

1. It is simply too difficult for the researcher to record all of the possibly relevant details of an event while on the run, without idealizing or stereotyping the event or relying on potentially faulty memories of the event.
2. Transcriptions and tapes allow us to revisit, check and refine interpretations, and to see the possible points of interpretive contact across the course of the entire event.
3. Close and continual examination allows us to move beyond the 'ordinariness' or 'obviousness' of the participants' actions, and towards an appreciation of the intricacy and artfulness of ordinary social experience. This is a particularly important aspect of the analytic mentality when the events are highly familiar to the researcher, as are, for the most part, everyday educational events.

In this chapter I offer some practical advice, examples and discussion concerning the analysis of interactions using transcripts developed from videotaped and audiotaped materials. It needs to be made clear that even these apparently straightforward steps of moving from the event to a tape of the event, and subsequently to a written transcript of the talk from the tape, involve a number of critical decisions that will influence the kind of analytic work that can be done and the kind of conclusions that are thereby made available. As we saw in the example of Wootton's work considered earlier, tapes leave certain things out and give primacy to other features of the event. Similarly, the production of a written transcript involves re-presenting what is heard of the audiotape itself, thereby, again, giving certain features salience and rendering others either unavailable or less important.

But first, a brief look at the different ways educational interactions have been studied.

Some background and a range of approaches

There is a long tradition of studying educational interactions. Prior to the mid-1960s, the details of ordinary everyday talk were not generally given much attention in research on education. Just as they still do, researchers studied the mental operations, capacities or traits of the ideal teacher and learner, the effects of idealized demographic variables (such as family background, gender, ethnicity, social class, disability), administrative structures, assessments or curriculum contents. One thing that these research activities had in common was that they largely ignored the ways in which the variable everyday details of life in homes, classrooms, teachers' staffrooms, churches, factories and colleges embody and give effect to policy, curriculum, learning, background, and thus to the characteristics of teachers and learners.

In recent years, Cultural Scientists have realized that to bypass the actual interactions that go on in educational events is to ignore a central source of explanation of the inputs and outcomes of educational practice. Even so, early efforts to examine talk in settings such as classrooms and homes tended either to under- or over-rely on the significance of the context of the interaction: on the one hand, regarding context as not particularly relevant to the purposes of the talk or to the ways in which it was conducted; and on the other hand, taking the context to determine and thus 'explain', somewhat mechanistically, the nature and structure of the talk.

Some studies characterized educational interactions, for instance, as stand-alone transmissions of information by experts/teachers without taking account of the peculiarly pedagogical nature and patterning of interaction; others glossed the details of the talk in a narrowly focused search for features that came from pre-marshalled theories of, say, learning or teaching, curriculum or assessment (Edwards and Westgate, 1994, describe and critique many examples of both of these approaches). Below I briefly mention a selection of the better-known studies of educational talk to give some flavour of the ideas that have had some influence in the field. These consist mainly of studies of classrooms, but the methodological and theoretical issues pertain more generally to the study of other educational sites.

Early studies that took seriously the significance of everyday educational interaction were reported by Amidon and Hunter (1967) and Barnes, Britton and Rosen (1969). These authors observed classroom lessons and took notes, with a view to offering teachers a relatively quick and readily applicable method of reflecting on and changing their talk in the classroom. To this end, they provided coding schemes that categorized teachers' and students' talk, focusing, for the most part, on types of questions and responses. One of the conclusions from these and other studies at that time was that teachers' talking styles, in particular their use of questions, resulted in what they described as a 'closed' interactional context, whereby, they argued, heavy constraints were placed on what students could say, and when and how they could say it. This interactional format – the 'closed' forms of teachers' questions and evaluations – they labelled 'teacher-directedness'. Many studies have since gone about documenting its prevalence. Several of these studies explored the implications for the use, valuing and development of students' knowledge in such interactive settings, such that

Edwards and Westgate concluded from their encyclopedic review of classroom talk that

> [classroom talk] is certainly not conducted normally on a basis of shared knowledge. Its outstanding characteristic . . . is one participant's claim to all the knowledge relevant to the business at hand. (1987, 124)

In progressivist and transformationalist critiques of educational practice, from the 1960s on in many countries, these observations about 'teacher-directedness' and teachers' 'claim to all the knowledge' were almost always couched as complaints. Teachers, including parents, were said:

* to talk too much;
* not to permit learners' creativity or free exploration;
* to be overly regulatory and constraining of students' behaviour in general;
* to be restrictive of students' cognitive and social development; and
* by some, to be effectively training in social and moral compliance.

So we can note the built-in moral context in which these findings were developed, 'found', and discussed. We can also note that the analysis itself places all of the agency for educational events at the feet of one category of the participants – the expert/teacher. Indeed, some studies of educational interaction analysed and reported only teachers' talk, as if the contributions of the students had no effect on the apparently fixed, pre-scripted talk of teachers. Equally significantly, some of the coding schemes developed allowed tallies of types of questions and responses such that these became disconnected from one another in the presentation of findings.

A number of research projects addressed the issue of the distinctiveness of educational interactions compared with other forms of interaction, speculating on how this might make it difficult for students from some backgrounds to participate. Willes (1983), for instance, examined transcripts to show how teachers attempted, in the early months of students' first year of formal schooling, to acculturate them into the particular ways of classroom talk, through corrections, paraphrases and close attention to the students' bodily movements and ways of talking. Her book was entitled *Children into pupils*, indicating that this process was the major institutional accomplishment of the early years of schooling. She also concluded that, in spite of all this evident work, teachers took a great deal for granted about children's interactional knowledge and about the 'naturalness' of the classroom as an interactive environment. Along with much regulation and correction, Willes observed little explicit guidance in many of the interactional expectations, and in the ways in which these procedures might be related to how young people could learn in the classroom.

These claims about a lack of interactional guidance and taken-for-grantedness were pursued in several studies that explored 'mismatches' between the talk of different kinds of homes and the talk of the classroom. The idea that some children are faced with unfamiliar or even impenetrable patterns of talk in school, compared with what they know about talking at home, is a powerful and recurring one in the literature on the relationships between schooling and social class, gender and ethnicity.

This 'mismatch' hypothesis – that aspects of the organization and conduct of schooling relate more closely to some home backgrounds than others, and that variations in educational achievement can be thus explained – has dominated much work on education and interaction (e.g., Bernstein, 1971, 1975; Tizard and Hughes, 1985; Wells and Wells, 1984). These accounts have explored and documented the proposition that it is the degree of contrast with the home that is the main explanatory point, rather than variations in the features of the educational experiences themselves, or the capabilities of teachers or learners.

A discipline arose in the late 1960s that aimed to reassess and re-present more dynamically the relationship among speakers, contexts, and educational experience and achievement (see Gumperz and Hymes, 1972). Sociolinguistics documented and examined these dynamic relations enacted in ('cued in', as it was expressed) the talk itself, aiming to show how the details of language reflected the changing and sometimes competing definitions of situations that speakers held. Sociolinguists thus put to serious work the notion from contemporary Sociology that 'interpretive frames' (as in Goffman, 1963, 1981), originating outside an institution such as schooling, are evident in the grammar of the spoken language, and that speakers cue one another into their definitions of what is going on in an interaction.

An important development within this line of work that is relevant to the study of educational interaction is the research and theoretical development offered by the functional sociolinguistic approach commonly referred to as the 'Birmingham School'. This approach focused on the functions of utterances in classroom talk, and aimed at a parsimonious model that could account for all of the talk at some level of generality:

> We insist on a relatively small number of speech acts defined according to their function in the discourse and combining in predictable structures to form higher units. (Sinclair and Coulthard, 1975: 11)

To effect this parsimony in their work, researchers in the Birmingham School, such as Sinclair and Coulthard, proposed a hierarchical analytic structure to account for educational talk, specifically focusing on classrooms. In this model:

- the lowest-level discourse unit is the act, a word or collection of words with recognizable function in the interaction (e.g., 'OK', 'That's right');
- these acts combine to form moves, which signal the function of the speaker's turn at talk (e.g., a response, such as 'Yes, that's right, cats' eyes look like that so they can see in the dark. Good.');
- moves combine to form exchanges in recognizable collections, such as a move that evokes a response, a response, and the evaluation of that response;

- in turn, these exchanges combine to form transactions which are, essentially, activity types or phases (discussions, reading aloud sessions, and so on);
- which themselves stitch together to form lessons in school.

This Functional-Linguistic approach to interaction has been developed in a number of directions since Sinclair and Coulthard's early work. Eggins and Slade (1997), for example, have refined and added layers of complexity to the application of these ideas to interaction in addressing casual conversation. But they also dealt at length with the issue of how language choices establish categories of 'knowers' in the talk and how this has consequences for the conduct of interactions aimed at learning. A number of other studies in this line of work have focused on educational interaction, including linguistic explorations of the ways in which knowledge and authority relations are constructed (see, e.g., Unsworth, 2000), and the linguistic features of student's writing for school (e.g., Christie, 1990).

While these studies have confirmed and sharpened conclusions from other research programmes, they have nonetheless focused on the application of the formalisms derived from functional linguistics rather than on an open-textured documentation and analysis of educational interactions. This is their strength and the particular agenda they set themselves. At the same time, as Drew and Heritage (1992) pointed out, such approaches, while significant in the ways they have advanced on other analytic approaches, have traded off an understanding of the detailed, distinctively mutual, interactive features of talk in teaching-learning activities in exchange for the preservation of the analytic formalisms on which they were based. The parameters that define the 'parsimony' of such approaches, at the same time, set the limits, in advance, on the forms of social practice that can be recognized. The aim, which is developed in the remainder of this chapter, is to strike on a set of rigorous and reproducible procedures that allow the events under study to be represented as knowable and conventionalized events, but, at the same time, as complex and purposeful in ways not necessarily anticipated by theoretical formulations and their attendant analytic methods.

This latter point about anticipation is significant. In educational research, much effort is put into evaluating and improving practice and policy. The approach developed here is 'applied' to the study of educational events, but not with an a priori, first-step goal of improving them. The first task is to understand them as everyday events. In critiquing cognitive approaches to classroom studies, Macbeth made the following points:

> Without saying so in so many words, we are left to understand that we know classrooms already and well enough to recommend their reform. . . . Rather, [the programme needs] to describe the methodic work of students, teachers and practitioners as they assemble the coherence of their tasks and understandings . . . there is . . . in the respecification of familiar affairs as their situated assemblage, the promise that we will come to know them differently. (1996: 281)

The goal of the outline that follows is to enable a different understanding of such highly familiar events as educational interactions. In general, the procedures outlined below derive from Conversation Analysis (henceforth CA). The remainder of the chapter spells out and illustrates some aspects of this approach. CA has been developed within Ethnomethodology, a form of Cultural Science devoted to the study of everyday social practice. Baker (1991: 163–4) has summarized three benefits offered by the application of CA to educational phenomena. Such an approach, Baker pointed out:

1. puts the study of educational events in the middle of actual, concrete practices, rather than in psychological or sociological processes that no one can see. Thus we make educational events directly observable and study-able.
2. emphasizes the view that learners need to work out what it means to 'learn' by actually participating in exchanges as speakers, listeners and witnesses. Similarly, teachers' understandings and evaluations of 'learning' 'can only come from witnessing particular instances of student performance' (1991: 163). So it is these actual instances that deserve close attention in their own right, rather than, in the first instance, whether or not they fulfil or fail to fulfil some theory of teaching or learning.
3. gives us some principled, publicly available methods of analysis for examining how actual educational events occurred and what, then and there, were the consequences of their occurring in those ways.

We now turn to some basic features of data collection, transcription and analysis, starting with some simple examples. The chapter concludes with a summary of the major ideas on which the following procedures are based. The approach to studying and analysing educational interactions sketched here generally applies to the procedures used in CA (see, e.g., Baker, 1997; Drew and Heritage, 1992; Fehr et al.; www.bekkoame.ne.jp/~mizukawa/EM/bib/bib-comp.html; Heap, 1997; ten Have: www.pscw.uva.nl/emca/ resource.html). Briefly, this approach involves a detailed examination of the conversational features at work in spoken interactions. In this approach, the 'focus is on the particular actions that occur in the same context, their underlying social organization, and the alternative means by which these actions and the activities they compose can be realized' (Drew and Heritage, 1992: 17).

Prior to exploring some of the ways in which transcripts can be used, we need a general format for the collection and analysis of interactional data. A template is provided by ten Have (1999a), who listed the following set of procedures as an idealized form of collecting and studying talk in interaction:

1. Create mechanical recordings of some kind, for example audio- or videotaped records.
2. From there, create a transcript and check this transcript for accuracy against the recording.

3. Select episodes or exchanges for particular study. These episodes or exchanges may be selected because they are: (a) a particular set of practices, for example the openings of lessons; (b) 'candidate phenomena' such as classroom discussions, or 'virtuoso moments' in which some particular interactional or, more broadly, educational accomplishment is evident in the talk.
4. Make sense of the episode initially in common-sense ways comparable with the ways in which the participants evidently make sense of what is going on, that is, how they know the actions are in fact interconnected.
5. Use the details of talk in interaction and the researcher's members' knowledge to provide explication of these exchanges.
6. Elaborate the hearings and look for what follows in subsequent apparent hearings.
7. Compare these explications with the explications of other kinds of events or phenomena in the setting or from other settings.

Much of what follows in this chapter is an elaboration of steps 4 and 5 above – making sense of and explicating data. But we begin with some ways of representing talk on paper.

Working with talk: conventions for getting from sounds to data

To begin our consideration of these matters, we consider the following non-annotated re-presentation of a small event in the world. Ann is three months old. Mother is changing her nappy. Example 6.1(a) shows the written notes initially taken from the videotape.

EXAMPLE 6.1(a) *What a nice little wind (adapted from Snow, 1977)*

'Note: Ann smiles and makes noises throughout.
M: Ooh what a nice little smile yes isn't that nice there that's a nice little smile what a nice little wind as well yes that's better isn't it yes yes yes there's a nice little noise gh, gh, gh, gr, gr, ooh you don't feel like it do you no I wasn't making that noise I wasn't going ah yes that's right.'

We can now revisit the tape and expand on what we can learn from the application of the following conventions, developed within CA. These conventions are summarized briefly below, but there are many other forms of annotation that could be applied, and you are referred to Jefferson (1984), Heritage (1984), and Button and Lee (1987) for a fuller set of transcription conventions.

*   // means interruption;
*   [means beginning of overlapping talk;

-] means end of overlapping talk;
- (talk) shows transcriber's best guess at difficult-to-transcribe talk;
- ((comment)) shows transcriber's comment about talk or about actions observed at time of talk;
- (x.0) means a pause of about x seconds; (.) is sometimes used to indicate a brief untimed pause;
- talk indicates emphasized talk relative to the surrounding talk;
- ta::alk means elongated vowel sound;
- = connects 'latched' or 'unseparated' or closely connected utterances;
- arrows indicate marked rising ↑ or falling ↓ shifts in intonation;
- punctuation marks are used to indicate intonation – a period shows a stopping fall in time; a comma shows continuing intonation; a question mark shows rising inflection;
- (   ) indicates untranscribable talk;
- words-that-are-run-together.

Using these conventions, we can re-present Example 6.1(a) in a new and more detailed form, as shown in Example 6.1(b). As you read this exchange, you should refer to the conventions listed above and try to 'bring the event to life' with the extra information that these conventions provide.

EXAMPLE 6.1(b) *That's better, isn't it? (adapted from Snow, 1977)*

1. A ((smiles))
2. M O:oh (.5) what a nice little smile (1.5) ye:::es, isn't that nice ↑ (1) there that's a nice ↑ little [smile.]
3. A   [((burps))]=
4. M =What a nice little wind ↑ as well. (1.5) Yes, that's better, isn't it? (1) Yes (1) ye:es=
5. A =v:::vk
6. M Ye:es. (1) there's a nice little noise (1.5) gh [gh, gh, grrrrrr]
7. A   [a:::::::::::::ah]
8. M O::oh you don't feel like it do you? ↑
9. A a:::::[:::a]
10. M   [No] I wasn't making that ↑ noise (1.5) I wasn't going a:::a=
11. A =a:::a
12. M Yes, that's right.

New understandings are made available when we revisit the videotape and apply the transcription conventions. Furthermore, this new information is crucial to the ways in which we may interpret what is going on here. For example, we now see that mother is not speaking monologically, but is actually responding to various kinds of sounds that Ann makes. Ann's noises do not function as 'background' at all. Both speakers initiate turns in a moderately co-ordinated sequence. One crucial purpose of such detailed transcription is to reveal what we now see as the *sequential* nature of talk as it unfolds interactively among speakers. We see as well that Ann sometimes produces her utterances at moments that we would describe as inappropriate spots to come into the flow of the talk, were she an experienced speaker. Our knowledge of three-month old children would lead us to interpret this as a result of Ann's relative inexperience as a speaker. Ann is a novice turn-taker, to put it mildly. That is evident from her occasional apparent disregard for the places at which her utterances would normally, and normatively, be inserted. Such places are referred to as 'transition relevant places', that is, places in the talk at which there could, and perhaps should, be a change of speaker, and at which the current speaker indicates that the possibility of a change of speaker is available. We see this in the change from turn 2 to turn 3 and again at the transition from 6 to 7.

Other fine points of the interaction come to light in this transcription. For example, Mother heard Ann's turn 7 as a protest or complaint. How do we know? We know from Mother's subsequent turn, in which she named it that way. She showed her analysis of what she just heard. We may hear that Mother's change of the sound in turn 6 interrupted Ann's apparent protest that had begun during that turn. Mother's final statement in the transcript in turn 12 was a confirmation that she heard Ann 'copying' the sound she heard immediately prior to the production of turn 11 – that is, that turn 11 was indeed a copying response to Mother's turn 10. In that sense, we can hear several of Mother's turns (e.g., 2, 4, 6, 10 and 12) as 'instructional' or, at least, acculturational – indicating her evaluative responses ('nice', 'right') to what she heard from Ann. Mother behaved as if she was modelling and evaluating Ann's talk – as if indeed she aimed to change it. We know this because she passed comments directly on her own success in this respect.

Educational researchers have found a three-part sequence – Expert Initiates–Novice Responds–Expert Evaluates – to be common in 'educational talk:

> the three-apart sequence is characteristic of the setting (classroom) only because it is generated out of the management of the activity (instruction) which is the institutionalized and recurrent activity in the setting. Thus, where the same activity is performed in other and possibly noninstitutionalized settings, as when parents instruct their children in the home, there also may be found similar three-part sequence structures. (Drew and Heritage, 1992: 40–1)

It is clear then that what we see here is that Mother was actually hearing Ann's contributions, not as simply noises, but rather as utterances, turns at talk. Mother co-ordinated a turn-taking exchange through her contributions. In a sense, then, one of the demonstrable functions of Mother's talk was to nominate that she heard Ann's contributions *as contributions* to an interaction, and, therefore, that the two of them were taking turns in the mutual production of an interactive event.

We may consider the question of whether or not Mother and Ann were consciously thinking about turn-taking in this exchange, but, effectively, we have nowhere to go in order to provide a principled answer to that question, other than back to the transcript or the tape. Mother, indeed, may have been thinking about this: she could have been thinking about the disgusting contents of the nappy; she could have been wondering why she is the one who changes the nappies more often than chance would predict; or she could have been thinking about what she might do once this chore has been completed. The answer, of course, is that we do not know, and even if we were to ask Mother at some later point about the contents of her cognitions at this moment, she would be able to offer merely a reconstruction of some sort. We must be clear that the consciousness we *can* study is the consciousness that is made public through actions, including *inter*actions. This is a consciousness that is co-ordinated, as well as responsive to, and an active, productive part of social life.

Mother and Ann did indeed produce an event that is recognizable as interaction. The timing and content of their turns depended on what they heard and saw from one another. Further, one of the participants, Mother, was actively shaping and evaluating the turns of the other. She did this by asking questions and by explicit evaluations. Mother and Ann used routines that our culture makes available, whether or not some conscious, computational thinking is going on about these routines. All this is made evident to us as analysts, just as mother's contributions are made evident to Ann and vice versa.

My main point in using Examples 6.1(a) and 6.1(b) has been to demonstrate the transcription conventions and to show how these can capture aspects of everyday, unremarkable social practices that are consequential to our interpretation of those practices. The accurate application of transcription conventions is a critical part of the claim for interpretive validity. As with all real-life examples, much goes on in Example 6.1(b). While transcriptions and interpretations can be endlessly revised, details such as pauses, emphases and inflections give us the grounds for testing our interpretations. In the sections that follow, we proceed through six 'analytic passes':

1. taking turns at talk;
2. building exchanges;
3. parties, alliances and talk;
4. interactional trouble and repair;
5. preferences and accountability; and
6. institutional categories and the question of identity.

Each of these builds on previous points, and each is aimed at consolidating a particular set of interpretations and the anchors these have to the actual events under study.

How to explicate? Six analytic passes

1. Taking turns

Studies of talk in interaction have demonstrated the importance of under-standing how turns are taken and allocated in any particular interactive event. In essence, the way a conversation proceeds – what it is about, how it unfolds and what might or might not be its significance – depends crucially on *who* it is that gets to talk, *when* they get to talk, and what the *consequences* of their contributions can be seen to be. One of the important initial contributions to this study was reported by Sacks, Schegloff and Jefferson (1974). These authors argued that turn-taking is not random or whimsical, but that it constitutes a 'system', and that this turn-taking system is a basic form of organization for conversation. There is a 'relative distribution' of speaking turns in conversation, analogous to how goods and services are distributed differently in different kinds of economies. For example, turn-taking can be allocated as the talk progresses, in informal ways, or pre-allocated, in more formal ways. Sacks and others found that the main characteristics of turn-taking systems in ordinary, mundane conversation are:

- in conversation, the speaker changes;
- overwhelmingly, one party talks at a time, and the 'party' may be a person or a group;
- occurrences of more than one speaker at a time are common, but brief;
- transitions from one turn to the next, with no gap and no overlap, are common. Together with transitions characterized by a slight gap or a slight overlap, they make up the vast majority of transitions;
- turn order is not fixed but varies (for example, if there are three speakers, then it will be rare to find that the order of the turn taking is A–B–C, A–B–C, and so on);
- turn size is not fixed, but varies (some turns are very long; some turns are very short);
- the length of conversation is not specified in advance;
- what parties say is not specified in advance;
- the distribution of turns is not specified in advance;
- the number of parties in a conversation can vary;
- talk can be continuous or discontinuous;
- turn-allocation techniques are obviously used. Current speakers may select next speakers (as when they address a question to another party); or parties may self-select in starting to talk;
- various turn-constructional units are employed. For example, turns can be 'bits' of statements or sentences or one word long or they can be whole sentences or more;
- repair mechanisms exist for dealing with turn-taking errors and violations.

For example, if two parties find themselves talking at the same time, one of them will stop prematurely and the trouble will generally be repaired in some way.

These points can be illustrated by a brief examination of a stretch of absolutely mundane, everyday interaction over the dinner table, provided below in Example 6.2. As with most of the examples used throughout this chapter, it is helpful to read through the example of interaction first, and later take into account the commentary notes provided. The aim is to get a feeling for the unremarkability of this talk and a general idea of what it may have been like as it happened. But keep in mind that the data under analysis relate to the *transcript* itself, not some speculation about what else we might have recorded that might have been going on. In this case, there are two points to this example: to observe the smoothness of the turn-taking system and the ways in which it is put to work without any apparent difficulty, effort or explicit attention on the part of the speakers; and to get a sense of what is left out of an event-in-action when it is converted into a transcript. The speakers were a mother (M) and father (F) and two children – Ben (B), aged 7 years and Kelly (K), aged 3 years. It was mid-way through dinner, and F and B had been discussing the games B played in the breaks at school. M, who had earlier helped B unpack his school bag, then directed the talk to B.

EXAMPLE 6.2 *You'll end up as bright as your dad*

Transcript	Comments
1. M So, what else did you do at school today?	The turn is explicitly handed to Ben.
2. B Mmmm	B acknowledges that it is his turn.
3. M Why didn't you get a library book? ↑	M hears the answer as uncertain and specifies a topic within her larger question.
4. B I've still got mine here=	B provides an answer.
5. M =Did you forget to take them back? ↑ (1)	The answer is quickly characterized as incomplete, that there is something unanswered.
6. F He got another award for his homework too.	F takes an unbidded turn, shifting the topic.
7. M Did you? ↑ When did you get another award, where is it? ↑	The shift is accepted; another question is put by M but not to the previous speaker, F.
8. B Umm, ( )	B provides another uncertain response.
9. F You can't get an award, because you'll end up being as bright as your dad=	F again takes an unbidded turn, again shifting the topic from M's question.

10.	B	=How many awards did you get when <u>you</u> ↑ were at school?	B quickly accepts this topic shift and asks a question of F.
11.	F	Only award <u>I</u> ever got//	
12.	M	//We were never at school//	M and F chop across one another's
13.	F	//When I went to school, mate I never did get//	turns but do not overlap.
14.	B	//I'm better than <u>you</u> ↑ then.	B chops across F's turn, indicating
15.	M	( )	the point of his question at 10.
16.	F	No, the teachers couldn't think of a superlative to describe my work.	
17.	M	No, they couldn't afford paper in ((name of town)), they'd never heard of a sawmill.	M continues to speak apparently to the children about F's education.
18.	B	Dad were you born in 1967? ↑	B continues to question F, shifting
19.	F	mm ↓	the topic again.
20.	M	Kelly was born in 1997.	M's unbidded turn hands a turn to K
21.	B	huh ↓	without shifting the topic.
22.	K	Mummy, I used to be a little <u>baby</u>.	K provides a contribution within the new topic.
23.	M	Were ya? ↑ and you'll-never grow-up if you don't eat all-your-vegies.	M comments and, without pausing for an answer, shifts the topic to the eating of dinner.

This segment of interaction, with 23 turns, took about 40 seconds to occur, and involved six topic shifts (school – library books – award – F's intelligence – years of birth – vegies), all apparently relevant to the contributions that they immediately followed. This shows 'sustained', even though shifting, relevance. We can note, in addition to the commentary above, that the turn-taking proceeded smoothly and without explicit indications of trouble from the participants, in spite of the rapidity of the exchanges and the shifting of topics. This shows 'one speaker at a time, with slight or no gaps'. There were no instances of overlapping talk. Interruptions caused previous speakers to stop their contributions, even when a turn was not taken by the participant to whom the previous utterance was apparently addressed (e.g., F's turn 6; F 'self-selected' as speaker here). The distribution, nature and length of the turns were fluid, and no speakers were held accountable for anything inappropriate about the distribution, nature or length of their turns. All of which is to say: this was a conversation.

Of course, we could say much more about this brief interactional event, such as noting the distinctive speaking roles that Mother and Father exercised in this stretch of talk. We may wish to comment on Father's unbidded entries – his 'insertions' – into the conversation at points at which his son was being questioned about potential problems to do with his day at school. We may also wish to comment on who it is that effects topic shifts, or on the nature of the relatively sudden series of interruptions that occurs around the middle of the segment (turns 10–14). Issues such as these will be revisited as this chapter proceeds, but the main point of this brief example and the commentary provided has been to bring to the fore the intricate but highly taken-for-granted nature of the ways in which we take turns at talk, to make those ways, those systematic methods, into a visible and interesting problem.

2. Building exchanges

Let's extend some of these ideas by examining a transcript of an interaction between a Mother and a boy aged two years and nine months called William, again developed from a video recording. We can see intuitively that this interaction is more evidently 'educational', but, as with the obviousness of turn-taking, the task is to establish, from the data, how that is, this time, here and now, and how we see it. We look now beyond pairs of turns, at the ways in which turns at talk are co-ordinated into larger collections, directed at particular topics or tasks within an interaction.

Mother and William are in a waiting room, and William has just brought Mother a book from a pile of books on the table. (Note: Upper case words are words read from the book.)

EXAMPLE 6.3 *There's only words*

1. M This one? What's this one? (1.5) ((points to word; W is holding book)) Say it.
2. W Colour (.) one ((starts leafing through book))=
3. M =coloured one (1) but what is it? (1) Caterpillar?
4. M ca/h/pilluh ↑
5. M Ye:es it 'tis too. What does it say?
6. W A/h/pool (1.0)
7. M It's an apple (.5) but what does it say? (2.0) ONE DAY . . .
8. W ((quietly)) (nn) day// ((looking at M))
9. M   //What does it say?
10. W I don't know
11. M Would you like Mummy to read you the words? ↑=
12. W =They don't need words. (.5) ((loudly, pointing to writing at the bottom of a page)) There's only words ↑
13. M Yes, those are words, but I think we start over at the front cover, don't we? ((pointing)) Start here (1.0) turn the page (.5) hmmm (.) turn another page (.5) ((quietly)) that just tells us the name of the book. It's called THE VERY HUNGRY CATERPILLAR (1) ((pointing)) what's that?=
14. C =don't know
15. M It's a su:un. Now we read the words on this page, see? IN THE LIGHT OF THE MOON A LITTLE EGG LAY ON A LEAF (1.0) look at it little egg on the leaf ((quietly)) do you want to put it on the table or not? (1.5) Now what do the other words say? ONE SUNDAY MORNING . . .

We can begin noting and commenting on the turns. The turn-taking was managed in a more orderly way here than we saw in the nappy-changing episode, and in a more focused way than in the dinner-time interaction. That is, we see longer and more purpose-driven 'stretches' or exchanges. William was a reasonably experienced talker, and tended to come in at transition-relevant places, even, as in turn 12, when he made an apparently agitated contribution. It is in fact Mother who provided the only interruption at turn 9. Further, we see that the participants brought off a fairly clear division of interactional labour in this interaction: Mother gave directives (1), asked questions (3, 5, 7, and so on) and offered confirmations and evaluations ('yes' in turns 5 and 13); William offered possible answers. We know this not only because of the internal grammar or vocabulary of the turns themselves, but as well because of what we see following each turn. The one occasion on which William did not simply answer questions is turn 12. Mother had been asking him questions and, up to his previous turn at 10, he had been providing answers. It is at turn 11 that Mother asked him if she should take over the reading of the words, and he responded with turn 12. This can be heard as an attempt to prevent Mother's taking over of the reading through an observation about the largely pictorial contents of the books. But Mother did not treat it (i.e., publicly hear it) as a resistance to the beginning of her reading. Again, it is important to recognize that we do not have access to William's internal intentions, only to those things that he made available, and to his reactions to how others heard his apparent intentions. At turn 13 Mother proceeded to take over the reading. We see as well the three-part exchange (question–response–evaluation/(dis)confirmation), mentioned earlier, in, for example, exchanges 3–4–5 and 5–6–7.

There are, therefore, a number of features that we can detect in this brief event in which a parent and a young child began what turned out to be a session in which a mother read a book to the child. We may like to apply a reading such as this: at the beginning of some sorts of informally-organized events, the parties involved need to come to some agreement, explicit or otherwise, about what the nature of that event is to be, and, as part of that, what their relative roles will be as they together accomplish the event. In the case of Example 6.3, we may wish to say that this negotiation takes place in the first 12 or 13 turns of the transcript. Mother and William needed to negotiate what kind of event this would be and what that means for the different interactional rights and respon-sibilities they would each adopt. William's statement in turn 2 that the book is a 'colour one' indicates his orientation to the pictures. Mother, on the other hand, persisted with questions about the words, and about his ability to 'say' (or is that 'read?') these words. When mother finally put the question about a formal organization of this event to William in turn 11 ('would you like mummy to read you words?'), William indicated that the words take up only a small portion of the page. The hearable implication of that is that the event could simply entail looking through the pictures, not necessarily reading the words. In turn 13 mother is heard not to pick up that inference, or the implications for the management of the turn-taking, and a particular kind of 'reading session' ensues.

Along with this interpretive reading of the event, we can note again some additional technical features in the ways in which these two speakers co-ordinate their activity. In transcribing text in this way, we make visible other details, for example, the pauses used by speakers. As with the other details we note here and in earlier examples, such as interruptions, overlapping talk and emphases, we do not take these pauses to be trivial or incidental features of the talk. We make that inference from research and from our own understanding of interaction: it is clear that pauses are not trivial – they carry meaning. One of the meanings they carry is that the speaker can indicate that the turn is over and that another speaker can come in at that point. That is, a speaker may make available a transition-relevant place with a pause. We see this in turn 1 in which mother asks a question and waits for about 1.5 seconds before speaking again. She makes a similar pause in turn 7 when, again, she appears to be inviting William to say 'what the words say'. We can contrast this with her statement in turn 15 in which she makes a similar question concerning 'what the words say', but, in this case, does not pause before continuing the reading herself. In this case we can take it that mother was allowing a turn for William in her turns 1 and 7, but did not make available a transition of speaker in turn 15 – the reading had begun and the two participants had publicly negotiated the interactional rights and responsibilities for this event, this time, for the practical purposes at hand, then and there.

There is an additional way in which we can see the 'educational' character of this event. Even though the vocabulary used by both participants is relatively simple, we can see that certain terms are used in a specialized sense. This is a feature common in much institutional interaction. Sometimes, as Drew and Heritage (1992) have pointed out, specialized vocabulary choices amount to the specialized language of the institution's core business; we might call these 'local jargon' terms. But there are also instances in which the use of a specialized meaning of a common term serves to highlight the institutional roles of the participants, or the categories they enact, in our case, expert and novice. For example, a crucial and contested meaning in the segment of interaction above is that attachable to the term 'say'. Mother asked William to 'say' the words (turns 1, 5, 7, and 9). William tried several responses to this before conceding that he did not know how to (turn 10). It turned out that 'say' referred, this time, to the reading of the words, not the appearance of the book (turn 2) the contents of the pictures (turns 4 and 6) or the repetition of the words Mother had just said (turn 8). None of these counted as 'saying', then and there, precisely because Mother repeated the question, so the 'right' answer (the answer for here and now) was still absent. She solved the meaning problem when she took over the role of reader ('that just tells us'; 'now what do the other words say?' and continued reading).

These participants, interacting in an everyday, non-institutional setting, and starting off just flicking through books, established a 'reading lesson' for William.

Such an event was organized through the accomplishment of Mother's expert status and William's novice status. Mother and William produced an educational event, regardless of how interesting or effective we or others may consider it. In fact, the event continued for another eight minutes or so in which William's only contributions were 'don't know', 'yes', 'no', and repetitions of words as requested by Mother. The interactional rights and responsibilities of these participants were established by the end of what we may regard as the negotiation exchange comprised by the first 17 turns of the transcript. The exchange structure thus is:

- turns 1–10: problem production (that William cannot 'say' the words);
- turns 11–13: negotiation (that William accepts that this means he cannot read the book); and
- the rest: reading (that Mother reads and William answers questions when prompted).

The session is thus acculturational in at least two senses: first, William learned something about reading; and second, William learned something about the structure of interaction in informal reading lessons.

So here we see a focused, explicitly educational event, in which there was an evident negotiation of the respective interactional rights and responsibilities among the speakers. This we hear commonsensically as associated with the roles of expert and novice, or teacher and learner, but it is important to note that the specific nature of these roles, and the rights and responsibilities that might flow from them, needed to be established, adapted, and enacted specifically from event to event. Who it is that takes what kinds of turns in the talk are not predetermined matters:

> [Conversation analysts] do not assume order or take it for granted, instead they discover it, make it available and then seek to describe the manner of its achievement. (Lee, 1987: 21)

The negotiations we see in Example 6.3 served to allow the event to proceed in a particular way. They are about establishing the mutually understood character of exchanges that will take place, and who will take responsibility for sustaining what courses of action as they play their various parts. Thus we can see that some of the talk is 'prospectively relevant', relevant to what will or can take place later, as the event unfolds. Such understandings may be contested or re-inflected each time, but their establishment is the basis of the co-ordinated nature of interactional events.

3. Parties, alliances and talk

When more than two people are involved in an interaction, as is common in many educational settings, we find that the interaction is organized in terms of groupings. That is, not all individuals get to speak in serial order. Even when only three people are involved in an interaction, we do not usually find that the talk naturally follows the sequence of: speaker 1, then speaker 2, then speaker 3, and so on, in a round-robin sense. Rather, as Schegloff (1995) has pointed out, the talk tends to be organized in terms of what knowledge various participants have of the topic at hand, and in terms of the local or institutional roles or categories of speaker that the participants take to be in operation at any given time (e.g., who is the expert, who is the novice). Groupings operate, however temporarily, within exchanges of talk; these groupings are referred to as parties (e.g., in Sacks et al., 1974, and in Schegloff, 1995).

Schegloff (1995) has given the example of a couple arriving at their hosts' house for a social evening. The arriving couple assumed that their hosts had not heard the news about a mutual friend's illness. The conversation on this topic therefore began with the arriving couple forming one party, the 'news givers', and the hosts forming another party, the 'news receivers'. As it turned out, one of the hosts had indeed heard this news, so the parties then realigned in order to inform the remaining person who was still in a position of receiving the news. These parties, then, can be shifted and realigned in the course of extended interaction depending on such categorizations as 'who has heard news', or 'who holds certain opinions on the topic at hand', or 'who has done their homework', and so on. Once the parties are aligned for a particular exchange, one of those parties can, to some extent, speak on behalf of the remaining individuals in their party, and can be heard by the others as speaking in that way, unless speakers signal otherwise.

The categorization of parties pertains to the structural elements of talk-in-interaction. These parties may be organized in three ways (Schegloff, 1995):

1. on the basis of alignments in the course of activities (e.g., those students co-presenting a report to the class);
2. as orientations to momentary co-attributes of participants (e.g., those students who have not completed the homework for the lesson); and/or
3. as arising from interactional contingencies that make relevant some groupings from outside the event of the lesson (e.g., those children with whom the parent is discussing a common previous experience).

As with many other features of everyday social life, we can most clearly see the operation of such structural elements as parties and alignments when something unusual or odd happens to make the interactional system more visible. Example 6.4 is a case in point. The excerpt shown in Example 6.4 (taken from Freiberg and Freebody, 1995) occurred in a classroom with students in their second year of formal schooling, aged about six years. At the beginning of the segment, the teacher responded to what she took to be repeated irritations caused by one student, Joshua. We can note in this series of exchanges how it was not only the teacher who took part in making Joshua's situation a problem, and how the students other than Joshua are recruited into the interactional format to position Joshua as the learner.

EXAMPLE 6.4 *What does breakfast do for us?*

1. T   Joshua stand up, give yourself a big shake, all over. (2.5) ((to another student)) Is your name Joshua? (1) Bigger than that, big milk shake, shake your head as well, I want to hear your brain rattling. (2) Alright then, sit down, did that wake you up a bit? ↑ (2) It didn't. ↓ Did you go to bed late last night? ↑ (1) Did you go to bed late the night before? (1) How come you're so tired? (1) Did you have breakfast this morning? ((J shakes head)) You didn't have breakfast? How come you didn't have breakfast, Joshua? ↑

2. J   I don't know ↓

3. T   Oo::oh, did you get up late this morning? Joshua, you'll have to get up that little bit earlier so you can fit breakfast in, you need your breakfast. What does breakfast do for us? Grade twos. Very important. What does it do for us, Mark? ↑

4. M   Makes our body healthy.

5. T   That's right, if we don't have breakfast we haven't got any food in our body to keep us going, it's like a car running without petrol. Does the car get very far without petrol? ↑

6. Ss No

7. T   No, it slows down until it stops. That's what your body is doing Joshua, it's slowing down. (1.5) Have you got big lunch? ↑

8. J   Nope

9. T   Joshua, look at me, have you got big lunch? ↑ (1) You haven't got any big lunch? ↑

10. S   He never has big lunch.

11. T   Sam, is your name Joshua?

12. S   No

13. T   ((to J)) Did you have morning tea?

14. J   No.

15. T   You didn't have anything for morning tea either? Go and get me your bag Joshua, let me have a look. Okay, the rest of us, what we're going to have a go at today, is we're going to read a Spring poem through, I've written out (the metre), we're going to hear a few more poems from (.) the book that we've been (.) the poetry book that we've been listening to, and later on we're going to have a go at writing our own. Tamara, on my desk, can you have a look for my (poetry) book? ((to J)) Didn't you have any morning tea at all? ↑

16. J   No ↓

17. T   How come you didn't have your morning tea today? ↑ (1) Did you make your lunch today? ↑ (1) Who is making your lunch today? ↑

18. J   No one ↓

19. T   No one, because you didn't make it. Did your sister get her own lunch today, or did Mum make it? ↑ (1) Okay. I've got a little bit of orange left,

you can sit outside and have that now. Umm, oh dear. Are you hungry? Come here, were you hungry this morning? ↑

20. J   No ↓
21. T   Were you hungry at morning tea? ↑
22. J   Yes.
23. T   So you were hungry at morning tea time. Did you tell the teacher on duty that you didn't have anything?
24. J   No.
25. T   You should always tell me Joshua, sit down here, have this, and I'll see about getting you something. (1.5) Have that, and then go downstairs and wash your hands after it, and then come back inside. Alright? Okay, Joshua's going to have some orange and then he'll come back up ( ). I think, we'll ask the Tuck Shop ladies to ring his Mum and ask about getting him some lunch. Right, now, yesterday, o:oh our last poem that we read yesterday, was . . . ((lesson continued)).

In the opening turn of this sequence, the teacher had Joshua stand, and she interrogated him about: getting to bed, why he was tired, and breakfast. Joshua's reply was silence and his turn 2 does not engage the topic. These announcements and the problem they were taken to signify were immediately made a public problem for the cohort by the recruitment of the recognizable question–answer–evaluation format (turns 3–5), a format that instated the matter as an educational topic, about which instruction could take place and from which something could be learned. The public nature of what was by then a problem was confirmed by Sam's bid for talk, which was named by the teacher as out of turn. More talk about Joshua's problem and the imputation of other members of his family ensued. The teacher's final turn quoted above indicates that her solving of this problem was indeed public conduct and conduct for the class to witness. Also public and, in this context, something to be learned, was recourse to informing the family, a move that the teacher named as coming from the class as a group: 'we'll ask the Tuck Shop ladies to ring his Mum and ask about getting him some lunch'. The 'we' here can be heard as 'the rest of us', from turn 15.

The exchanges we can consider in this sequence:

1. turns 1–3: The Problem Production (that Joshua's behaviour is a result of inadequate food);
2. turns 3–14: The Object Lesson for but also with the rest of the class group as a party;
3. turn 15: The Reminder that the lesson will continue when the problems here are solved;
4. turns 15–24: The Interrogation of Joshua;
5. turn 25: The Resolution for Joshua and the group.

The teacher's work in having the other students produce the relation of Joshua's perceived and named state to his learning (3–5) gave substance and justification to the intervention and simultaneously instated it as a reasonable intervention by the *group*. So the class group as a collective, and the teacher as its organizer, took it that they could jointly act out commentary on possible deficiencies in the backgrounds of individual members.

Features of the context and of the participants may also be locally highlighted and made relevant in the completion of any, however momentary, purposeful interaction:

> there is a set of procedures by which participants, any number of participants, can organize the allocation of participation among themselves, on that occasion, honoring whatever relevant aspects of the occasion or the participants they find themselves constrained or disposed to honor. (Schegloff, 1995: 32)

Considering these interactional alignments as relevant to the institutional 'work' done by a participant or party of individuals makes us realize that such institutional roles or categories (e.g., teacher–learner; expert–novice) function primarily as resources for interacting in certain ways, for distributing inter-actional rights and responsibilities. In the case of classroom interaction, for instance, our own experiences and the large body of research available on this topic indicate that much talk is organized around a two-party system: a teacher and the students-as-a-cohort. That is, often the teacher takes every second turn at talk, and an individual student's answer may be taken to be somehow representative of the state of knowledge of the other party – the students – as a whole. But the shifting party formations in educational events are part of the repertoire of teachers' and learners' cultural accomplishment (Macbeth, 1994). They are not in the sense of being applied in a fixed, mechanistic or entirely predictable way, but as reasonable and reasoned ways of managing changing conditions in the immediate context of the business at hand.

4. Trouble and repair

When speakers come to recognize that they are not working with comparable versions of what is going on in an interaction generally they attempt to repair immediately, that is, to establish or to re-establish a successful interaction that can be collaboratively understood and thus sustained by all participants. If one or more participants do not recognize that their talk is causing trouble for their interactants or they do not recognize their own part in the collaborative production of 'interactional trouble', attempts at repair may prolong the trouble. Interactional trouble can be prolonged when one speaker does not hear the other's turns in talk as indicating trouble and does not locate the source of the trouble in their own course of action. Failure to recognize the source of the 'trouble' in their own course of action is most persistent when the course of action reinforces or sustains the attributes of the relevant participant categories, for example, in the production of conventional student-like or teacher-like behaviour.

Example 6.5 indicates a number of these features. This was part of a reading lesson given to young students, aged about six years. The teacher was reading from a book and asking questions as she went along. (Recall that words that are directly read from the book are shown in upper case.) The story in the book concerned a cat that travels around the house eating whatever it can find. Prior to the segment shown below, the teacher had read the words on each page, and asked a number of questions about those words, the contents of the story, and inferences that students might draw from the text and the pictures.

EXAMPLE 6.5 *I thought we'd never get there*

1. T   You ready? MUM WENT SHOPPING AND GOT OF POT OF PEPPER.
2. S   ((quietly))Yummy
3. T   Is he still looking greedy? ↑
4. Ss   ((chorus)) Yeh.
5. T   Look at the lady, she knows now. He's thinking, I wonder what's in that little pot there, do you think that greedy cat can read?
6. Ss   No ((one: yes))
7. T   If you were a clever cat you could read, what clues would you find, on the jar, the ↑↑ ((pointing to pepper pot))
8. Ss   ((chorus)) Pepper pot
9. T   Tom, what clues would you look for on a pot of pepper? ↑ Max you're being silly. (1) If you were a clever cat and you could read, what would you discover ↓ (.) Vorisio? ↑
10. V   That pepper makes you sneeze ↑
11. T   Well how, no no, do you know that by looking at the actual pot of pepper ↑, would it say, this makes you sneeze? ↑=
12. Ss =((laughter))=
13. T   =No, we know that though, Vorisio, we know that it makes you sneeze, but what could you find ↑, what clues would you find on the label per[haps]? ↑
14. S   [oh oh]
15. T   Vorisio ↑, oh Ahmed? ↑
16. A   It doesn't taste good ↑
17. T   Well before you even tasted it (1) that's the next step, but before you even opened it up and tasted, or sniffed it or (.) did anything with it. Phillip? ↑
18. P   You'd read um pepper pot ↓
19. T   Oh, I thought we'd never get there. What-would-we-read ↑ (.) we'd-read ↑↑=
20. Ss+T =Pepper pot

Note the explicit production of the parties of teacher and whole class group through the routine of chorusing in pairs 3–4, 5–6, 7–8, and 19–20. Note also that the parties change at turn 9 when the teacher re-puts a question to which she had already heard a chorused answer. But what we note perhaps most dramatically is the trouble. The teacher named this trouble as remarkable in her last turn in the transcript. How did this happen and what were its consequences?

The teacher first drew on the fantasy that the greedy cat written about in the story knows that food comes in jars (turn 5: T. He's thinking, 'I wonder what's in that little pot there') she then asked the students the question 'Do you think that greedy cat can read?' All but one student answered 'no' to this question. The teacher continued with the fantasy (not shared by the students) that a cat can read if it is a clever cat. The next question in turn 7 (T: If you were a clever cat and you could read, what clues would you find, on the jar?) is intelligible as a question about reading only if the students thought of the cat as a reader and believed that the cat knows: that food is found in jars; that some things in jars are inedible; that labels on jars indicate what's in the jar; and that having read the label, recognizes that pepper is not palatable.

The students' previous answers show that they did not connect the cat, its greed, its knowledge that the contents of jars may or may not be edible, the label as a key to the contents of a container, and the literacy skill of decoding that was signalled in the prefatory question. The students' answers to the follow-up question, which was also not explicitly about ways to decode words, also demonstrated that they did not understand the logic at work in the teacher's statements and questions about the cat. Vorisio's answer in turn 10, 'that pepper makes you sneeze', was his answer to the question of what he 'would discover' were he in the situation of the cat character in the book – a greedy cat that gulped things down without checking what they were. The teacher's questions in turns 11, 13, and 17 can be heard as attempts to repair the trouble caused by her failure to hear that the students did not hear her question in turn 5 as signalling that she was changing the topic from the story about the cat to the topic of reading. Her earlier attempts to signal a topic shift to reading were simply not heard as that by some students.

In turn 11 the teacher indicated that the acceptable answer was available *by looking at the actual pot of pepper* and that the answer that was sought was said on the pot: would it say, 'this makes you sneeze'? In turn 13 she included the information that the key to contents is found on the label. In turn 17 the cat's usual incautious eating practices were excluded: 'Well before you even tasted it? That's the next step, but before you even opened it up and tasted, or sniffed it or, did anything with it.' So finally all of the propositions necessary for the production of the answer are at least available: the cat can read; it is not like the greedy cat in the story; it wants to find out what is in the pot before it gulps it down; it knows that the information about the contents of the jar is on the label on the outside of the jar. So now Phillip can answer the question.

It is only at the very end of this entire exchange that the students, not cued into these early relevances, discover that the question was about reading. The answers provided by Vorisio and Ahmed are perfectly reasoned answers about what would be discovered by a cat about to have dealings with a pepper pot. What the students' need to know is apparently bypassed on the grounds that they either already know, and that the process of the pedagogy will draw this knowledge to the surface, or that the completion of the routine will bring with it an appropriately timed discovery of the desired knowledge.

This example shows, among other things, that teachers and learners work on the premise that the purposes of an exchange can be discoverable through participation in the interaction, in this case, through the question–answer–evaluation cycle. The teacher's continued resistance to explicating the point of her questioning in this segment indicates that the purposes of an exchange can be sequentially enacted and that trouble of this kind can be pushed through rather than repaired by explicit intervention. The provisionality of the students' contributions was often, as in many classroom transcript studies, made public by the upward, questioning inflection with which the answers were offered (turns 10 and 16, but note that Phillip's answer was given with a downward inflection, suggesting his certainty). In these kinds of exchanges, the provisionality of the students' contributions, their 'informed guessing', was not only about the right answer of itself, but also about what is going on in the talk, about what kind of exchange this is, and what kind of response will count as an acceptable contribution.

This teacher set a question in train and tried to provide clues to how it might be answered, rather than hearing the students' answers as calling for adjustment of the question itself or the background framing of the question. The questioning sequence was given a privileged status, and students' answers were heard not as reasonable analyses of the immediate question at hand.

In summary, we recognize, as the students themselves evidently do, the institutional nature of the structure of this exchange: questions–possible answers–evaluations. The students' close attention to the special inferences called for here is part of the acculturational work done by such exchanges. For instance, in

5. T   . . . do you think that greedy cat can read?
6. Ss No ((one: yes))
7. T   If you were a clever cat you could read . . .

The students needed to hear turn 7 as an evaluation (a correction) of the chorused answer in 6. That is, they needed to hear that it was to be taken, for the discussion here and now, that the cat *can* read, and that this will be relevant to the ensuing talk. So when this comes along:

9. T   . . . If you were a clever cat and you could read, what would you
         discover ↓ (.) Vorisio? ↑

the 'discovering' is to be heard as 'discovering-relevant-to-reading'. The sustained and reminded relevance to reading needed, from the teacher's actions, to be the frame for the answer. The repair was conducted through continued questioning; therefore, in this setting, continued questioning was to be heard as re-putting and reformulating the point of the exchange. This reformulating occurred even when the question was exactly re-posed, because it was re-posed in the light of previously unacceptable answers. The students were, in part, being acculturated into knowing that, and similar things about institutionalized interaction, not by being told explicitly, but by needing to attend closely to exchanges such as these.

So the trouble and repair itself is an instance of institutional practice whereby certain limitations on the nature of participation, in this case, limitations on the teacher – sticking to her questioning and evaluating – are taken to be demon-strations of the activities bound to the category 'teacher'. Such practices, which in this case prolonged the interactional trouble, have been termed 'ceremonial' or 'ritual' practices – the implication being that they are somehow unreasoned or unreasonable habits. It is, however, important to start with the assumption that they have 'reasoning' behind them, however conscious, and however much you may agree with any given actions. They can have various, not just negative consequences. For example, the teacher declined to clarify, or just answer, her own question other than through further interrogations. By doing this she showed the students that they need to attend to the often subtle cues that marked the sustained relevance at work in teachers' talk.

5. Preferences and accountability

Exchanges are formed when certain kinds of contributions come together in sequences of pairs: greeting–return greeting; question–answer; charge–rebuttal, and so on. When the first part of one of these recognizable pairs is heard, the next contribution is held to be the second part, even when it may not imme-diately (perhaps grammatically) seem so. It may also be that, following a first pair part, a contribution is made that is not a direct or apparent second part, but which will be heard as an insertion into the talk prior to, and necessary for the completion of the pair.

Speakers are accountable for providing the second parts of pairs, or at least for showing in their next turn why it is that they cannot or will not provide the next part. Interactions thus have a moral order, a micro-morality, to which participants can be held accountable. This accountability derives from the turn-taking system outlined earlier and from the variations to that basic system on which institutional interactions, such as classroom talk, operate.

Speakers are also accountable for the kinds of second pair parts they provide. Again, we know this not from a theoretical position, but rather from what can be observed ordinarily in talk. For invitations, for example, acceptances are preferred; for suggestions, agreements; for directives, acquiescence, and so on. When dispreferred second pair parts are provided, we typically see softening of some sort. Institutionalized interactions have preference systems that pertain to the manner of response and the acceptance of certain category-relevant contributions, relating, in some cultures, to politeness to superiors, positive affirmations to requests from teachers, provision of personal information to doctors, and so on.

We can contrast cross-generational interchanges in apparently non-educational settings, say, in homes, by looking at the systems of preferences and what happens when dispreferred contributions are made. These, in the case of school education, relate to distinctive versions of being, say, a child or a learner. We see variety and complexity in the adult–child, expert–novice positions developed and enacted in many 'on-the-fly' interactions. The point at issue in this section is the interactional options we see exercised by parents (adults – potential experts) and by young people (children – potential novices) across various interactional sites. The following is a clear and condensed illustration of the varying moves enacted in running conversation and the interactive positions they offer the participants.

The scene in Example 6.6 (taken from Luke and Freebody, 1997: 216–17) includes mum (M), dad (D) and a six-year-old child, here called Cherry (Ch) having a discussion over afternoon tea. The family are waiting for Cherry's friends to arrive to take her to a tennis lesson. Cherry, who is near the end of her first year of formal schooling (aged 5–6 years), has been saving up for something that costs a hundred dollars:

EXAMPLE 6.6 *You should know*

1. D   How much have you got there? ↑ (2)
2. Ch I've got thirty-two dollars mummy. ↑ I've never had thirty-two dollars.
3. D   What's thirty-two from a hundred? (1) What's thirty-two from a hundred?
4. Ch No, but daddy. Daddy//
5. D   //Work it out this way, come on.
6. Ch No I got (this much) in the bank at the moment (1) I'll have it in next year.
7. M   No, but how much have you got to save up? ↑
8. D   You've already got thirty-two. How much (to make) a hundred? ↑
9. M   One hundred take thirty-two? ↑
10. Ch No, but mummy, I'm learning how to (take away) next week. I only got//
11. M   //What? ↑ thirty-two, you wont have thirty-two 'till next week?
12. Ch Next time we (get)//
13. M   //Well okay, we'll just take a hundred dollars, and thirty-two.
14. Ch (hmm ↓)
15. M   One hundred dollars take away thirty-two dollars, what have you got left? ↑=
16. Ch =I don't know ↓ (.) why? ↑=
17. D   =You should know.=
18. Ch =Why? ↑

19. M   Can't you work it out in your head?
20. D   What's two from zero?
21. Ch No.
22. D   What's two from zero?
23. M   Never mind, never mind. Okay here they ((other children)) come.
24. D   Write it down. Write it down. A hundred take away thirty-two.
25. Ch I don't know. ( )
26. D   Hey, get a piece of paper.=
27. Ch =No.=
28. D   =(Get some) paper and write it down.
29. Ch No. (.) If you'll be quiet I might be able to.

In this obvious attempt to achieve the child's compliance, we see issues of relevance at work here (e.g., Cherry's resistances in turns 4, 6, 10, 21, and 27, and her defence that she has not covered this topic in school yet, in turn 10). This event involved a complex set of conventions:

1. about who can speak, when, and how;
2. about what (Cherry's 'why' questions were not answered as 'why' questions; they were heard as failures to comply);
3. and about who can determine what kind of interchange this is (e.g., Cherry's questions as to 'why' she can know and should know, as in turns 16 and 18).

There are forms of address used by Cherry when she wished to resist the other speakers' courses of action (turns 4 and 10) as a polite softener when the event still seemed negotiable (up to the unsuccessful recourse to the sequence of the school curriculum in 10). Turn-taking rights were negotiated (e.g., only parents interrupted, in 5, 11 and 13). As in many interactive events, these features were not static or predetermined: the event may or may not have ended up with a written 'take-away' procedure; the relationships were also fluidly constructed, most dramatically evident in Cherry's admonition to her parents to be quiet in the final turn quoted. (You may appreciate knowing that Cherry went on to bring off a topic shift later, an inquiry about the time of her tennis lesson, and the take-away was not completed.)

As with earlier examples, this interaction shows the participants acting out a negotiation of what kind of event this is to be. Mum and Dad orientated to a joint party 'teacher' but Cherry's contributions did not display an acceptance of her potential rights and responsibilities as a 'learner'. Cherry resisted 'doing student' and even her provisional acceptance of the task at turn 29 was presented in a form that indicates resistance ('if you'll be *quiet*' – a strongly dispreferred move for the learner in an educational activity).

Needless to say, Cherry's contributions are interpretable independently of the issue of whether or not she is capable, in the end, of doing the take-away task. The trouble evident here is to do with the accomplishment of a conversation versus an educational event. The nature and formation of parties, and the

attendant interactional rights and responsibilities of those potential parties, are
what is at stake:

19. M   Can't you work it out in your head?
20. D   What's two from zero?
21. Ch No.
22. D   What's two from zero?
23. M   Never mind, never mind. Okay here they ((other children)) come.

Orientating to the interactional expectations that embody the party 'learner'
in an educational event is foundational to accountable participation. But
such orientations are not predictable or predetermined. They intersect with
the procedures familiar to members of a culture from everyday, mundane conversation. However, the speaking rights and responsibilities that are practised,
and the inferences that participants can reliably draw, prove in some cases to
be unproductive or even counter-productive in institutional interactions.

6. Institutional categories and the question of identity

In casual conversations, speakers orient to their responsibilities to provide
preferred second-pair parts to exchanges. They orient to this even when they
do not provide a preferred contribution. Declining an invitation, for example,
is often conducted by various softening procedures such as pauses, apologies
and explanations for the decline, and suggestions of other possibilities for
acceptance. The word 'no' may never appear in all of this, even though it will
be clearly 'heard'. So the speakers' accountability to interact in preferred ways is
oriented to just the same.

As we saw earlier, institutional interactions such as educational activities are
enacted with particular limitations on and opportunities for interacting for all
participants concerned. That is, institutional interactions entail particular parties:
participants are accountable for engaging in particular kinds of sequences of talk
– doctors ask questions and suggest explanations, patients answer questions and
ask for clarifications; attorneys ask questions in court, witnesses answer, judges
mediate and make rulings and so on. By the same token, institutional settings
make other moves less preferred for the various parties to the talk. Participants
are held accountable for institutionally dispreferred contributions. We can see
then that a person's engagement as a party to an educational activity – doing
teacher or learner – does not involve simply a description of that participant; it
entails that participant's place in an institutionally known moral order, a set of
rights and responsibilities to which participants need to display their orientation,
and for which they can be held accountable.

Example 6.7 shows a number of these features. As you read through it,
consider the interplay of preferred and dispreferred moves you observe,
and consider also the ways in which these signal the kinds of momentary

identities-for-this-interaction. The talk took place between a seven-year-old child ('Esther') and her mother over breakfast.

EXAMPLE 6.7 *Go to your dictionary!*

1. M I was reading an article the other day in a magazine about breakfast cereals and they said that ((brand 1)) are pretty bad because they've got heaps of salt in them, and ((brand 2)) are bad for you because they've got nothing even worthwhile ↑ in them=
2. E =Except for the games=
3. M =Except for the games ↓ ((M laughs)) But//
4. E //That's worthwhile=
5. M =There's no fibre in them and there's a bit of sugar and salt in them so they're not really good for you.
6. E And ((brand 3)), with four vitamins and iron
7. M Yes, but they're also got (.) ((brand 3)) are about 36 percent sugar.
8. E That's almost half sugar ↑ ↑
9. M That's right and ((brand 4)) is not better, so the one that they say is the best is ((brand 5)) oats, porridge.
10. E Eww yuck =
11. M =The next best is ((brand 6))
12. E I think I prefer breakfast bars. ↓
13. M ((brand 5)) breakfast bars? ↑
14. E ((brand 5)) breakfast bars, made out of breakfast=
15. M =Yes and they've got a loads of sugar in them.
16. E No they don't ↓
17. M Yes they do, what do you think they stick to? They stick them together with honey and sugar.
18. E They use glue, no, food glue.
19. M Ri:ight ((sarcastic))
20. E Beau::utiful
21. M This is something that only you know about (.) that nobody else knows about ↑
22. E No::o, it's in the dictionary.
23. M Show me.
24. E Food glue, go to your dictionary, ( ) three months ago and they (invented) breakfast//
25. M //This is another case of Esther knowing best is it?
26. E Oh mu:um ↓
27. M Esther knowing best. ↓ O:oh listen, listen, don't do this please.

Note the contrasts in structure between this interaction, on the one hand, and those with William and Mum, Joshua and the class, Cherry and her parents, and the teacher and Vorisio and Ahmed. While Esther's and Mum's interactions displayed some features traditionally recognizable as child–adult interaction, the interactive options they both exercised at different points constituted an intersubjectivity beyond those boundaries (e.g., turns 5–7 and 11–13). The deployment of irony and counter-assertions throughout shows a readiness to use the standard adult–child positions as objects of play. Esther 'did child' (2, 10, 26) and 'did adult' (4, 16, 22, 24) in the one brief exchange, demonstrating the multiplicities afforded her by differing interactive options. It is also worth noting that Mum opened this exchange with a call to the authority of literacy ('I was reading an article the other day in a magazine'). This may have been an invitation to discuss and change Esther's eating habits (we do not know); if it was, it is clear that Esther was happy to persist in the 'informal discussion' format and was careful not to permit any moves into the lesson format. In the end, the always potential charge–rebuttal format along with the production of the expert–novice categories were deflected by Esther by an equally authoritative recourse to literate sources ('it's in the dictionary'; 'go to your dictionary').

Esther's manipulations of Mum's moves were thus both playful and functional. In making those manipulations, she showed clearly evidence for the observation made earlier that children need to develop a well-tuned set of ideas about what adults take children to 'be' in order to take part in their own acculturation.

In summary, Esther made a number of dispreferred moves in this interaction: Her 'eww yuck' as a response to Mum's suggestion about 'the best' in turns 9–10; and her contradictions of Mum's statements at turns 16 and 22. At the conclusion of the quoted segment, Mum holds Esther accountable, in her turns from 21 to the end, questioning Esther's rights in exercising this claim to knowledge in this interaction. This interaction teeters on the brink of being an educational event, but the foundational categories for such an event – teacher and learner – are never brought off by the concerted actions of the participants.

Example 6.8 below (taken from Freebody and Power, 2001) shows us a different angle on this issue. It is a transcript of a discussion conducted entirely in a sign language in an adult training college. The six students are deaf and the teacher is bilingual (English and Australian Sign Language, called Auslan). The transcript was produced through a series of back-translations, from a double-camera, split-screen video. One of the 'virtuoso moments' in the corpus of these lessons concerned the variations in the participation of the students. These students varied in the degree and duration of their schooling as children and in their proficiency in Auslan. The lesson dealt with the giving and understanding of directions – how to get around using maps and asking people. The teacher began by asking the students to give directions for various places that they each frequented. One student, S4, had difficulty at the beginning of the lesson, and was asked to describe, to S2 and S3, how she came to this class, held next to a suburban church.

EXAMPLE 6.8 *It's simple*

1. S4 ((to T)) I would get off at the train station and walk to where I need to be. It's simple. ((looking at S2 or 3)) You know that

2. T   Now, can you explain that to everyone?
3. S4   ((Looking at S2 or 3)) So have you never been there before to that church?
4. S3   No.
5. S4   Well how would you get here?
6. S3   Me?
7. S4   Yes.
8. S3   It doesn't matter how. I don't know where it is. (3.5)

S4 claimed that the students to whom she had been asked to explain these directions must obviously already know. We can note a number of particular features in this extended transcript. First, we note that, rather than doing a display for the whole group, S4, in turn 1, directed her answer specifically to the teacher as if it were an answer to an actual request. She then indicated, at the end of that turn, to the other students involved in this exchange, that she has registered trouble in that these students already know how to get to the class. In turns 3 and 4, the target student, S4, asked a direct question of the student to whom she was supposed to be explaining, and that student indicated a hypothetical answer in turn 4. Again, in turn 5, the target student registered her surprise, apparently treating the interactive routine as a factual exchange. Again, S3 indicated an attempted repair in turn 8, to the effect that 'it does not matter' what the actual answers to these questions are. (Note that in this transcript, 'hn' and 'hs' indicate 'head nod' and 'head shake' respectively.)

EXAMPLE 6.8 *continued*

9. T   ((hs)) If you met up with ((pointing to students 3–1)), none of them knowing know how to get to the Church, just pretend they ((pointing to S3–1)) didn't know how to get to the church. How would you explain to them? They've never been there, so they don't know where. Just pretend.
10. S4   So you're lost? ((to S3))
11. S3   Yes.
12. T   They don't know. They are lost ((points at S2, S3)). They are lost. You have to explain ((hn)) ((points to S3)).
13. S4   Are you looking for other people?
14. S3   No, I'm asking you to show me where to go to get to the church, all the directions I need to get there.
15. S4   There are different ways, but they are wrong. You can go to the left or right.
16. S2   [((laughs, looks at T))]
17. S3   [Huh, ((Looks to T))] [I don't understand her.]
18. S2   [That was so wrong.]
19. T   ((Laughs, looks at S3)) Poor thing, you are totally lost. You ((points to S4)) said go to the right, go to the left and to the right, he ((points to S3)) got lost. Poor thing.

And later

32. T   ((Looks at S4, points to S3)) Can you try one more time to explain it to him? So explain it one more time.
33. S2   She didn't understand.
34. S4   It's hard
35. T   ((Looks at S4)) It's hard? Oh, ((Looks at everyone, laughs)) it's hard. All right. ((points at S4)) It's okay.
36. S2   ((Looks to T)) No confidence. I was right. Wasn't I right?
37. T   That's right.
38. S2   Good, good, good. ((points to S4)) What would you do if you were ever lost? How would you get help from ((points to S3)) on where to go?
39. S4   I have never met him ((points to S3))
40. S2   ((sighs, as in 'I give up')) Yeah. ((flat, resigned posture))

The extended pause following turn 8 is responded to by the teacher with a head shake, indicating a recognition of trouble. The teacher then re-posed the task, emphasizing the 'pretending' nature of the exchange. Throughout the following turns (10 to 16), S4 continued to interact in terms of actual presupposed knowledge. The trouble came to a head, and was announced as such, in turn 18 by one of the students. However, the teacher recovered the reasonableness – the explicability – of the exchange in turn 19 by 'losing' S3 in this virtual topic of discussion and by blaming this problem on the confused nature of the directions given by S4 in turn 15.

When the task was again picked up by the teacher at turn 32, one of the students indicated potential trouble in the following turn by naming the student as not understanding. We can hear the teacher's contribution in turn 35 as indicating her abandonment of this particular task in the case of S4, through the use of the readily recognizable exchange boundary marker,' it's OK', signalling an ending. In turn 36 one of the students offered an account of the problem with S4. This account resorts to an explanation concerning 'confidence' rather than other aspects of the student's ability to understand the signs of her experience in the world. The teacher confirmed this account in turn 37, so that we can hear the following turn by the student who offered this account (turn 38) as an attempt to bolster the target student's confidence and specify the task. This, again, led to trouble on the part of S4, who registered the inappropriateness of the task on social grounds in turn 39. The student who attempted this re-posing of this task indicated that the exchange can (and perhaps should) be closed.

We can see that, independently of teacher's and learners' capabilities, or of their confidence, there were certain specific interactional and thus relational moves made in the course of the construction of the corpus of propositions for a lesson for which not all students were equally prepared. Whether or not this particular target student had previous experience in such hypotheticals in this setting is not known. To some extent, it is not relevant. The critical thing from an analytic point of view is to note the attempted repairs of the trouble, and to note as well that the student's difficulties, and the interactive trouble that was signalled by the other participants, arose not out of any knowledge base or capabilities specifically to do with signing the language or knowing the 'facts of the matter'. Rather, that difficulty arose directly out of the student's inability or unwillingness to position herself socially within the interactive routines (in this case, 'hypothesizing') upon which this phase of the lesson was entirely dependent.

Summary and conclusions

Drew and Heritage (1992) listed four features of the approaches to talk-in-interaction as outlined in this chapter that have a particular relevance to the study of talk in institutional settings:

1. *A focus for the activity*: We begin with a detailed consideration of the interactional accomplishment of particular social activities, rather than with prefabricated explanations such as 'culture' or 'identity' or 'syntax', 'grammar' and so on.
2. *The significance of sequential analysis*: Organization of practical social action is assured and secured through an architecture of intersubjectivity and moral accountability (Heritage, 1984). Activities, in this sense, are about the public management and co-ordination of consciousnesses: 'the sense of an utterance *as an action* is an interactive product of what was projected by a previous turn or turns of talk and what the speaker actually does' (Drew and Heritage, 1992: 18; emphasis in original).
3. *A conception of context*: Talk-in-interaction is both context-shaped and context-renewing. It is not productive to begin with a 'bucket' theory of context (where things happen inside a context), but rather by viewing context as the members of a culture view it – as transformable, and as both the project and the product of their actions. Talk is both reflective of and productive of the context of its occurrence. That is, speakers do not merely act out roles predetermined by community or institutional contexts, but can specify, re-inflect, and transform the context through the talk.
4. *A comparative analysis*: To see the consequences of distinct features of talk in different settings, it is useful to use the features of mundane, conversational talk as a benchmark. Other features can then be related to the particular work of the institution, including the nature of the relationships and the core business of the setting.

We turn now to collecting the main points, made at various places throughout this chapter. These can be thought of as a set of propositions (adapted from Freiberg and Freebody, 1995) on which this approach to analysing talk-in-interaction is based:

- We study records of actual interactions, not idealized, intermixed, stereotyped, invented, speculative, possible or remembered interactions. This is because of a belief in the particular value of understanding actual educational practice. We do not rely on substitutes for actual, naturally occurring interactional data such as: what we are told in interviews; what we code or summarize from observations; intuitively invented instances of possible interaction; or artificially produced data, such as role-plays or laboratory simulations.

- We view interactions as structurally organized through turns at talk. Everyday activities, including educational activities, are organized in some way or another. Interaction is not just an additional feature of human activity that helps the organization of daily life; rather, interaction is itself a major part of the action, and interactional events are organized in recognizable, structured ways. It is the nature of the structures that reflects and at the same time constructs the nature of the activity in the world. Talk is action; action is organized.

- Perhaps most significantly for educational researchers, interactions are mutually accomplished. They are brought off by the various speakers and listeners involved, even in a highly structured and 'stage-managed' event such as a classroom lesson. These are not accomplished, or even 'mainly accomplished', by one of the speakers alone.

- How something is heard – the work it is taken to do in the talk – is available, the intent of the speakers is not. While we may believe we recognize a teacher's or learner's intent, analysing talk does not equate to describing purposes. We need rather to look to how the participants themselves display explicit clues to what they take to be going on.

- Sequences of talk need to be viewed by the analyst as they are used by the speakers – *as* sequences and *in* sequence. Specifically, this means that:

  – any utterance has the potential to be heard in many ways, and may be taken to have potentially multiple functions and hearings in a sequence of interaction: 'The big question is not whether actors understand each another or not. The fact is they do understand each other, that they *will* understand each other, but the catch is that they will understand each other regardless of how they *would* be understood' (Garfinkel, 1952: 367; emphases in original);

  – the work done by an utterance, then and there, depends on *how it is heard* in sequence – its location in the course of jointly-produced action; indeed an utterance can be heard as projected by previous turns at talk, from the other speakers and from the speaker in question (Macbeth, 1991);

  – a speaker's analysis, understanding, and/or appreciation of a prior turn at talk will be displayed in that speaker's current turn. Thus, speakers publicly display and sustain an updated shared, intersubjective understanding of what is going on and how they may contribute;

  – a description of an utterance that is warranted is one that takes account of the point at which any utterance occurs within a sequence of talk;

- there is an over-riding assumption among speakers that everything said is pertinent to the business at hand – 'sustained relevance' – unless explicit markers to the contrary are evident in the talk. Thus, insertions that may appear to be tangential or irrelevant, however embedded and extensive, are heard by participants as being within the frame of sustained relevance, unless otherwise indicated by the participants themselves;
- therefore, no interactional detail can be dismissed in advance as digressive, irrelevant, disorderly, or accidental;
- speakers work with a retrospective–prospective sense of occurrence, taking account of what has already been said and what may be said in the future of an interaction as they interpret one another; and
- current utterances look forward to later utterances, and these retrospectively display the hearing of utterances and may legitimate previous utterances, and interpretations (e.g., a question asked earlier).

• In linked talk, we find a set of prevalent normative systems (or organizations of rules). These include, for example, question–answer–positive/negative evaluation or comment; invitation–acceptance/refusal; assessment–agreement/disagreement. Specifically, this means that, when the first part of one of these recognizable systems is heard (e.g., an invitation), the strong tendency will be for the next contribution to be heard as fulfilling the second part's role (i.e., acceptance/refusal).

• Speakers show through their talk that not all kinds of contributions are equally preferred. Pauses, apologies, excuses, indirectness, or one or more of a variety of 'softeners' are used when a dispreferred contribution is made. For example, we see that acceptances are preferred to refusals, agreements to disagreements, and positive evaluations to negative ones.

• In much talk, especially in institutional talk, the participants are working interactively towards the visible completion of a task (Drew and Heritage, 1992). The structure of this discourse-action is built around directive-compliance sequences, in which components of the task are sequentially described, requested and implemented by the different parties to the talk (e.g., teacher and students).

In considering these propositions, we can see how it is that macro-sociological concepts such as 'power' or 'control' can be documented in the details of everyday talk in and out of educational activities. We cannot presume or predict these, nor can we simply take it that such enactments are unwarranted or unreasoned – 'power for power's sake'. The aim is to locate the moves social actors make in the sequences in which they make them, and through which they make sense of one another, at the same moment as they accomplish together a mutually recognizable social practice of some sort – a reading session or a classroom lesson.

This chapter has been aimed at providing a brief introduction to some ways of analysing interaction as social practices in educational settings. Six analytic passes have been suggested and illustrated, but there are many other analytic moves and angles that could be pursued. You are referred to the suggested readings to explore these further.

The logic of the six passes rests in the end on their interconnectedness and the accumulation of insights that are provided at each pass. Such a cycle of analyses can lead towards understandings of how it is that educational activities are brought off every day, and how they may or may not, in the details of their execution, match up with the formulated aims and aspirations of educators. Natural and Social sciences often treat the nature of relationships and inter-actions as effects of social and institutional conventions, structures, expectations, roles and so on, Cultural sciences, in contrast, turn the explanation the other way around, aiming to show how the orderliness of particular social activities is shown in 'the collaborative ways in which members manage their conduct and their circumstances to achieve the orderly features of their activities' (Zimmerman and Boden, 1991: 7). Analysing the details of this management and orderliness can provide rich and grounded accounts of such educational issues as 'quality teaching', 'effective intervention', and 'equitable and excellent teaching and learning'. That is, the goal here is not to begin with a predeter-mined sense of what may be good, bad or indifferent about current practice, or even of what current practice is, but rather to explore in detail what members of a culture routinely do. A central goal for the educational researcher, therefore, is to study the ways in which educational events are 'achieved and made recognizable in and through the practical actions of members of society' (Psathas, 1995: 66).

Educational activities are different in important ways from mundane conversations and other institutional practices. These differences are visible in:

- the ways in which turn-taking is managed;
- the construction of purpose-built exchanges;
- the development of purpose-built parties to and alliances in the interaction;
- the kinds of interactional troubles and repairs that the participants encounter and use;
- the systems of preferred and dispreferred contributions to the interaction; and
- the production and display, through these and other routines, of activities that are relevant to the categories that the 'doing of educational activities' entails – minimally, teachers and learners.

In educational activities, individuals draw upon, disclose and reconstruct specific, relevant features of their biographical and institutional identities in accom-plishing social activities such as, in this case, teaching and learning in homes and classrooms. In interaction, the focus is on how certain subjectivities – forms of consciousness-for-this-event – are jointly constructed. These intersubjectivities locate speakers in cultural and moral reference groups, and project, in the case of schooling, learners' possible future educational trajectories, their success or otherwise at 'doing teacher' and 'doing learner'.

The analytic passes shown here represent the reflexive nature of educational activities, as well as the reflexivity involved in documenting and analysing them. Participants' actions are informed by their shared understandings of the practices that are relevant to the categories into which the core activities of the institution place them – teachers or learners. Their practices in turn constitute their membership of that category, or their refusal of the category and thus of the activity, as we saw in some instances in this chapter. Their practices may reproduce, modify, or challenge the relatively stable patterns of practices so recognized in such settings, but nonetheless, even in this variety of ways, the event is mutually recognizable as 'educational' to these participants, then and there, and recognizable precisely through their orientation to these categorizations.

Educational researchers are also members of a culture, so pursuing such analyses is not simple or straightforward. As members of a culture, researchers themselves have a strong sense of the relevance of social structure, of how our societies are organized and how that is powerfully relevant to how we do the business of education. To pursue the goal of examining the conduct of education as cultural practice, it is necessary therefore to be able to engage in certain analytic practices, as part of our working with educational data. This is the force of 'analysis' rather than 'commentary': not to presume the relevance of social structures in advance, or to privilege, from the outset, our own understandings of that relevance, either for the particular set of events that we are studying or among those who collaboratively constructed those events. That is, in Psathas's words 'the problem is how *not* to reify social structure' (1995: 54–5; emphasis in original). The people who are parties to the educational events that interest us clearly take their behaviour to be constrained by forces or structures that are external to them (e.g., conventions for how parents and children talk together in everyday family settings). The researcher's over-arching question is not simply 'what are those forces and structures?' but, more specifically, 'in what ways are the parties reproducing the very structure that is commonsensically believed to be external and constraining?' (Psathas, 1995: 55).

Concerted actions build and rebuild social order in and through educational events. It is not the other way around – the social order does not produce their activities, nor, therefore can it explain, of itself, those activities in any productive way. Qualitative examination of the details of educational activities, informed by a theory that emphasizes co-ordinated production of recognizable and accountable events, amounts to an exploration of how people produce social order through teaching and learning events – of how people re-accomplish the structures and patterns of domestic and institutional life through the organization of their educational activities. In that sense, in the close analysis of educational interactions practitioners do not begin by presuming what is normal, proper, or good. However, it is clear that such analytic work is highly relevant as a device for allowing educators, including parents, classroom prac- titioners, curriculum and assessment developers, and policy makers, to view the ways in which their goals, their specific objectives and their rhetoric relate to everyday practice.

Beginning with the details of interactions as they comprise naturally-occurring educational activities can avoid pre-emptive interpretations of what goes on. It provides us with three things: It offers a brake on simply finding what we already knew/hoped/feared to be happening, and it gives us an opportunity to discover new phenomena or to re-see familiar events in a new light. More importantly for the researcher, however, it places on us the burden of empirical proof in a domain in which we may feel very much at home – the most analytically dangerous domain in which to conduct research. Schegloff put the issue like this:

> the lively sense we may all share of the relevance of social structure . . . needs to be converted into the hard currency of defensible analysis. . . . It is not for us to *know* what about context is crucial, but to discover it, and to *discover new sorts* of such things . . . to discover them in the members' worlds, if they are there. (1992: 106, 128; emphases in original)

When you study institutional practices such as educational activities, you probably feel that you know a lot about what you see already, including a lot about what matters in these activities, what is important, and what is peripheral. Analytic work of the sort illustrated in this chapter offers a way of testing that knowledge, of putting the sort of activities that you know so well, and in which you have so long participated, under a new microscope.

DISCUSSION TOPICS, QUESTIONS AND EXERCISES

1. When at home (or any other setting that you frequently visit), invite a friend, partner, relative etc. to participate in the following brief activity. First, record a short conversation of no more than 10–15 seconds in length using an audio tape recorder. Immediately following the conversation write down everything that you remember about the conversation. Include as much detail as you can recall – your 'co-conversationalist' can help you (if you can persuade them!). At a later time, transcribe the events recorded on tape using the conventions outlined in this chapter. How do your notes made immediately following the conversation compare with your transcription of the audio tape recording? Were any details from the notes missing in the transcript and vice versa? Which approach do you think provides a more accurate 'picture' of the event? Why?

2. Below are two transcripts of what might be considered 'educationally relevant' interactions from 'not-so-obviously-educational' contexts (here 'obviously-educational' is taken to mean 'an instruction activity of some kind'). Read each transcript and then perform the tasks that follow:

TRANSCRIPT 6.1

1. A [[ohohuh ((noise))]
2. B =to play with him if he's being left out ?or something from what he (says)
3.   (4.0)
4. C you've? always got someone to play with here?
5.   (1.0)
6. A yeah
7. C yeah (1.0) it mightn't be the one you've chosen in your mind ((noise)) but there's always somebody there (0.25) because you've got a good way of asking people and you are a fine? boy to them
8.   (0.25)
9. A yes
10. C you are
11. A but but Ta I wanted Tarrant to be my friend and he keeps keeps saying no no no
12. C mm do you know what I say to those sort of things?
13.   (0.25)
14. A what=
15. C =you need to find a friend who'll say yes? and that means you've found a kind friend (1.5) doesn't? it (1.5) there's plenty of other kids (.) remember there's Jason (1.0) [Wayne (—)   ]
16. A   [yeah I I I'VE BEEN]
     ASKING EVERY KID
17. C Lachlan
18.   (0.5)
19. A but they all say no
20.   (6.0)
21. C next time you come we'll see who can play with you where do you want them to play in the sandpit or somewhere different to that (0.5)

TRANSCRIPT 6.2

1. A Has this got a good (.) story l::ine? (.) to it?
2. B I don't know [I haven't read any=
3. A   [You haven't read it
4. B =[of them yet
5. A [Oh yeah
6. B [Hmm (0.5)
7. C [Hmm
8. A okay (0.5)
9. B yeah (0.25) too busy on the weekend ((laugh voice))
10. C RIGHT
11. B ((short laugh)) but ah (0.5) YEAH BUT GENERALLY from (.) what I can tell just by looking at (.) [you

12. C   [Mm
13. B =know the words and [that (0.5)
14. C   [Mm
15. B you know she's had a pretty good go at that for her
16. C Mmm ↓

   (a) Characterize the participants' actions during each turn at talk. What
       are the participants doing with their turns at talk (i.e. asking or
       answering questions, complaining, rebutting, storytelling etc.)?
       Remember to look at the prior and following turns (rather than simply
       focusing on the meaning of the words in the current speaker's turn) as
       clues that show how the participants themselves make sense with
       and from each other's turns at talk.
   (b) Do the participants display a preference for performing particular
       actions (making particular contributions) and avoiding others?
   (c) Look for places where 'trouble' occurs (usually found at places where
       a participant accounts for a prior action). What kind of trouble is this
       (i.e. a dispreferred contribution of some kind e.g. speaker provides
       'other than' a second pair part for a first pair part etc.)? How is the
       trouble resolved?
   (d) Identify any parties or alliances that occur between A, B and C in each
       interaction. How would you characterize these groupings (around a
       topic, issue, action, set of actions etc.)?
   (e) Look at the distributions of types of action among participants. Do
       particular actions that are performed unproblematically by one or more
       of the participants present 'trouble' (as oriented to as such by the
       participants themselves) when performed by others? If so, what might
       this tell you about the nature of the interaction: What kind of event is
       this a transcript of? Where might it occur? What might the institutional
       identities of participants A, B, C be (i.e. teacher, student, parent,
       child, researcher etc.)? What tasks are they trying to achieve?

Source: Transcript 6.1 is an excerpt (used with permission) from:
M.J. Leiminer and C.D. Baker (2000) A child's say in parent–teacher
talk at the preschool: Doing conversation analytic research in early
childhood settings. *Contemporary Issues in Early Childhood*, 1 (2), 135–52.
http://www.triangle.co.uk/ciec

7

Conducting and Analysing Interviews

'Do you suppose she'll interview me?'
'Never in the world. She'll not think you of enough importance.'

Henry James, *Portrait of a Lady*, 1881

The deceptive complexity of interviews

Just as educational practices operate in and with continuously changing cultural configurations, they also reshape and redirect those configurations. Both formal and informal educational activities can reflect, adapt or reconstruct cultural practices. One of the ways in which changes over time, and local, community and social variations can be documented is through an exploration of the accounts by which members of a culture construe the significance and nature of educational practices. As they do this, people also describe the relationships among educational practices on the one hand, and, on the other, considerations such as social order, work, individual differences, human and cultural development, and so on. A common and apparently straightforward method for documenting these accounts is through interviewing. But is interviewing as straightforward a procedure for data collection as it may first appear?

To explore that question I first tell a story about a famous interview study that opened up many of the issues with which contemporary analysts of interview techniques are concerned. I then deal with the fundamental realization that interviews are special cases of talk – co-ordinated interactions – and the consequences of that realization for a rigorous treatment of interview materials. I proceed to show some ways in which interview materials can be approached with an eye to the internal structure of the speakers' accounts of the world – the categories they use to carve up social experience and the descriptive and moral implications of those categories. Finally I deal with the significance of the ways in which speakers use certain strategies, such as the implication of rights and responsibilities, category use and list formations, to build up the fundamental explanatory structures they deploy in order to dramatize and add weight and credibility to those structures. The overall aims of the chapter are to provide a set of cautionary notes about the naïve treatment of interview materials, and to outline a set of analytic procedures. These procedures are aimed at allowing researchers to draw reliable conclusions that do not sell the reader short on the diversity of people's views on complex issues, and that do not sell the people who are the objects of study short on the artfulness and sophistication with which they can convey those views.

A final prefatory point: most approaches to interviewing in educational research draw a distinction based on the degree of latitude given the interviewees. Thus we commonly see a three-part taxonomy: structured or fixed-response, semi-structured and open-ended interviews. *Structured or fixed-response* interviews are those that restrict the domains of relevance of the talk to a predetermined set of questions and thus, by inference, a set of possible answers. Any materials outside of that domain of relevance are not sought, not recorded, and/or not taken into account in the compilation or analyses of the data. Structured interviews aim to keep the focus of the talk tight, the data collection focused and efficient, and the compilation of data straightforward. *Semi-structured* interviews begin with a predetermined set of questions, but allow some latitude in the breadth of relevance. To some extent, what is taken to be relevant *to the interviewee* is pursued. This means that the interviewer will follow particular lines of talk with ad hoc follow-through questions. The talk is typically then tabulated or transcribed in full and the researcher may decide what to analyse in depth, depending on the patterns and themes that emerge. The researcher may also find that the issues guiding the research in the first place need to be adapted, re-tuned, or even changed comprehensively in the light of the statements of the interviewees. Semi-structured interviews aim to have something of the best of both worlds by establishing a core of issues to be covered, but at the same time leaving the sequence and the relevances of the interviewee free to vary, around and out from that core. *Open-ended* interviews are further along this continuum, in which perhaps only a few highly general questions or issues are put to the interviewee who is free to answer and direct the talk. Such approaches aim to make the interview session less artificial, even if in doing so they can make the interview data less directly comparable across the group of people interviewed for a project.

But however structured the format of the interview or the intentions of the interviewer, the participants are engaged in interaction, and the relevance patterns of interaction will obtain. Interviewees will provide their analyses of what they hear in their talk and will proceed to answer in terms they deem, at that moment, to be relevant to the specific question, to the ongoing and developing context, and to their understandings of their interactional rights and responsibilities. Indeed, as we will see, the force of the prior structuring of an interview format weighs more significantly on the interviewer. He or she may need to re-put questions that have been effectively answered, or to name as 'digressions' statements or lines of interpretation produced by the interviewee, or to re-install or shift topics, perhaps with some degree of interactional aggression. As with all interactions, these moves become part of the context and relevance patterns of an interview, and need to be taken into account in any serious attempt to analyse 'what happened' with any fidelity.

This chapter takes these issues into account, rather than allocating them to the status of 'noise' or 'static'. It is no longer theoretically or empirically warrantable to treat interviews as transparent windows onto people's stable, self-contained knowledge or beliefs about a topic. This observation was presented most forcefully in a classic interview study from some years ago, which is worth some extended attention at this point.

A tale of two veracities

Beginining with the innocent aim of exploring the working lives of internationally eminent biochemists, Gilbert and Mulkay (1984) found themselves caught in a maelstrom of conflicting opinions, dismissive attitudes, and a professional environment riven by two warring camps, built around opposing theories about a particular scientific phenomenon. The fact that top-flight scientists could be in such protracted and comprehensive dispute over an apparently minor empirical and theoretical matter puzzled Gilbert and Mulkay to the extent that they engaged in a series of formal and informal interviews. This led them to a number of realizations about the nature of conflicting opinions, dismissive attitudes and warring camps. For our purposes, however, it also led them to critique contemporary approaches to interviews as a research method, and to rethink interviewing, and how people provide accounts of their own and others' activities more generally. This rethinking, which resulted in the writing of something of a minor classic in the sociology of science, took them well beyond standard ideas about the data collection and analytic routines with which they were familiar.

Gilbert and Mulkay came to a number of critical realizations. They pointed out that the usual sequence of events for the conduct of interviews is:

1. the interview questions are prepared, based on theories prevalent in the area under study;
2. the participants are interviewed;
3. the analyst looks for broad similarities among their answers to pre-prepared questions;
4. these answers are taken at face value, and the 'common' or frequent answers are located and gathered;
5. these 'common' answers are taken to be accurate, partly because of their prevalence; and
6. the analyst constructs generalized, idealized versions of these participants' accounts, and presents these versions as the conclusions yielded by the analysis.

Gilbert and Mulkay noted the odd mixture of premises from Natural and Human Science on which this familiar routine is based. For instance, there is an underlying interest in the perceptions of participants, but an overlaid assumption that it is what these perceptions have in common, rather than their distinctiveness, that constitutes the notable 'findings'. Further, what is taken to be 'in common' is to a large extent determined by the researcher's theoretical premises, set up in advance, and by the ways in which these direct the contents of interview questions. Thus, participants' specific statements in interviews are subsumed under more general concepts and reshaped into idealized accounting procedures. The analyst identifies those segments of participants' talk that are to be taken by the reader, presumably because they are regarded so by the analyst, as representative of generalized processes – idealized 'sayings' – at work 'out there'. By direct inference, the reader is taken to share the analyst's lack of interest in:

1. where the questions came from and how they gave particular shape to the interview event;
2. how all interviews are jointly constructed by all parties;
3. the specifics of interviewees' accounts; and
4. the accounts that are marginal, that is, 'non-representative'.

Particular statements about particular people or actions are thereby generalized to entire groups and to entire classes of action by the interview's data collection and analytic routines.

Part of the challenge they issued to these traditional assumptions and methods arose from the fact that Gilbert and Mulkay found that they could document, in their interviews with the scientists, two distinctive interpretive repertoires: a formal or scientific repertoire and an informal or contingent repertoire. The scientific repertoire was a way of talking that is familiar to us from our knowledge of the Natural Sciences. These Sciences entail and trade on a reliance on controlled studies and verified theories, a respect for formal experimental routines, and a belief in the discover-ability of the fundamental 'facts of the matter'. The contingent repertoire concerned itself with assumptions about the malleability and multi-interpretability of supposedly standard scientific routines, about scepticism concerning the definitiveness of the 'facts of the matter', about the significance of interpersonal dynamics among scientific researchers and their students, and about the politics of scientific activity. On the last point, here is a selection of the factors that were given to Gilbert and Mulkay by the scientists to explain the opposing camp's mistakes: reluctant to make the effort; disliking of new theory; extremely naïve; feeling their status threatened; too accepting of the views of their 'gurus'; being American and therefore thinking in a woolly fashion; generally irrational, cussed and pig-headed; and stupid (Mulkay and Gilbert, 1982). 'Hard' science indeed.

Gilbert and Mulkay came to a number of significant conclusions, some about science and the scientists they interviewed, and some about the conduct of interviews and how interviews should and should not be interpreted. They concluded that the accounts that people produce in interview settings are not literal descriptions of independent social realities, nor are they simply neutral outcomes of standard, 'normal' interpretive procedures to do with questioning and answering. Rather, they characterized interview accounts as means by which participants make available to us and to one another versions of the state of their belief as it is appropriate to the specific interpretive occasions in which they find themselves.

Gilbert and Mulkay's book became an important contribution to the Natural Science community and to the history and sociology of interviewing as a research technique. The fact that it concerns a Natural Science community that prides itself on its transparent and consensual research techniques adds to the weight of its implications.

Starting points

Atkinson and Silverman (1997: 305) have pointed out that interviews are among the most widespread of methods for collecting data in social science. The premise, however, that interviews, particularly open-ended interviews, offer 'an authentic gaze into the soul of another' and the 'dialogic revelation of selves' is now taken by many qualitative analysts to be not only incomplete or potentially misleading, but downright untenable. It is based on the romantic idea that people's understandings of their experiences, as people transparently articulate them in interviews or anywhere else, are primordial, authentic and portable from 'telling to telling'. It is these 'tellings' that are the basic grist to the social-scientific mill, independently, as Gilbert and Mulkay found, of whether the interviews are structured, semi-structured or open-ended in their intent. So a point to note at the outset is that the stories told and the views conveyed in interviews are not 'any more authentic or pure a reflection of the self than any other socially organized set of practices' (Atkinson and Silverman, 1997: 322). Nonetheless, interviews can provide insight into individuals' constructed social worlds and into the ways in which they convey those constructions in the particular interactional setting of the interview (Silverman, 1993).

It is the significance of this interactional setting that Baker (1997) pointed to in calling for a reconsideration of interviewing, to see it not so much as a 'data-gathering', but rather as a 'data generating' method. The interactions that make up interviews are dynamic, not static, forms of social action: in each interview, all participants, including the interviewer, re-encounter and re-produce social order in and for the site of the interview itself. Baker (1997: 131) listed three key concepts in a consideration of interviews as data–generative activities:

1. Interviewing is best understood as an interactional event in which members of a culture draw on and rebuild their shared cultural knowledge, including their knowledge about how members-of-certain-kinds routinely speak in such settings.
2. Questions are a central part of the data and are best viewed not as neutral or uninterested invitations to speak; rather, they shape the grounds or the footings on which the participants can and should speak.
3. Interview responses need to be treated as accounts rather than as straight reports; we can understand interviews as events in which all parties (interviewer/s and interviewee/s) work to give accounts of themselves and the topics of talk.

Baker (1997) showed that speakers, as competent cultural practitioners, construct versions of truth around the categories and their associated attributions that develop in the interview. So rather than evaluating interviews as more or less successful, or well or badly conducted, this approach examines the capabilities of the researcher to describe accurately the ways in which the interview participants, including the interviewer, together make sense in generating meaningful accounts of the experiences they describe.

So we approach interview data in two ways. In one pass, we can study the interview session as a particular interactional event, and proceed to examine the practical actions that the parties engage in. Here we ask how the interview is structured, and explicate its social organization (e.g., see Hester and Francis, 1997). That is, we treat the interview as an instance of specialized, distinctive talk, but as talk nonetheless. In a second pass, we can investigate the content of interviews as the reflections of social order that the speakers construct. Here we ask how the accounts of the speakers are put together as possible descriptions of their social experiences. Again, these accounting procedures are practical social actions, but we can see them as well as jointly produced instances of 'practical sociological reasoning' on the speakers' parts. That is, we can treat the interview as the formulation of accounts. These two passes form the basis of the sections of this chapter, but note that this analytic distinction is in part for convenience rather than a reflection of how interviews directly work or, even less so, what speakers are thinking about or planning. The approach takes it that, as with conversation, speakers show one another clearly what it is that they are taking and putting as relevant.

Interviews as talk

In much educational research, we still find results from interview studies reported either without any of the direct speech of the interviewees, or without any reporting of the actual talk that went on between interviewers and inter-viewees. Sometimes we see apparent monologues, excerpted from dialogues or multi-logues, even though the most obvious thing we can say about interviews is that they are conducted through interaction – talk that is telephonic, or direct, or written down. Ignoring that, and reporting apparently 'monologic' talk in fact adds to the illusion that 'this speaker thinks this', for-all-time and in-all-spaces, independently of the local contingencies of the event then and there.

We will see that the interactional features of interviews include the kinds of turn-taking procedures and troubles and repairs that reflect and rebuild institutional identities. We will also see that some specific ordinary-talk features are used more or less frequently than in conversation, but even the management of these rests on a bedrock of everyday interactional practices.

Interviews as specialized talk

In the previous chapter, a series of passes for analysing talk in interaction was outlined. To explore some of the particularities of interviews, and to develop an understanding of the interactional rights and responsibilities that are in operation there, we begin with a simple example. Here are the opening turns in a fixed-protocol, structured interview, an interview that follows a set of questions available in written form to all participants during the conduct of the interview, with the parents of 'Donny', aged six, by a researcher working as part of a team on an educational research project.

EXAMPLE 7.1(a) *'and he's male?'*
(Ir=Interviewer, M=Mother, F,=Father)

1. Ir When was Donny born?
2. F Donny was born on the first of April, and he's six years old and it's '99 so we're going back to '93=
3. Ir =And he's male?
4. F Yes male.
5. Ir How many brothers and sisters?
6. F Donny has one older brother who is <u>three</u> years older than he is and one sister who is three years <u>younger</u> than he is.

7. Ir What are their ages?
8. F   Luke is (.) will be 10 (.5) Luke will be 10 on the 16th of January, 2000
        (.5) and Olivia is three now but she's just (1.5) she's just three. That's
        silly of me I'm very//
9. Ir   //That's alright, we don't actually need those.
10. F   She's three a couple of months ago (.5) just had a birthday.

How is this visible to us, even thirty seconds or so into the event, as an
interview and not a casual conversation? There are at least five features of the
interaction that alert us to the possibility that the talk so far is part of an
interview:

* the stems of questions were repeated in answers ('school–style' as in turns 2
  and 6);
* one person only questioned throughout;
* this questioner explicitly nominated what was and was not relevant (in
  turn 9);
* a question may be weird, but nonetheless taken to be part of the pre-set
  protocol, and responded to acceptingly (turn 3); and
* the answerer apologized and corrected himself following hearable 'mistakes',
  for fumbling over information that it was, then and there, his apparent
  responsibility to know about (in turns 8, 10).

A few turns later:

EXAMPLE 7.1(b) *'he likes to just play'*

20. Ir Has Donny got any health problems?=
21. F   =No.
22. Ir Has he had any//
23. F   //No, absolutely not.
24. Ir What are the main things that Donny does on the weekend?
25. F   On the weekend he plays video games, umm, harasses me to play with
        him, umm, (1) he likes to just play with his, like, bigger brother, go down
        to the park and kick the soccer ball around. Umm, (.5) he likes to read,
        he likes to, (.) he's trying to learn to read, he's been trying very hard, he's
        ahh, (1) Donny has not been a fast learner, we've, (.) we've had some
        learning difficulties with Donny, he ahh, (.5) he actually had help when we
        were living in ((another town)), Donny had help and assistance one day a
        week (.5) a special, specialized person, (.5) we're always helping him to
        learn because he was a, (.8) he had learning difficulties.
26. Ir What materials and what method did this person use?
27. F   (Lots of) questions (.) that (.5) that, specialized teachers, they, they
        encouraged him with maths and with reading=
28. M   =At pre-school=
29. F   =At pre-school yeh.

We can note F's emphatic statement concerning Donny's lack of health problems, that emphasis marked in his immediate, latched answer in turn 21 and in his interruption of Ir's next turn, at a point before the question was posed, with an upgrading of his answer to the original question ('//No, absolutely not'). F thus strongly accentuated a view of Donny as not having 'health problems'.

We see also a further set of relevances brought into play here by Father (in turn 25) – the issue of Donny as a 'student' and thus themselves as the 'parents-of-student'. The parents knew in advance that the interview was to be about education, conducted by educational researchers, and Father shifted the weekend hobbies topic to reading and learning difficulties, and received from the interviewer a confirmation of this shift in the form of an 'educationally interested inquiry' (in turn 26). Donny's emphatic lack of 'health problems' was then a context for viewing another, educationally relevant set of 'difficulties' that he has.

A few moments later:

EXAMPLE 7.1(c) *'I didn't refuse to believe'*

38. M I was a little bit dubious about it because I thought 'out of all
       the families at this private kindergarten why is it our child
       who needs this help?' you know?
39. F Myra refused to believe that our child could//
40. M   //No I <u>didn't</u> refuse
       to believe, no I thought 'well that's possible' (.) but they were a private
       school. He was, he wasn't slow but they umm, they didn't have her
       entirely with Donny, when they led me to believe that it was just for
       Donny and then when I used to go there I'd find this teacher with other
       children too.

This was Mother's first significant entry into the interview (apart from her prompt to F in turn 28), and her first mention either by the interviewer or by Father. Father's statement concerning Mother was directed to the interviewer; it is about Mother, not to Mother, or with Mother. So it is not just in terms of the actual content of the statement (in turn 39), with which Mother disagreed, but also in terms of the interactional structure of Father's comment, that we can see the grounds for Mother's dis-alignment with him. She then explicated the grounds of that dis-alignment in pursuing her concerns about Donny's teacher. And then:

EXAMPLE 7.1(d) *'trees and butterflies and god knows what'*

48. F Yes (.) the boy was in his big brother's shadow (.5) very
       much so.

49. Ir So he just needed more attention?=
50. M =More attention than one teacher could provide for the whole class.
51. F Since he's come, since he's come here ((to this suburb)), it's been a totally //
52. M   //He's blossomed=
53. F =He's blossomed, yes. He's changed dramatically (   ) He's come ahead a phenomenal amount. (1)

And finally:

54. Ir We were talking about what Donny does on the weekend. What does he do before school in the morning?
55. F Video games, tele//
56. M   //No he doesn't play video games, they're not allowed to I won't let them.
57. F He tries to.
58. M He likes to watch cartoons.
59. Ir Before he goes to school he's got what two hours or something to get ready?
60. M Two hours yeh. Yeh, he just get's ready, they boys usually get their own, often get their own breakfast in the morning.
61. F They're very independent the boys. Yeh and they want to walk to school.
62. M ( ) you know I leave everything out they just get themselves organized and they like to leave early.
63. F They like to get to school forty minutes early if they can so they, like to get themselves ready and off they go and they, it's twenty minutes walk and they go through the back tracks and stuff, it's not main road, so they, they, so I'd say they have to leave here at eight o'clock to get forty minutes of playing kicking the footy round and so on and so forth, ((to M)) wouldn't you?
64. M They play on their way to school, yeh they like to leave here at eight o'clock. So they usually get //
65. F   //They're just adventurous they like to look at the trees and butterflies and god knows what all the way to school.

Mother and Father took distinct courses of social action here, sometimes co-ordinated, sometimes not. In a sense, they positioned themselves distinctly on the matter of Donny. There is a sense in which Mother and Father presented a different version of Donny and a different angle from which they view and thus can characterize him.

From a conventional content-based analysis, the interviewer has learned that Donny:

• is six years old;
• is male;
• has two siblings – a brother aged nine and a sister aged three;

- has (absolutely) no health problems;
- plays video games and soccer on the weekends;
- reads, or at least 'likes and tries to read';
- has a learning difficulty;
- needs 'more attention';
- watches cartoons before school; and
- is considered 'independent' by his parents.

But much that we have been shown in this interview is left out of this content analysis. From examining the interactional structures familiar to us from our consideration of talk in the previous chapter, we see particular inflections of these that give shape to the talk as 'an interview'. The participants – Interviewer, Mother and Father – all bring off this recognizable interactional event through their use of particular interactional moves. But they do not accomplish this simply by presenting these 'facts' about Donny. The three speakers shift the relevances at different points; the two interviewees display temporary alignments and dis-alignments; each 'works up' a different Donny for this interview; thus, each displays a distinct orientation and relationship to Donny – Mother managed his preparation for school and his leisure time (turn 56: 'I won't let them' [play video games before school]; Father announced that they do, and was interrupted and corrected, and let the correction stand); and Father described their 'healthy' adventurousness, as previewed in his early emphasis on Donny's lack of 'health problems'. It is the interactional features that show us precisely where and on what counts the interviewees align and dis-align.

Turning to the interviewer's turns, we find they consist of elaborations, lead-ons, and reinstatements:

3. Ir =And he's male?

9. Ir //That's alright, we don't actually need those.

49. Ir So he just needed more attention?

54. Ir We were talking about what Donny does on the weekend. What does he do before school in the morning?

59. Ir Before he goes to school he's got what two hours or something to get ready?

These moves co-ordinate the talk, and shift, instate and reinstate the topics, linking back to prior talk and forward to next talk.

Thus, we can apply the six passes described in the previous chapter to give a sketch of features of the talk in these interview segments:

1. There is specific and visible management of the turn-taking, and, through this, the relevances in this talk.
2. Sequences of a utterances are mutually composed in the completion of question–answer exchanges.

3. There is the moment-to-moment formation, dissolution and a reformation of parties and alliances.
4. We see explicit indication of the accountabilities acted on by each of the participants with respect to their rights and responsibilities in the interview.
5. The participants talk into being a variety of institutional categories – a mother and a father, a family, and, significantly, a family-for-Education; that is, they act out and describe themselves as acting on their rights and responsibilities as parents in this educational interview.
6. Finally, we see something of a division of the relational labour: Mother positions herself with respect to her duties concerning Donny's maintenance as a school student, partly through her expressions of concern; Father portrays a version of Donny as a healthy, fun-loving and resolutely 'normal' boy.

Interviews as troublesome talk

We have seen the ways in which interviewees need to co-ordinate their talk to fulfil their rights and responsibilities in interviews. We have also seen how speakers can align in their talk, dis-align, and then repair such that they are speaking coherently as a single party once again. This we may consider a form of trouble and repair. Because of the special rights and responsibilities in which speakers engage in interviews, however, there are other particular kinds of trouble that can occur. We consider a few of these below: the trouble with questions; the trouble with answers; and the trouble with question–answer sequences.

The trouble with questions

Consider the following from an interview conducted with members of an isolated farming community. Prior to the interview, the farmer, Bill, was told that the interview concerned the provision of educational services to remote rural and farming communities. The interview itself was structured by a series of questions, written and shown to Bill to guide the interview. A number of these questions concerned the kind of communication and media contact that these community members engaged in – the number of newspapers they read per week, the amount of television they watched, and so on. Each of these questions simply asked for a straightforward nomination of the number – of newspapers, hours, and so on. Up to this point, Bill had provided brief answers that consisted of such numbers. Then this exchange occurred (from Muspratt et al., 2001: 161):

EXAMPLE 7.2 *'You can't go down'*

1. Ir   So, how often do you listen to the radio and watch TV?
2. Bill   I have the radio going all night because I don't sleep very heavy and
         I wake up and (.) I used to wake up and just lay there and sometimes

I would get up to read a book or read the paper and that annoys the wife (.5) so I just listen to the radio (1) we are under extreme pressure (.) every waking thought is how you are going to survive (.) you are in a survival mode (.) you have got so much investment and you have a lot of money tied up and you have worked your whole life to get there and you can't go down without putting every single effort (1) if we could get a break in the <u>wea</u>ther, it would make it a bit easier but we have got this far and we have done pretty well (.5) we've got to <u>change</u> (1.5) you know, I am very good with sheep, and I have got to go away. You know (.5) there is just no money in them and you are just making a loss in them. I'm doing two men's work and there is not much sense in that.

The trouble for the interviewer, of course, lies in the fact that this is Bill's 'answer' to the question. This direct answer is given in his first utterance – he has the radio on all night and, by implication, every night. The interviewer can then make some notional estimate of how many hours per week Bill listens to the radio. The problem in considering this estimate of the number of hours as 'the answer' is that it is clearly not the significant part of the answer for Bill. The issue of the number of hours he spends listening to the radio is the platform for his disclosures about his anxiety, his workload, and whether or not he and his family will 'go down'. Bill's attention could be brought back to providing a more precise answer to the question of the number of hours he listened to the radio, but the more significant question for the interviewer is 'what is the research status of Bill's disclosures here?' Is it to be set aside as irrelevant or just part of the 'static' of the interview process? Is it to be pursued for further collaboration and worked into a significant finding of the research project?

What Bill has presented is deeply relevant to him within the context of this interview – an interview with a person from the city, apparently interested in rural and remote communities and the circumstances in which they live. Bill produced this answer as an artful response to an apparently banal question concerning his everyday habits. This is not to say that he was dissembling or exaggerating; rather it is simply to acknowledge the choice that he made, at that moment in the interview, to offer these significant disclosures. He has taken a particular course of action in this answer which may or may not turn out to give particular shape to the events that follow in the interview. The length and relevances of his answer are warrantable from the question asked him, in particular the 'so' preface used by the Interviewer, which links the question to what has been said earlier and provides an acceptable context for a continuation and extension of topics dealt with so far.

While the substantive trouble is told by Bill, the interactional trouble is presented to the interviewer: she has rights and responsibilities as an interviewer, including the prosecution of the list of questions guiding the interview, but also rights and responsibilities as an interactant, then and there. Clearly these are not static: Bill's insertions of his troubles into his answer to a comparatively unexciting question attests to the significance he accords those troubles.

The trouble with answers

All interactional events are co-ordinated mutually by the speakers. As we saw above, they have the choice to determine the issues that are relevant to their questions and answers. Questions themselves can become the object of interest in the talk, again presenting apparently unforeseen troubles to the interviewer. Consider the following, a segment of an open-ended interview between an educational researcher and a school teacher in a disadvantaged community. As the interviewer made clear prior to the interview, the project was concerned with the relationships between the home life and school life of students in a variety of communities.

EXAMPLE 7.3 *'it's a sticky one'*

1. Ir The conflict between home and school, does that ↑ happen often?=
2. T =Yes, heaps↑ of times this year (.) just enough to be concerned. We have an ongoing thing with one of the children with that. They don't believe they have to be grown up here because they're not (.) they're treated as very young at home. Whereas we expect the opposite here.
3. Ir So is that with just taking responsibility↑ or is it //
4. T //with their learning. Oh↑ most definitely. They won't problem-solve. They won't get up and have a go at anything. They will sit back and let someone else work out their problems for them even within their work so that they will sit beside a stronger person, because that person will get everything right on their work and they will just take down the information. So they won't actually go out and actively seek information out for themselves.
5. Ir I guess that we're talking about impacting on their learning and development↑
6. T And literacy↑ development, very much so. A self-esteem type of issue I guess it comes down to.
7. Ir So you see literacy and self esteem very much? ↑=
8. T =Oh, most definitely. If they think they can do it they can do it. If they think they've got problems with it they've got problems with it. But which comes first the chicken or the egg? Do they get the problems first and then the literacy doesn't develop or (1) is the literacy not developing so (1.5) I lost the train of my thought (.5) What comes first=
9. Ir =What you started saying is they are coming here and you can't tell which is the problem yet because they are not trying and not doing it or because they haven't got the language to do it.
10. T Very good, I'm glad you're here. Exactly yes.
11. Ir So coming from the other end, what comes first? Is it that they are not being given the language at home or is it that they are not being encouraged to try and learn?↑
12. T Mmmm, that's right. ↓ (1.5)

13. Ir It's a sticky one=
14. T =Yes, and it is one that you forever battle with.

In this case, the question asked by the Interviewer, in turns 5 and 7, became the object of the discussion, rather than a question to be directly answered. Questions can be talked about in terms, for example, of their significance, their pervasiveness as issues in education, or their perennial intractability. Again, we see here the trouble for the interviewer arising from the status of these characteristics of the question, compared with the status of the question as something requiring an answer. What kind of conversational object is the question jointly produced across turns 6–9? In turn 13, the interviewer conceded that the question will not be answered, but that it was worth talking about as a difficult issue for educators. In the final turn in this segment, the teacher confirmed that, and added that it is a perennial matter of concern. Again, we see the interviewer faced with her rights and responsibilities as an interviewer, as opposed to those pertaining to her general interactional rights and responsibilities in this talk.

In Example 7.3, T gave definite and strong agreements to the first four questions: 'yes, heaps of times; oh, most definitely; very much so; oh, most definitely'. This definiteness can also be seen in the strength of the agreement markers that the interviewee uses – the interruptions and immediate flow-ons from the interviewer's questions (=s in turns 1–2, 3–4, 7–8, 13–14), and the harmonized inflections, matching the upward, inquiring tones of the interviewer (↑s and emphases in turns 1–2, 3–4, 5–6, 7–8). This close latching and tonal harmonizing signals that the speakers stayed 'in tune', keen to agree and closely attending to and accepting of the relevances that were developed by one another. This continues to turn 12, at which point the '↑' is met with a '↓'.

The critical juncture here is the hearing of turn 11. As it is spoken, it could be heard as a re-posing of the question raised by the interviewee, or as a reformulation or reminder that this is indeed the question that had been raised. We see in turn 12, as confirmed by the interviewer in turn 13, that this was to be heard as a reformulation of the question. That is, it is this question itself that is the definite answer to the original set of inquiries in turns 1 through 9.

As with Bill and the radio, what was presented and enacted was a particular kind of problem. In this case the problem concerns the topic of the talk, and this is further visited as a problem on the structure of the interactions themselves.

The trouble with co-ordinating sequences of questions and answers

In conversations, we expect certain pairs of moves to be adjacent (e.g., questions–answers). These are the fundamental mechanisms of co-ordination and the construction of a shared ground for operation. As we have seen, interviews put particular twists on some standard conversational features. One further twist concerns the feature noted above about the combination of talk-about and acting–out the accounts under construction. Consider Example 6.5 in which an educational interviewer and a teacher discussed the community surrounding the school and its role in literacy education:

EXAMPLE 7.4 *'There's actually like a barrier'*

1. Ir   What about the school and the surrounding community? Does the school and the community interact?↑ Do they have much to do with each other?↑

2. T   Not that I know of. ↓ I'm not really familiar with the community, I just commute. ↓

3. Ir   How long have you been teaching here?↑

4. T   It is a year now. I really don't know the//

5. Ir   //We are talking about the social (.) do the <u>par</u>ents and friends come along to the schools functions (.) like that? ↑

6. T   Not that I know of. ↓ We've invited parents to several things and not many have turned up. Maybe three or four out of the double teaching area ((about 55 students, so a potential 110 parents)). A very low show for the parents but then a lot of them are working or busy with small children, lots of them have small children. (.) It's hard for them to get away.

7. Ir   What about the community generally?↑(.) is it interested in literacy education or (.5) interested in schools or (.5) what happens in the school?↑

8. T   I don't know.↓

9. Ir   You might get some idea from participation like the <u>inter</u>est that are actually shown by coming here. What sort of <u>feed</u>back do you get from the kids about how their parents see school?↑

10. T   I don't get any feedback really. ↓

11. Ir   (2) Kid's don't talk about when they send <u>home</u>↑work home or anything?↑↑

12. T   No ↓ the homework just comes back without any comments.
↓ There's <u>act</u>↑ually like a <u>barrier</u> between school and home, I've noticed but then again I've only ever really taught in this area and it is just the general trend. ↓

13. Ir   What about resources in the school //

14. T   //I think the school is well resourced. I just think it's disorganised↓

Here we see a less harmonized exchange than we saw in Example 7.3. The interviewer posed a series of questions, but, effectively, the interviewee passed on giving definite answers ('Not that I know of. I'm not really familiar; I don't really know; not that I know of; I don't know; I don't get any feedback'). In addition, we see a lack of harmony in the tonal features noted in the transcript, with upward inflections and emphases from the interviewer met with a lack of emphasis and downward inflections from the interviewee throughout the transcript.

In turn 12, the 'definite answer' was produced with force; the passes to the first five questions served to punctuate and dramatize the force of this statement. In that sense, the previous passes and the blocking or negating tonal disharmonies served as an accelerating and increasingly upgraded prelude to the forceful and definite answer given in turn 12. That is to say, these passes and disharmonies formed part of the substantiation given by the speaker to her final definite answer, and they give it weight, force, and drama. We return to the matter of substantiation procedures in a later section, but it is notable at this point that interviewees and interviewers alike have a variety of 'load-bearing' interactional moves available to them in the conduct and production of interviews. We might not find all of these resources listed in the 'guide-to-good-interviewing' texts, but it is clear from the examination of transcripts that such resources play a critical part in the ways in which speakers add force and coherence to their participation in interviews.

Discovering your interview-ability

We have seen that, in interviews, each party has a distinctive set of rights and responsibilities that need to be co-ordinated with the other(s) in order for a recognizable 'interview' to come off. Further, these rights and responsibilities vary depending on whether the interview is designated to be structured, semi-structured or open-ended. A primordial aspect of this co-ordination relates to establishing and confirming the 'interviewability' of the interviewee. An interview is based on some particular ground on which this person is interviewable, and this interviewability needs to be located – found and worked up. Generally, interviewees are interviewed because of their membership in a certain category. One of the particular strengths afforded by interviewing as a research technique is that the researcher can plan to interview a variety of persons, sampled across a range of categories that the project takes to be explanatory or at least relevant categories – principals of schools, parents, teachers, males, females, people in urban, rural or remote settings, and so on. So one set of rights and responsibilities that serve as the resources for an interviewee is not just to talk, but to talk-as-a-speaker in and for the category that seems of interest to this interview.

An interviewee will work with a knowledge of 'what-I-am-for-this-interview' as a resource for making appropriate sense in the interview setting, for drawing on their immediate rights and fulfilling their immediate responsibilities as interviewees, then and there. But, of course, any given interviewee may be characterized as belonging to any number of these categories (a teacher may be a parent, may be a researcher, may be an administrator, and so on). It is usually the case that, unless the speaker explicitly signals otherwise (e.g., 'speaking as a parent . . .'), it is the category that the interview calls on that becomes the starting point for the common ground on which the speakers can interact. This is not to say that interviewees will not express 'individual' views, but only that part of being a member of our society is knowing what interviews are, why it is that we might be interviewed on some occasion, and that there is a relationship between that knowledge and how we can be appropriately heard.

Locating the self for this interview

In this section, I use some examples from an interview study of deaf adults in educational settings (reported by Freebody and Power, 2001; the discussion below draws directly on this paper) to illustrate the variety of moves speakers can make in establishing their 'interviewability'. We observed three distinctive ways in which the respondents (Deaf Students, DSs) answered an opening set of questions on the level and origin of their Deafness. First, a number of speakers immediately adopted the official and technical designations that have been applied to them in the course of their diagnosis and treatment for Deafness or hearing impairment. Examples 7.5 and 7.6 display this feature. (Note that these interviews were conducted entirely in Australian Sign Language (Auslan), and the transcripts were produced by a series of back-translations by English-Auslan bilinguals.)

EXAMPLE 7.5 'In terms of diagnosis'

1. Ir   In terms of diagnosis, what type of hearing loss do you have? Is it severe, mild, profound?
2. DS It's a mild hearing loss, I think, about 50 per cent loss in the right ear and 25 per cent loss in the left ear.

Here the interviewer provided a category solution to her first question in her own first turn. The three categories of hearing loss were offered as the terms in which the answer can be provided, and the interviewee indeed used those categories, adding further technical information about her knowledge of the degree of loss in each ear. In that sense the interviewer, at the outset, provided an interpretation of her very first question in the first part of turn 1, and the interviewee not only complied with the categories offered but elaborated on the technical discourse traditionally used to describe degree of hearing loss.

EXAMPLE 7.6 'I am profoundly Deaf'

1. Ir   Were you born with a hearing impairment?
2. DS I was born Deaf.
3. Ir   Do you know what degree of hearing loss you have?
4. DS I am profoundly Deaf.

In this case, the interviewee not only responded with a statement about her condition at birth, but elaborated on the interviewer's descriptor 'hearing impairment' – she upgraded the categorization from hearing impaired to Deaf. In exchange 3–4, we see the interviewee, unprompted, adopt the technical designation for the category of her Deafness.

These two examples of opening exchanges, while containing visible points of negotiation and refinement, nonetheless display a direct and explicit acceptance of interviewers' technical taxonomies for Deafness. At the very outset of the interview, in these cases, the particular nature of 'the Deaf person to-be-interviewed' is established in terms related to publicly available technical usage. There were, however, instances in which this use of official descriptions was not evident. In these cases, the speaker generally arrived at such official descriptions at some point later in the talk, but took a certain route to get there – either story or a re-categorization. Example 7.7 is an instance of a narrative aimed at explicating the cause and, by inference, the nature and level of the impairment.

EXAMPLE 7.7 *'my mother was telling me'*

1. Ir   Okay, do you happen to know any of the details of your hearing impairment, like is it mild, severe or moderate?
2. DS Well, my mother was telling me that because of the tests, they just never knew what caused my hearing impairment, so I've come to the conclusion that it must have been Rubella. That was what my mother had, but that's my theory.
3. Ir   Right, okay. Do you know what degree of Deafness you have? Would you describe it as a mild loss or moderate loss?
4. DS Severe in one ear and profound in the other.

In the opening exchanges of this interview, the interviewer again provided a hearing frame for her initial question in the first turn ('like is it . . .?'). This frame consisted of three technical categories. The interviewee responded with a narrative drawn from her mother's account of the causes of the impairment, and her own considerations about that. It is this narrative and explanation of origins that the interviewee took to be relevant to 'the details of [her] hearing impairment', as requested in the first question. The interviewer acknowledged the relevance of that with standard tokens ('right, okay') and re-put the taxonomy question in technical terms. This last question, as in the examples above, was answered without any queries for clarification and with the addition of a new category, 'profound', indicating that the speakers know-in-common the official descriptors that apply to hearing loss. The interviewee's choice to insert other narrative moves along with or before the naming of that descriptor forms part of how she located a particular history for herself prior to the official categorization.

As a final example of the mutual location of the Deaf interviewee by the speakers early in exchanges, consider the opening exchanges from another interview, shown in Example 7.8.

EXAMPLE 7.8 *'I'm just a person'*

1. Ir   I just want to talk about your level of Deafness. Were you born Deaf or did you become Deaf later?
2. DS   Born Deaf.
3. Ir   Would call you yourself hearing-impaired or Deaf person, hard of hearing, or how would you refer to yourself?
4. DS   I'm just a person. I call myself, I'm in the middle.
5. Ir   Oh! So (.5)
6. DS   I'm not really Deaf or hearing-impaired. I'm in the middle somewhere.
7. Ir   Do you happen to know what the level of your Deafness is mild or moderate?
8. DS   It's profound B.

This is a complex exchange. The interviewer opened the topic of 'level of Deafness', but immediately followed that with a reformulation of the question in terms of the onset of Deafness. There are two possible hearings of combined moves in talk such as in turn 1. The first is that the question about onset was an insertion into a larger exchange concerning level; that is, that in determining the issue of level we need first to determine the issue of its origins. The second hearing is that the second question was in fact a self-solution of the first issue; that is, that the speakers could resolve the issue of level of Deafness by turning to its origins – that these questions are made, for practical purposes, then and there in the interview, into equivalents. Such hearings are resolved moment-to-moment by speakers, since there is usually no a priori method for determining which hearing will turn out to be the preferred one.

Here the interviewee, as usual in such double requests, answered the second part first and waited for further elaboration from the interviewer. In turn 3 the interviewer specified the question of level in terms of the ways in which the interviewee would describe himself, with the provision of a number of commonly available descriptors. What is noteworthy here is the respondent's move in turn 4. The categories offered by the interviewer were not initially accepted. Rather, the speaker focused on his own descriptions of himself as 'just a person', and 'in the middle'. The interviewer registered surprise and invited the speaker to continue, and turn 6 provided an elaboration whereby the typical labels were said not to apply to him. In turn 7 the interviewer tried again, this time using a softened approach ('do you happen to know'), and again offered the technical categories for describing Deafness, with which, this time, the speaker complied in a way that is sufficiently unproblematic to indicate his appreciation of the category-form that was sought all along. Exchange 7–8 clinches the category-identity – the specific 'interviewability' of the speaker.

It is often early in an interview that local working identities are accomplished as resources for the immediate practical tasks of talking, implying and inferring, as the interview proceeds. This local identity, for this occasion, is a resource on which both speakers can proceed intelligibly. The interviewee's talk is the object of primary curiosity in the interview and both speakers can now operate on a shared appreciation of what sort of interviewee this is.

In the examples above we can see techniques these interviewees used to effect their locally relevant self-categorization-for-the-interview. In the production of these identities, a categorization such as 'Deaf' or 'hearing-impaired' can allow for certain 'typified' assumptions and predictions about the person to become operative for the interview. One of the outcomes of this, however, is that the particular histories and cultural habits of the individual can be subsumed under the typification. An outcome of the strategies shown in the latter examples above is that speakers generally ensured that some aspects of their biographies found their way into the event (Jayyusi, 1984: 25). Speakers used a variety of techniques to differentiate and 'biographize' their identities. Each drew on narrative resources in the course of the talk, rather than allowing that identity to be assumed as typical from the category 'Deaf' or 'hearing-impaired'.

Freebody and Power concluded that 'Deafness' was enacted in three distinctive ways by this group of speakers: as a disability, as a potential logistic impediment – something that just made it harder to get around – and/or as membership of a particular cultural community. We could say that, in some abstract sense, or in some undefined or imaginary space, all or none of these may be somehow 'true'; but to accomplish the practical work of the interview, it was generally from one of these discursive devices that the interviewees derived the resources for a form of self-presentation that was both coherent and relevant, then and there. That choice had implications for the ongoing conduct of the interviews, for what kinds of stories they told about themselves, for how they described themselves as adult students and learners, and for how the interviewers' questions were 'heard'. But it also had implications for the kinds of conclusions and recommendations that might be drawn from this research. Thus it had implications for how the research may contribute to the public understanding of, in this case, Deafness.

More broadly, such understandings have implications for what we take ourselves to be doing when we conduct and analyse interviews. These understandings lead us away from the view that there is a definitive, singular, authentic person, stable through time and across place, whose knowledge and views we can 'reach in for', if only we produce the right set of questions and ask them in the right manner and setting.

The problem of interviews: mundane becomes exotic becomes 'typical'
We have seen how interviews entail the participants' acting on particular interactional rights and responsibilities. As we saw above, one of these is an acknowledgement that one of the speakers is the 'object of curiosity'. In interview settings, the phenomenon or person of interest needs to be interactively negotiated, located and characterized, variously from site to site. By asking questions about mundane aspects of the interviewees' everyday lives, their 'curiousness' as

persons-of this-category (e.g., Deaf) is foregrounded. The interviews reported in Freebody and Power (2001) show many examples of this process, an instance of which is shown in Example 7.9.

EXAMPLE 7.9 *'Sometimes I don't worry'*

1. Ir   Do you read books?
2. DS   Oh, yes my husband reads a lot of books. But I don't have a lot of time. It's difficult.
3. Ir   What about with your children, do you sit them beside them and read books?
4. DS   Yes, if there is easy English words, if there is baby words, for the kids, yes.
5. Ir   Do you read well?
6. DS   Oh, yeah, but hard words I have trouble understanding. Sometimes when I'm reading a book I might look in the dictionary, to find out what the words mean.
7. Ir   Now when you are reading and you don't understand what a word is, you will get the dictionary and have a look?
8. DS   Yes, that's right, so I can understand.
9. Ir   So, when you are meeting hearing people, and your husband is with you, he talks with the hearing person and then tells you what the hearing person has said. What about if you're on your own.
10. DS   Well, if my husband is there I would talk through him. It's easier for me. But if I'm on my own, I'll read, I'll write.
11. Ir   What happens if there are long words?
12. DS   Oh, I'll write things down on the paper, if there are long words and I don't understand what they are saying, I'll ask, and they will explain it to me. They might write more.
13. Ir   When you are reading a book and you are reading away and you find a word that is difficult what do you do?
14. DS   I look in the dictionary.
15. Ir   Do you do other things or do you always look in the dictionary or sometimes do you not worry about it?
16. DS   Sometimes I don't worry about looking the word up. I look in the dictionary, but a lot of times I ask my husband. He gets fed up with me asking what words mean.

As Freebody and Power argued, the intricate combination of circumstances that the interviewer set up to interrogate this Deaf person shows the ways in which the mundane can be made exotic. Many of the answers given by the speaker here could also have been given by a hearing person learning to read or attempting to expand their reading repertoire. It is clear that this speaker's reliance on her husband relates directly to her limited reading and writing experience. However the routines she claimed to use to overcome this, largely through the use of literacy practices, are rendered 'curious' by the degree of

intrusiveness of the interviewer's questions and the pursuit of a range of hypothetical difficulties – strategies that characterize the standard semi-structured
interview protocol.

A direct outcome of this 'exoticizing' methodology is the further alienating
and compartmentalizing from the ordinariness of social life of the category
of interest, in this case, Deaf people. It can thereby further de-historicize the
individual of interest. By collecting sets of apparent generalizations, and then
abstracting them to the point on their applicability across the entire sample,
the representativeness of each apparent display of the category 'Deaf', while
apparently robust, can amount to simple stereotyping. The ironic catch here is
that such techniques – analyses that abstract and collect statements and transform
them into generalizations – make it seem as if it is the members of the category
of interest who stereotype themselves.

Procedures for substantiating the self

In considering interviews as talk, there is a final set of interactional resources
that are relevant. As the one whose talk is the focus of curiosity and interest in
interviews, the interviewee also has the option to provide markers about their
status as holders of certain views. We saw in Example 7.1(d), for instance, Mother
cuts into Father's commentary concerning whether or not Donny plays
video games and watches 'tele//' in his morning preparations for school ('they're
not allowed to I won't let them'); similarly, in Example 7.3 above, the Teacher
substantiates her views on a question by nominating a specific example ('we have
an ongoing thing with one of the children with that'); and in Example 7.4 above,
the Teacher making moves on the issue of her credibility on the matter at hand
('then again I've only ever really taught in this area'). These are all ways in which
speakers support, qualify and give more precise weight to their statements –
substantiation procedures. So part of our analysis needs to concern the question:
What substantiation procedures are used by the speaker to support the accounts
they give? So far, we have seen five general kinds of substantiation procedures
used in talk:

1. 'shared understandings', in which the speaker takes it as commonly
   understood and accepted that their accounting procedures are self-evident
   ('everybody knows that . . .');
2. anecdotal evidence, in which stories from the past are presented as iconic
   narratives that support the account ('we have an ongoing thing with one of
   the children with that');
3. dramatic techniques, such as direct quotes, or enlivened re-enactments of
   events, heighten the impact and immediacy of the anecdote ('I thought "out
   of all the families at this private kindergarten why is it our child who needs
   this help?" you know?');
4. official discourses, in which research or policy documents, or media accounts

are presented as substantiation ('50 per cent loss in the right ear and 25 per cent loss in the left ear'); and

5. personal or professional experience drawn upon to support a generalization ('I've only ever really taught in this area').

These resources, more of which we encounter as the chapter proceeds, are significant in that they signal speakers' credibility-commentaries on their statements about the topic. But they can also indicate the authority source to which the speaker orientates. We can think of substantiation procedures as analogous to an economy, in which speakers down- or upgrade their moves according to the significance and credibility with which they would have their statements heard.

Interviews as building accounts

We turn now to the accounts that people give in their turns at talk in interviews. How do we develop a rigorous way of documenting these accounts while staying close to the actual raw material of the interview transcripts? The method outlined here leads on directly from observations in the previous chapter about the ways in which people draw on their institutional and cultural identities – their biographies, experiences, and the explanations for events that make up public life. Importantly, it is not just the events that make up public life; it is also the explanations for those events that make up the common ground on which social order becomes both possible and understandable.

When we consider the kinds of statements that people make in interviews, it is clear that interviewees take as their interactional responsibility the task of providing explanations and accounts, and of substantiating those and making them coherent within the specific context of the interview. Natural and Social scientists working in psychology, anthropology, sociology and education have traditionally used social and cultural categories – relating to class, gender, age, ethnicity and so on – to explain the kinds of materials they find in interviews. The methods outlined here treat these categories themselves as resources that are available, and that may or may not be drawn upon, by speakers in interviews. It is the reasoning practices, including categorizations, attributions and explanations, used by speakers in the context of interviews, that constitute part of the 'facts' of the interview, the 'facts' conveyed by the interviewee in concert with their co-speaker/s.

An analytic framework that addresses these issues directly is called Membership Categorization Analysis (henceforth, MCA). This set of procedures sets out to document social organization by investigating the actual 'raw material' of human interactional behaviour, the ways in which categorizations, attributions and explanations are deployed by speakers as they reflect on and reconstruct social orders for the purposes at hand in the interview (Heritage, 1984: 235). For our purposes, these orders include accounts of the purposes, aims and procedures of education, of who has the right to it, the responsibility for it, who does it well and otherwise, and so on. Versions of educational order and their relation to social order and cultural practice are thus directly made available to us as we document the categorizations, attributions and explanations used by speakers in educational interviews.

Membership Categorization Analysis

We begin our consideration of MCA with an illustration. Example 7.10 below took place in a referral interview between a teacher (FT) and an Educational Psychologist (EP) (provided in Hester, 1992: 159; and reproduced as shown there, with some minor modification to the transcription conventions to fit with those used in Chapter 5). They are discussing various children whom they had referred to the School Psychological Service, a special education service provided by local education authorities in UK at that time.

EXAMPLE 7.10 *'a very good bully'*

1. EP   So:o the:e what is the nub of the problem?
2.   Truancy doesn'[t sound like it]'s
3. FT   [well that's not] no it['s n]ot=
4. EP   [no]
5. FT   =that's no it's really it's thieving for a start
           that brought things to light but she's a very
           good bully
6. EP: Mm hmm

First, we see the familiar question–answer exchange here; we see FT overlapping the talk to dismiss truancy as the nub of the problem, and EP confirming an acceptance of that; and we see the provision of the problem (in turn 5) and a confirmation of the acceptance of that in (turn 6). But we see as well an *account* of why this student has been referred to the Service. MCA is a way of documenting and explicating that accounting.

Put simply, MCA is a way of explicating how speakers draw on and reconstruct common cultural sense in specific situations. It aims to document the categories, classifications or social types that people use to describe persons ('bully'). These categories can be linked together to form *membership categorization devices*, or collections of categories (a referred school student). A number of research applications of MCA have shown some of the ways people use categories and collection devices in their talk and when they provide accounts. For example, people tend to operate as if it is adequate to use a single membership category to describe a member of some group or population ('she's a very good bully').Accounts also rely on understandings about *category-bound activities*, activities that are predictably done by persons who are referred to through a particular category ('thieving for a start') – rights, expectations, obligations, habits, knowledge, typical haunts, needs, and other attributes and competencies. These categorizations and attributions are the building blocks for the *explanations* of the topic at hand.Together they form reasoning practices – ways of making the talk 'reasonable', not necessarily logical or correct in some abstract sense, but 'having reason' then and there, at that point in the interview. In Example 7.10, FT's account presents a categorization and attribution in a mutually confirming relation: FT points out that it was the 'thieving' that 'brought things to light', thus showing that the categorization was valid. The attribution signalled this category, and more, 'bringing to light' as the warrant for the categorization.

MCA focuses on explicating these aspects of how speakers use categorizations of people, attach certain attributes to those categorizations, and thereby produce orderly sensible accounts of everyday experience:

> the fact that someone is male, or is middle aged, or is Jewish is, by itself, no warrant for so referring to them, for the warrant of 'correctness' would provide for use of any of the other reference forms as well. . . . That is the problem of relevance: not just the descriptive adequacy of the terms used to characterize the object being referred to, but the relevance that one has to provide if one means to account for the use of some term – the relevance of that term relative to the alternative terms that are demonstrably available. (Schegloff, 1992: 49–50)

What we have found in our examination of interview materials so far, just as we found with everyday interactions in the previous chapter, is that interviewers and interviewees organize and co-ordinate the understandings that are produced in the course of the interview. One of the ways in which we can approach this co-ordination is by documenting a number of critical moves the speakers make in the construction of accounts. MCA leads us to ask these questions:

- What *categories* of people do speakers use in their description of the topics?
- How do these categorization moves rely on, call on, or make relevant certain meaningful collections of categories, or *Membership Categorization Devices*?
- What *attributions* are made or assumed to be relevant about members of these categories?
- What *explanations* – that is, cause-effect sequences – are enabled by this combination of categories and attributions?
- What procedures do speakers use to *substantiate* the relevance of these categories, attributions and explanations to the topic at hand?

In this section I offer a brief introduction to a method of analysing interview accounts in these ways, relying on illustrations to build up an understanding of this form of analysis. (Eglin and Hester, 1992; Hester and Eglin, 1997; Hester and

Francis, 2000; Jayyusi, 1984, 1991; and Lee, 1991; Leiter, 1980; Speier, 1970 give more detailed and technical introductions.)

Categories

When we examine interactions and interviews, we find three kinds of categories used to describe the members of a culture (following Jayyusi, 1984: 21ff):

- self-organized groups (for example groups with proper names such as Hell's Angels or Presbyterians or School Principals or Headmistresses);
- individual descriptor designators (such as drop outs or bullies); and
- type categorizations (often references to members of semi-organized groups or references to descriptions or attributions of people).

We start our exploration of interview analysis using MCA with an example taken from an interview conducted by an educational researcher from an urban university with a farmer (discussed in Muspratt et al., 2001: 162–3). This farmer, Pam, and her farmer-husband, Steve, had lived in this relatively remote rural area of the country for a long time. In the course of discussing her views about education, she mentioned how rapidly the local community had changed in recent times.

EXAMPLE 7.11 *'A real family situation'*

1. Ir   What are the main changes you've noticed living in this community?
2. Pam I have noticed a big difference out here. (.5) We used to have a real family situation and all of a sudden the families are going away, and we actually have got very few situations where, (.) like next door we have a fellow who is trying to start up a wood carving business in town but he is not a farmer, he is just (.) using the house etcetera, and his <u>children</u> go into <u>Hawks</u>nest [town 40 kilometres away] and I think there is a farm manager down the end. (1) There used to be a lovely family next door but it is rented out to alternate lifestyle people. We found marijuana growing in our rainforest and Steve was <u>most</u> upset to think that somebody would be capitalizing on our land, making a fortune. The po<u>lice</u>man said they are probably making about a quarter of a <u>million</u> dollars every year.

The interviewee's immediate answer to the question was that the community ('we') 'used to have a real family situation and all of a sudden the families are going away'. In elaborating this answer, Pam deployed a number of categorizations and explicitly attached attributions to some of them. We can also recognize that the segment concluded with a substantiation procedure, an anecdote. We can begin an analysis by tabulating these moves made by Pam, as in Table 7.1.

TABLE 7.1 *Categorizations, Attributions and Substantiation procedures from Example 7.11*

Categorization	Contrasting categorizations	Attributions	Substantiation procedures
'real family' 'lovely family situation'	• fellow who is trying to start up a wood carving business in town	• not a farmer • just using the house etcetera • children go into Hawksnest	
	• farm manager		
	• alternate lifestyle people		Anecdote and reported speech: • Steve • somebody • policeman

Table 7.1 shows the *explications* produced by Pam in her answer. There is, as well, a set of *implications* necessarily entailed in this talk. We are to hear that 'real' and 'lovely families', as there used to be in this community, are not 'using property', not sending their children out of the community to school, not 'just managing' a farm, and not 'capitalizing' on other people's land. Pam constructed her account of the change by way of negative attributions – those who are here now were necessarily characterized in terms opposite to those who were here before – 'real family' and 'lovely'. That is, while unsaid, the necessary inference is that 'real and lovely families' work and live off the property, send their children to the local school, are farmers – own and manage and work the land – and do not capitalize on other people's land. From the stated negative attributions that Pam constructed, we get a clear sense of the core features she takes to be positive attributes of community members and the extent and qualitative nature of the changes she has seen around her.

MCA begins with the proposition that members possess common-sense knowledge of social structures and that this knowledge results, in part, from the organization of categories that are available as interactional resources for the conduct of any particular occasion. The aim of MCA is to show that this methodical activity both follows and re-validates a set of clear cultural conventions. Membership categories are defined as descriptions of types of persons. Further, membership categories can be grouped into membership categorization devices – MCDs. To see how MCDs work, consider the Example 7.12, spoken by a shopkeeper, Ron, who also happened to be the former mayor of the town, in a small remote rural community.

EXAMPLE 7.12 *'The man of the house'*

1. Ir   The unemployment situation in town, how do you see that, as a
          business in town?
2. Ron   I believe it's a problem and I have been quite vocal on unemployment
          lately. When you have all this violence in the home and mothers bashing
          children (.) I really believe if men had work and they went to work every
          morning and they came back in the afternoon, we would cut that violence
          by about 80 per cent. (1) I think it all comes to idleness, and if a man
          (.5) a father (.) you know there is so many defacto relationships (.5) the
          man of the house is sitting around home all day, it creates problems in
          as much money, and if there is ever going to be a row in a household it
          starts over money, not enough of it, and he will want to smoke and want
          to go and have a drink and his wife doesn't have enough money to buy
          milk for the children. Then there is a row, and that leads to violence,
          because he is too idle.

Two initial points to note: First, the interviewer's question positioned Ron's
answer in terms of his status as a business operator. Second, Ron's first moves
were to express his concern about this topic and to refer to the significance
of his public status (a public figure, whose 'vocal' statements have substance in
this community). These initial moves of Ron's are substantiation procedures,
designed to give weight and reasonableness to his subsequent statements.

Further, Ron's concern with unemployment was immediately named as a
concern with domestic violence, the case of violence by mothers on children.
This, in turn was named as a problem with unemployed and thus unoccupied
men. The inference was also made available that this problem itself is associated
with the public status of 'the man of the house', with the speaker making
plain his inability to name the man as a 'husband' or 'father'. This problem was
elaborated in moral terms: the 'man of the house' wishes to use the money for
recreational, legal drug use, and the mother is left without 'enough money to
buy milk for the children'. In this respect, the non–normative status of the
domestic relations are posited as the category problem that fuels the violence.
The 'man' is not fully attributable as 'husband' or 'father', and thus 'will' act
neglectfully or detrimentally to the interests of 'wife' and 'child'. The categorizations of people deployed here are, in order: *mothers, children, men, man, father,
man-of-the-house, his wife* and *children.* The membership categorization device
from which these categorizations are drawn, and that they construct we might
term Family. But this term is nowhere used in the interviewee's talk. Some
general proxies for the collection do appear – 'in the home' and 'in a household.'
Indeed, we can see, from this use of proxies and from the speaker's insertion and
immediate removal of the Standardized Relational Pair to mother and wife ('and
if a man (.5) a father (.) you know there is so many defacto relationships (.5)
the man–of–the–house') that the status of the MCD Family in this community
was made into a problem in this talk.

This problem arises as a central feature of Ron's talk because of one of the standard, cultural rules that apply in all interactions. This rule, or 'maxim' (Sacks, 1992), concerns the use of categorizations. Ron, for instance, opens his account with a statement concerning 'mothers bashing children'. One of the findings from studies of interaction is that, if two or more categories are used to categorize two or more members of some population, and those categories can be heard as categories from the same MCD, then we hear them that way: we hear the 'children' as the children of these 'mothers', not somebody else's children. That is, we hear both of these categorizations as drawn from the MCD collection Family. MCD Family 'collects' these categories. One of Ron's points, a point that organizes the moral order of his statements, is that the other categories conventionally collected (the Standardized Relational Pairs) under Family – specifically, Father-Husband – do not adequately apply in the domestic arrangements he is talking about.

One feature of talk that this shows us clearly is that description, the action of selecting categories and attributes, has not only empirical, 'descriptive' consequences. Descriptions are actions that also have consequences for the moral relations, the moral orders, that are constructed by the speakers and within which the accounts are produced (Jayyusi, 1991: 241–2).

As with Pam's descriptions of the 'real family situation', Ron's account goes on to illustrate the kinds of activities that are to be heard as associated with the idle-man-of-the-house (money spent on smoking and drinking, rather than on the mother's priorities of buying milk for the children). These attributions are then strung together into a cause–effect account of, in this case, where the violence comes from. Ron produces a sequence of if–then propositions: idleness, sitting around, money on smokes and drink rather than milk, row, violence explicitly attributed back to the original idleness. This is the account: a composition of categorizations, attributions, cause–effect connections and inferences that set limits on the generality of these connections. It is this account that Ron has us hear as the answer to the question about unemployment – the idleness, shortage of money, violence cycle in domestic arrangements 'so many' of which do not have the standard, expected categories of people, nor, therefore, the standard, expected moral order.

Membership Categorization Devices, in Sacks's (1992) words, are inference-making machines, meaning that members of a culture are able to draw inferences from the use of membership categorizations and devices such that, when an MCD is named, a number of possible categories can be warrantably inferred. The reverse also applies: when categories are named and they can be collected from common cultural knowledge into an MCD, then the material, social and moral orders that apply to that MCD can be inferred as relevant. This is what Ron did so artfully in his talk: he named then un-named the usual categories of MCD Family, those pertaining to the male adult, to interrupt any inferences that the hearer may make about the moral order of domestic life in his community.

It is important to emphasize that these structural relations between categories, Membership Categorization Devices, attributions, and explanations are not fixed models of knowledge in the sense that some theories emanating from, say, cognitive psychology may characterize them. Taking an example from the interview with Ron, the membership categorization 'children' can form part of several possible devices: Family (with parents), Stage of life (with adults), School (with teacher), depending on the particular context of use. Speakers draw inferences from MCDs within the interactional sequence of events at hand, then and there, such that for any given MCD a variety of possible categories can logically and accountably 'go' with it on any occasion. As members of a culture, speakers operate with 'presumed commonsense knowledge of social structures' (Hester and Eglin, 1997: 3), and this common-sense knowledge both allows and results from the organization of categories in particular interactional instances.

In summary, we can consider the issue of the categorization of people in talk in these ways:

- for any given person many varied categorical descriptions are possible ('man-of-the-house' 'real families');
- as people talk in interviews, they necessarily accomplish 'who' they relevantly 'are', and 'who' the person(s) they are describing relevantly 'are', at any moment in the interview, from among all these possible categorizations that they could draw on;
- membership categorizations are maintained insofar as the speakers continue to orient to those categorizations – to make them relevant then and there, and thereby to accomplish those categorizations as reasonable.

The analytic task, therefore, is to show from the details of the talk:

1. what is relevant to the accomplishment of the interview;
2. which categories, out of myriad possible membership categories, are mutually accomplished by a given interviewer and interviewee at any moment in the interview; and
3. what are the consequences for the explanations and moral evaluations made or necessarily implied by speakers of those categorizations.

The warrant for the claim that a particular person is a member of, for instance, the category 'real families' is not that the analyses show that this is what a person's category might actually be, but rather that the analyses demonstrate that, for the participants in the interaction, the account depends on persons' membership of that category, then and there.

Consequently, to categorize and thus accomplish the person as, say, an instance of the category 'bully', for the purposes of the talk requires that participants in the talk take that 'identity' as relevant to the talk. The selection of 'bully' relies upon those participants drawing upon the current interests, their biographies and the physical and moral features of the scene. Categories are therefore not simply analytic devices for researchers but are fundamental sense-making resources for members in everyday interaction, including in interviews (Schegloff, 1991; Wilson, 1991).

There are two other technical analytic features of Membership Categorization Analysis that need brief commentary. The first of these relates to a particular form of 'asymmetry' in accounting procedures, and the second is to do with the functions of lists in talk.

Symmetry and asymmetry in accounts

One of the ways in which accounting procedures can work using categorizations is to set up a number of contrasting or adjacent categories that do not operate in the same ways from occasion to occasion. For instance, categories of persons can be described as behaving the way they do because of the conditions in which they operate and the reasonable choices and practices that they exercise; other categorizations can have their behaviours explained in terms of their membership of a category, as 'that type of person'. When we find these two kinds of explanations given – which we may call, in the first case, contingent accounts, and in the second case, typed accounts – we have an instance of asymmetery in the accounting process. Related to that, we may find the same phenomenon accounted for in contingent or typed ways.

For instance, as reported in Freebody (2001), the phenomenon of parents' showing close attention to their children's educational progress can be accounted for in distinctive ways depending upon the relationship between the person doing the accounting and the culture of the community in which the phenomenon is observed. In that study teachers in schools in poverty areas were observed to account for some of the migrant parents' attention to their children's educational progress in terms of the cultures to which those parents belonged – 'that's just what they do in that culture'. This had the consequence, in the accounts of many of these teachers, of not allowing the children to develop independence and maturity as students. Similar kinds of parental diligence and attention were accounted for in more contingent ways by teachers working in schools and communities more congruent with their own cultural backgrounds. These parents had their diligence described in positive terms, with the consequence that the children were able to develop as effective and motivated learners in school. This distinction between explanations based on reasonable contingency and those based on categorization alone provides us with a significant move in documenting the ways in which speakers accord differing degrees of rationality, normality and moral acceptability to the various categories of people found in their talk.

Lists in talk

Finally, it is important to give some brief attention to the ways in which people use list formations in their interview accounts. Lists are surprisingly common, and they perform a number of significant functions. Lists can be of categories of persons, or they can deliver a category (in the sense that the list: apples, peaches, bananas; can deliver the category fruit). The items that are defined in a list are selected by speakers both for their internal adequacy (their immediate sense and recognizability) and to deliver up a particular course of social action that the list is to achieve in the talk, then and there. One of the things that has been noticed in list formations in talk (a technical treatment of which is in Jayyusi, 1984) is that lists seem to serve a certain iconic purpose in talk; they often entail an assumption that has been called the 'etcetera procedure', whereby the hearer is invited to make the relevant inferences of expanding on the generality of the point being made. In this sense, lists, like categorizations and typed accounts, cover over the specifics of people's practices, the ways in which people behave differently, and the different rationalities that people use in their behaviour. Consider the following example, spoken in an interview between an educational researcher and a doctor in a remote rural village. In discussing this example, we draw together some analytic features already discussed, as well as introduce some issues to do with the uses of lists.

EXAMPLE 7.13 *Golf, kangaroos and drunkenness*

1. Ir   So what are the main issues for you in living in this community?
2. Dr   I would stay here if there was another doctor in town. I spend probably rostered 3 hours a day at the hospital and the rest of the time, probably 8, 9 hours a day in the clinic and then there is all the after hours stuff which is split fairly evenly between the two, so you have very long days. Social isolation is one thing that is driving us away and education for the kids is the next thing that will drive us away and the after hours workload. So if you had another doctor where you could split work and I'll disappear this weekend and you cover, and I'll cover next weekend. You could probably handle it for a lot longer. Which is why doctors in little towns last about 2 to 3 years.
3. Ir   What do you mean by social isolation?
4. Dr   Either through background or education status, I mean even the teachers are too young, they are half my age, they may sort of have a similar sort of educational background we just have different life experiences. There is no one really that you can talk to, and most of the people that I do get on well with are 60 plus it is a really strange set up. You will find that in town, I have seen with the patients that there is a big chunk of people below the age of 15, a big chunk 60 and above, a smaller chunk that are 25 to 45, and a tiny little that are 20 to 30. I have noticed that between 20 and 40 they are virtually not in town. There is a handful of people, and that is it. On my weekend, if you don't play golf or if you don't shoot kangaroos or get drunk there is not much to do. You are privileged because you are the doctor, this is the community perception, but it is a privilege that they sort of begrudge, not all, but particularly the young, they

begrudge that as it is sort of inherited, that right. And it just reflects the answers there ((pointing to survey questions)) that 'literacy isn't important, literacy does not dictate the sort of career you get', it is as if these people haven't had that, therefore it is not important.

These are complex answers to apparently simple questions. This speaker responded to the question: Would you like your children to stay in this community? His first recourse was to the problem of the work load. He then mentioned, in the middle of work-related talk, the problem of 'social isolation', a point queried by the interviewer. The speaker then drew on background and stage-of-life as two MCDs that explain his social isolation. In this community, a number of people drew our attention to the unusual age distribution in the town, and the problems that leads to in terms of the range of activities and initiatives available. This speaker orientated to his perception of the age distribution in the town as a source of social isolation: those with similar educational and cultural backgrounds are significantly younger than him and there are very few in his age group.

The social isolation is further elaborated in the speaker's final comment, an answer to the question: What do you do in your leisure time? He invoked his lack of a social reference group again, drawing on class-related issues to do with prestige and its perceptions and cultural consequences. The first section of this final comment comprised a list of three activities: 'if you don't play golf or if you don't shoot kangaroos or get drunk there is not much to do'. How to interpret this list composition presents an analytic problem. Jayyusi (1984, Chapter 3) has made a number of critical observations concerning the use of lists in talk. First, lists can be collections of categories of people, or they can in fact deliver categories: that is, it is sometimes the case that the collection itself operates to allow the interpretation of some higher order categorization of people. Second, sometimes the order of the items is important; sometimes the items act cumulatively or reciprocally on and with one another. In the case of this list, are these three types of activities to be taken to refer to three types of people, to none of which the speaker relates? Or are the activities to be heard, cumulatively and sequentially, as offering a characterization of the one category of person encompassing all of the people in the village? If the latter hearing is preferred, then the sequence is artful in the context of the speaker's self-described social isolation in that it progresses from an acceptable activity with some class connotations ('playing golf') to a dubious and clearly rural activity ('shooting kangaroos') to a clearly morally unacceptable activity ('getting drunk'). The list delivers a downgrading of the community's activities. In the cumulative, sequential hearing, the neighbourhood as a whole is taken to be variously involved in all of these activities, affording the speaker's earlier conclusion that 'there is no one really that you can talk to'.

Thus, the earlier context of talk lends some common-sense support for this cumulative, sequential interpretation of this list. But the speaker's artfulness also extends to the provision of designedly ambiguous list formations. Both interpretations are technically available, and thus the speaker can formally fall short of, or at least equivocate in naming the whole town as getting drunk.

Third, Jayyusi insisted on the fundamentally interactional nature of list formations in talk. Like all communicative formations, lists comprise items selected to furnish the course of social action that the list aims to achieve in the talk, and to install an element of relevance to things said earlier and to be said later. In this case, the list is placed between a question about the speaker's leisure activities and his statements concerning his class position in the town. Immediately following the list is a series of observations that can be heard as 'internal quotes' silently attributable to the do-ers of the activities presented in the list: 'You are privileged because you are the doctor, this is the community perception . . .' and so on. So at the one time, the list can be heard as offering an explanation of why the speaker has 'not much to do' in leisure time, and as a bridge into an account of the community's 'begrudging' him his social position. This allows that 'begrudging' to be itself heard as an account of social isolation and lack of reference group.

We see that the speaker's third move in this final comment, recalling that it is an answer to the question 'What do you do in your leisure time?' is to relate the current talk to the question of literacy, discussed earlier in the interview session. What has been collected and then transferred onto the question of literacy and this community is a fundamental reasoning routine: the townspeople's view of his social privilege was named as the same logic that leads them not to value literacy. The view that the speaker does not deserve a position of privilege ('it is sort of inherited') comes from the people's lack of world experience in precisely the same way ('it just reflects the answers there') as the view that literacy is unimportant. The speaker thus characterized the resource he offers the town as a person and a medical practitioner as benightedly undervalued and indeed spurned. Here, then, the geographically local community is seen not only as empty in terms of resource-related information but also as alien and culturally hostile. Further, that hostility is seen to arise from the community's unacceptable cultural standing, made available through the apparently exhaustive list of preferred activities, and their ignorance of valued practices and attributes, such as literacy. So valuing medical practitioners and literacy, as sets of everyday activities, were together reconstituted as 'dividing lines' that demarcate 'other' groups of people and offer a ready index of social hierarchies, an index that reflexively sustains a particular moral organization of the local community.

Conclusions

One of the simple messages from the discussion in this chapter is that what is said about a certain phenomenon or event in interviews cannot be taken as a reliable proxy for the observation of that phenomenon or event. This is not because people tend to mislead interviewers (although at times there may be good reasons why they might), but rather because phenomena and events do not relate directly, finally and comprehensively to one fixed account. There are many ways to tell the 'truth' about something, and the ways that are chosen and mutually built up over the course of an interview have far-reaching consequences for what can be reliably concluded about speakers and the topics they address. We have seen that both interviewer and interviewee need to work to construct a common ground whereby the interactional and often moral rights and responsibilities of each, as part of what we commonly understand in our culture about interviews, can be productively co-ordinated.

That crucial understanding raises a number of other issues that have been central to the interests of this chapter. A documentation of what the interviewer does is central to an understanding of the contents of an interview. The interviewer's courses of social action give shape to an interview. For educational researchers to claim validity for their interpretations of interviews, they need to show:

1. how each speaker, including the interviewer, provides guidance for the preferred kinds of accounting – the MCDs, categorizations, attributions and reasoning practices – that constitute the interview's interests and relevances;
2. how these forms of guidance are visible in the interactional features of the talk – in the management of the turn-taking, the exchange structures, the production and repair of trouble, and the institutional and biographical characteristics of each speaker that are called into play for this interview here and now; and
3. how the interviewer provides designations, explicit or otherwise, of *who the interviewee is* for this interview (a farmer, mayor, doctor, family member, Deaf person, student, parent rich, poor and all the rest), and explicit norms for accounting. These then become part of the factual and normative framework of the interview, its empirical and moral 'centres of gravity'.

The premise of an interview is the construction of a mutually intelligible platform for formulations that are informative-for-that-occasion. In that respect, both interviewer and interviewee show one another their appreciation of one another's domain of the interest and forms of intelligibility. We may at first glance regard negotiations around those estimations as 'playing the interview game' or 'saying what the interviewer can, wants to, or needs to hear'. Even if we take the hard form of that argument, our data are still informative: what are revealed are the formulations, by this particular group of people, of what they take to be culturally available accounts of the lives of people in the category of person that makes them 'interviewable'. But even the soft form of this argument can be challenged. Unless we make the assumption that spoken formulations are transparently and generally true, and true, as they are spoken, in a wide variety of contexts, we would still need to make inferences about what is made available in other interactive social settings. This raises two serious challenges to the naïve acceptance of the proposition that there is a core of formulated truth with which the speaker is 'playing': first, the ways in which things are spoken of in other settings is always an empirical question; second, such a view assumes that the opinions, life histories or accounts of these people exist in some other truthful state outside of the social contexts of their formulation.

Qualitative researchers in education need to take seriously the demands for reliability and validity (Silverman, 1998). This requires a diligent focus on the empirical details of an interview. What aspect of interviewees' accounting practices may prove to be common or prevalent across a group cannot be determined in advance. A group of parents living in remote rural areas, for instance, may or may not show commonality in the categorizations they install to describe the people around them; they may attach common or distinctive attributions to those categorizations; they may deploy common or different explanatory or substantiation moves. It is these commonalities and variations that are the facts of the matter for that interview study.

We conclude by revisiting Gilbert and Mulkay's study of eminent bio-chemists. One of the ways we can re-specify their findings is to say that they found asymmetrical accounting procedures: the activities of the scientists' 'in-group' were accounted for in terms of contingent rationality – 'there are good, local, then-and-there reasons why "we do what we do"; "they do what they do" for reasons to do with the category to which they belong and the attributions that are readily and consistently attachable to that category'. What is sustained and rebuilt daily through the use of such asymmetrical accounting is a particular moral contrast, a moral relation that, even apart from the content of the attributions, renders the activities of the members of one category 'reasoned and reasonable' and the activities of the others non-contingent, non-reasoned and explicable, to put it bluntly, in the terms of strings and puppets. Agency and purposefulness are thus differentially distributed through account-ing procedures. This is a powerful way of downgrading members of certain troublesome, 'sundry' or 'deviant' categories, and thus its careful documentation can be one of the significant outcomes of interview analysis.

As common as they are in history's most interviewed and most interviewing of societies, interviews can nonetheless be seen as an odd way of finding things out about educational practice. In the everyday business of education, in whatever context, members of a culture not only act with one another; they show through their actions what it is they take themselves to be doing and how their actions are to be interpreted and acted upon and with. They provide, in their actions, visible accounts of teaching, learning, childhood, adulthood, expertise, competence, apprenticeship, and all the rest (Garfinkel, 1967).

The activities that people produce and manage every day include, of course, interviewing and being interviewed. Interviews, then, can be considered to give us 'naturally occurring' data. But the view developed here gives us important new ways of considering how people conduct themselves in interviews as instances of cultural practice, how they find ways of telling the truth-for-then-and-there, how they establish consistency and relevance, and how they attend to their co-speakers to enact and validate their rightful participation in the interviewing event.

These considerations appear to make the business of conducting and analysing interviews more complex and tentative than the naïve understandings that have guided much work to date. Another way of looking at that increased complexity, however, is to appreciate the enhanced purchase on validity and reliability that comes along with the less grandiose but more empirically defensible aims of understanding interviews themselves as cultural practices *about* cultural practices. Such enhanced validity and reliability give interview studies the potential to have more direct impact on educational practice and policy; they give us, as researchers, a more interesting and challenging intellectual task; and they install a view of the objects of our study – the people we interview – as artful, reasoned and sophisticated cultural practitioners.

DISCUSSION TOPICS, QUESTIONS AND EXERCISES

TRANSCRIPT 7.1 *A very short, short story*
(Ir=Interviewer, Tr=Teacher)

1. Ir   Do you want to talk to us about the poorer//
2. T   //right, poorer ones
      generally (.) generally they don't have much writing for a story
      basically they have maybe (1.0) ((makes noise)) one
      paragraph I know this one's probably an exception (1.0) u::m
      (.) yeah it's an exception for a poorer one she usually writes a
      bit less (0.5) but um (.) this one (.) this student [ha:as]
3. Ir   [Mm]
4. Tr   (.) u::m (1.0) whose name's Alison, her writing you know (.)
      she generally struggle (.) [can]=
5. Ir   [Mm]
6. Tr   =struggle with her writing
7. Ir   Mm
8. Tr   She's generally quite capable like I feel (.)
9. Ir   Mm
10. Tr U::m (.) like (.) she's (.) not necessarily from a (0.5) non-English
      speaking background but she is from overseas she's
      just arrived from New Zealand (.)
11. Ir Mm Hmm↑
12. Tr this year (.) and um (1.0) found it a little bit hard to adapt in
      the first term but generally she's fit in
13. Ir Mm
14. Tr since then (.) in terms um two and three. Her general wr-
      writing yeah tends to be um, you know, she tends to have
      poor punctuation or grammar or spelling umm, you know,

tends to rush through things and tends to (.) basically try and achieve or do things a short a time as possible
15. Ir   Mm
16. Tr   yeah.
17. Ir   So the structur:res? (.)
18. Tr   Yeah not not really suitable for a (.) it's like a story (.) [(you know)]=
19. Ir   [Mm]
20. Tr   =It's a very short short story
21. Ir   Mm

1. Consider the rights and responsibilities displayed by each participant in their turns at talk, specifically those which enable you to recognize the transcript as 'an interview' (and not, for example, 'an instruction activity'), and then answer the following:

   (a) Who is it that: asks questions; answers questions; opens topics; introduces issues and focus points; produces accounts and formulations; accepts, rejects, acknowledges, evaluates the relevance of matters at hand etc.
   (b) Can you find any turns or sequences of talk where participants' rights and responsibilities are distributed differently. As an example, examine turns 14 to 17 and consider whose task it is, in general, to 'provide an account of the salient features of poor writing'. Consider also the design of this exceptional case. How do the participants accomplish this sequence without disrupting the sequential organization of the interaction (so that it remains recognizable as 'an interview')?
   (c) From this segment, what implications do you see, if any, for people's understandings of teacher–pupil relations?

2. Establishing and maintaining the interview's 'footing':

   (a) How does Tr orient to the initial task-at-hand (nominated by Ir at 1) 'talk about the poorer writers' (i.e., what does Tr do when asked this question)?
   (b) What procedures does Tr use to substantiate his account of 'poor writing' in general?
   (c) What procedures does Tr use to substantiate his account of ((student)) as 'a poor writer' and as 'an exception'?
   (d) Which of the features listed by Tr as 'salient features of poor writing/writers' does Ir take to be relevant to the task-at-hand (talking about poor writers)?
   (e) What features do Ir and/or Tr consider not to be relevant? How do you know?

TRANSCRIPT 7.2 *Too much structure . . .*

1. Ir   Now year five they're supposed to have done the narrative
        genres?
2. Tr   Ye::[eah
3. Ir   [supposed to be consolidated [right?=
4. Tr   [yep
5. Ir   =by [this=
6. Tr   [yep
7. Ir   =time ↓ (.) so what's happened (.) do you [reckon what's
        your]=
8. Tr   [u::ummmm↑]
9. Ir   =best guess (.) on this
10. Tr (4.0)
11. Ir you can speak   [anonymously]
12. Tr   [As far as a narrative]
13. Ir ((laughs))
14. Tr As far as the narrative is concerned, I think they are given too
        much (2.0) structure [and not enough creativity]
15. Ir   [okay that's what you were saying before] yeah
16. Tr yeah
17. Ir yeah
18. Tr U:::::[um
19. Ir   [but ↑
20. Tr [( )
21. Ir [( )
22. Tr [(particularly the narrative)]
23. Ir [the structure should have] come out to you right? I mean (.)
        [complication
24. Tr [yeah
25. Ir resolution
26. Tr yeah↓ (.) Yeah they didn't hhh <u>I d- I didn't</u>↑ I think maybe
        too that teachers tend to use too (0.5) technical words (.) with
        the kids like they say (.) like this is – especially I used first
        steps when I went back to model this again with the kids
27. Ir Yeah
28. Tr and um I just photocopied straight off the plan to do a narrative
29. Ir Yeah
30. Tr and the words on it were really (1.5) too hard for the kids in my class (.)
        um I can't remember what they were but it was like orientation um
31. Ir (enhancing, synthesizing) and   [(all that stuff)]
32. Tr   [ye::::::::::::::ah] and stuff
        like that and (.) and I just blacked out those words straight
        away said 'put a cross through those and put' you know um
        'introduction (.) and tell me who's in the story (1.0) and
        where it is' (.) and then I said [u::::m
33. Ir   [mm hm↑

34. Tr you kn::ow (.) 'and and tell me where it's taking place (sort
        of) set the scene for me introduce it all to me tell me where
        it's happening' [and
35. Ir   [Mm
36. Tr hhh and then I said 'and then you wanna' (.) I said 'some
        problem's going to arrive↓' (.) you know, or- or 'tell me
        something that you need to be able to fix up you've run into a
        problem what sort of problem is it [describe it,
37. Ir Mmm
38. Tr how are we going to fix this problem'. Lots of them found
        problems fixing the problem like that   [solution=
39. Ir   [Mm Hmm
40. Tr =stage
41. Ir Mm Hmm↑
42. Tr That=
43. Ir Mm
44. Tr =totally blew them they all fixed it by saying (.) 'And it was
        fixed'
45. Ir Mm
46. Tr like no::o sort of (1.5) um (1.0) over[coming]=
47. Ir   [yeah
48. Tr =it
49. Ir Mm Hmm (.) yeah
50. Tr Like
51. Ir Yep
52. Tr [no::o]
53. Ir [yeah] (1.5) actual resolution
54. Tr Yeah

Exercises:

I's question 'they're supposed to have done the narrative genres . . .
so what's happened?' (turns 1–7) makes relevant R's prior claim (not
transcribed) 'I found these [year 5] kids couldn't do a narrative'.
R responds to I's question with an account of 'why these kids couldn't
do a narrative', that is 'they are given too much (2.0) structure and not
enough creativity' which she later reformulates (produces a different
explanation). Identify the turn(s) where R's reformulation occurs and then
answer the following questions:

(a) Why does R reformulate her account?
(b) Do you think R had an idea that her initial formulation would cause
     'trouble' prior to speaking it? How do you know this?
(c) What might I's challenge to R's initial account (turns 18–25) and R's
     subsequent reformulation tell us about I's local identity-for-the-
     interview? Consider I's use of technical vocabulary 'complication' and
     'resolution' (turns 23–25), I's position concerning the account (and
     later reformulation), and possible inferences drawn from R's initial

account ('they are given too much structure' – from where? by whom?).

(d) Again, what substantive procedures (anecdotal evidence, dramatic techniques, official discourses etc.) does R use to formulate her second account? Consider R's claim that 'teachers tend to use too technical words' (turn 26) and 'the words on it were really too hard' (turn 30) and the actions of both participants in design of turns 30 to 56.

(e) In both accounts, R employs a variety of substantive procedures, descriptions (of her classroom practice) etc. to construct (deliver) a version of herself as 'teacher' – normatively as 'a good teacher'. From the transcript, write a list entitled 'R's general categorical features of a good teacher for-the-purposes-of-this-interview and for-the-task-at-hand' (i.e. 'A good teacher is someone who . . .').

8

Analysing Educational Texts

What are texts?

A number of approaches to the analysis of texts are outlined in this chapter. The opportunity is also taken to illustrate two points that have been mentioned earlier: that quantitative and qualitative analyses may interplay in the conduct of a research project; and that grammatical analyses can offer principled lines of analysis in adding substance to Membership Categorization Analysis. This chapter can offer only a brief introductory sketch to those matters, and the interested reader is referred to references cited throughout the chapter for a more complete introduction.

Here the term text is taken to refer to crafted, communications – visual, graphic and electronic representations of language and objects. That is because it is not only printed documents or even electronic or printed representations of language that are prevalent in educational settings, where the term *texts* includes maps, diagrams, photographs, posters, magazines, school textbooks, literary works, notes, students' exercises and assignments, signs, report cards, vision statements, class notes, institutional regulations, websites, public signs, teachers' lesson preparation plans, letters between schools and homes, and all the rest. Having said that, the bulk of the examples used in the discussion below are graphic-based, due simply to the printed nature of this text.

A point that will recur throughout this chapter is that texts have an indeter-
minate, slippery relationship to the realities they depict. We can begin to view
this in operation by taking what seems to be a simple example, in what seems
to be a straightforward, non-linguistic format, of how the processes of representation function in various textual formats. We know that the earth is a sphere;
we know that the land masses on the earth are distributed in certain ways upon
that sphere. We can consider the ways in which texts represent choices in ways
of showing reality by exploring briefly how it is that the land masses on the earth
can be represented in two-dimensional textual form. How does the Earth
become a text? What, in short, is a map?

It turns out that there are many ways of showing the land masses of the earth
in two-dimensional format. Two of the most common ways are termed the
Mercator Projection and the Peters Projection. These are contrasted here to
illustrate the following propositions about how texts represent reality and
experience:

- all texts embody a number of purposeful choices about how reality is to be
  displayed;
- these choices have consequences for what it is that a text can afford about
  that reality; and
- these consequences are not only to do with interpretation; they also have
  implications for the varying opportunities people have for appreciating that
  this text is not a definite, unchallengeable representation of that reality.

Consider first the most familiar depiction of the land masses of the earth, the
Mercator Projection, shown in Example 8.1. It was developed in order to make
navigation easier for trade purposes ('mercator' is Latin for 'merchant'), by
choosing to make the imaginary boundaries formed by latitude and longitude
to be perfect squares and to be the same size across the map.

EXAMPLE 8.1 *The Mercator Projection of Earth*

Since the earth is a sphere, there are the two principal distortions Mercator
makes in the interests of navigation. First, the actual latitude–longitude
boundaries (that is, those on the planet itself) are nowhere perfect squares, and
the closer we get to the poles, the less they look like squares; second, the surface
masses within a latitude–longitude boundary will actually vary systematically
depending on how close the area is to the poles. What the Mercator Projection
does is blow up beyond their actual size those boundaries that are close to the
poles, and shrink by comparison those closer to the Equator. So, Europe, being
about 9.7 million square kilometres in size, appears larger than South America,
which is in fact about 17.8 million square kilometres; Scandinavia, about 1.1

million square kilometres, appears larger than India, which is about 3.3 million square kilometres; Greenland, with about 3.2 million square kilometres, appears larger than China, with 9.5 million square kilometres; Russia, 22 million square kilometres, appears vastly bigger than Africa, 30 million square kilometres, and so on. This typically results in the Equator and the Tropics being represented well 'below' their actual location on the sphere (as shown in Example 8.1), so that the relatively larger land masses of the far northern hemisphere can be shown in more detail.

One person who took some of these distortions to be problems was Arno Peters, who developed the Peters Projection shown in Example 8.2. This projection has a different set of purposes, preserving the actual sizes of land masses and retaining true orientation (north–south–east–west) from land mass to land mass. Note that the preservation of actual land mass sizes and the maintenance of exact north–south, east–west orientations are not incidental outcomes of the Peters Projection. They are explicitly why this representation of the planet was developed. Good for comparing land mass sizes, but less useful (and indeed a bit tricky) for navigating, at least in the seventeenth century.

EXAMPLE 8.2 *The Peters Projection of Earth*

We can also note a number of features of both of these representations of the planetary sphere. We see that both represent the centre of the map at the Greenwich Meridian, rather than at the International Date Line, that both omit

the continent of Antarctica, and that both represent what we call the Northern Hemisphere at the top of the page. Each of these issues has consequences for our understandings of the physical features of this planet and, in particular, of the land masses on it. Representing the International Date Line at the centre of the map, for instance, would result in a large proportion of that central area taken up by the Pacific Ocean. As it is, the island nations of the Pacific Ocean do not appear at any point on either of these representations of the earth. It is not that they are 'too small' to represent; there is actually no space for them on the page.

This brief example of how experienced reality comes to be represented in textual format, in this case, two-dimensional print format, gives us a starting point for a consideration of how texts are necessarily 'purposeful distortions' of, and abstractions from, that experienced reality:

1. texts need to look from somewhere (visually, conceptually, motivationally, ideologically);
2. texts shape experienced reality into the form that makes it usable for some activity – that is, texts both arise from and afford certain practices;
3. this shaping process necessarily results in 'purposeful distortions' – omissions, additions, and systematic mis-representations; and
4. these distortions have consequences for textual depiction and thus our understanding of reality. So what we can do, and what we do, with texts about some phenomenon in the world reflexively shape our understandings.

As an example of these consequences, the New Internationalist characterized the contrast between the Mercator and Peters Projections in this way:

> Traditional maps, of which the Mercator . . . is one example, have tended to show countries incorrectly in proportion to one another, to the advantage of the European colonial powers. . . . By setting forth all countries in their true size and location, [the Peters Projection] allows each one its actual position in the world. . . . The peoples of the world deserve the most accurate possible portrayal of their world. (New Internationalist, n.d.)

So even in attempting to depict visually an object as familiar as the land mass distribution on the earth as accurately as possible, the transfer from a three-dimensional, spherical representation, in the form of a globe, to a two-dimensional representation, suitable for print or electronic communication, has necessitated certain crucial decisions. These decisions can find their way into history as unremarked conventions, but they nonetheless have significant implications for how the object under study is 'read off' by those who are variously positioned by the representational process. So much more the case, then, when complex objects, concepts or experiences are represented by the even more abstract symbolic resources of language.

Why texts?:

> Schooling is a matter of mediating the relationship between children and the printed text. (Olson, 1977: 66)

Olson's comment represents the strong case for why educators should be urgently concerned with texts – what they are, how they function, and how they can be analysed in principled and productive ways. The representation of knowledge in texts makes education, as we know it, possible. Further, the exchange of texts makes communities, societies, cultures and states possible. What Olson's comment reflects, however, is a mid-twentieth-century view in two contrasting senses: it tends to ignore oral and visual texts that make educational practices possible in non-literate and pre-literate societies. That is, it tends to be a 'post-print' conception of educational practices. In another sense, looking from the future, it tends to overstate the case for print in the face of electronically mediated texts, and the reliance of even standard print materials on increasingly complex visual representations.

It is important that educators understand and can work in principled ways with texts. In contemporary societies especially, a critical understanding of cultural practice and social organization depends fundamentally on an understanding of how texts operate. This is because societies are made possible by the production and exchange of written, oral, electronic and visual textual materials: communications produce recognizable communities, and communities are made possible, at any given moment, and over time, by shared understandings of communicative products.

In all communities and societies, texts mediate and embody:

- the identities and practices of individuals;
- relationships among individuals;

- relationships between individuals and the institutions that bear on their lives; and
- relationships between individuals and the civic and community bodies that give shape to and regulate individual and collective experience.

Specifically for our purposes, educational practices, however informal and local, are made possible by texts. It is important for educators to recall, however, as Ong (1958) showed, that the ways in which texts are used in contemporary educational settings, both formal and informal, are not accidental. They have histories, and those histories are histories of victories and defeats – certain ways of organizing education, of thinking about what knowledge and learning are, and of conceiving the nature of learners' development and expertise – all of these that we now recognize have come to predominate because of their, potentially temporary, defeats of other contesting ideas and practices. The printed-set-text hold on much twentieth-century institutionalized education is not accidental, nor is it simply a natural product of inevitable forces.

Texts are cultural artefacts, producible and recognizable by cultural members as acts that communicate meaningful content. That a member of a culture can produce and recognize a meaningful text is explicable in terms of the cultural history that has gone before and the ways in which that member can draw on that history to enact the cultural practices relevant to the particular communicative context into which the text is to be or has been delivered.

There are at least three good reasons why educationists should be particularly interested in the ways in which texts operate and how they may be analysed in principled ways:

1. contemporary educational practice, like other cultural practice, is saturated by texts as resources for learners;
2. public educational arrangements are defined and regulated by texts; and
3. public educational activities are challenged, changed and legitimated by texts.

The first of these relates to the most obvious function of textual materials in educational practice, and that is that they are used as sources for learning; in most cases, students' actual achievements are gauged through their production of various kinds of text. Thus we find, as Olson argued, that, for the last hundred years or so at least, schooling has been centrally and increasingly about exposing young learners to texts and enhancing their abilities to manage, that is, use and produce, certain kinds of textual materials.

A second reason for considering the place and significance of text in educational activity relates to the institutional administration of formal education through schooling of various kinds. A wealth of policy documents, curriculum guidelines, syllabus outlines, and educational resources regulate the field on educational practice as it is publicly arranged through public institutions. In most countries, some form of schooling is legally mandated, and governed by sets of legal regulations embodied in texts. In addition, the details of the administration and conduct of public education are micro-managed, partly because of public schooling's reliance on motivations relating to equity, and partly because public education is an expensive governmental operation, requiring increasingly fine degrees of accountability. Thus it is that education, in its formal, mandated embodiments, is regulated by and through texts.

Finally, it is largely through texts that these two aspects of education as public activity are co-ordinated and legitimated. The relationship between, on the one hand, the institutional practices of schooling and the needs of communities, and on the other the regulation and education of individual students' lives, is given body and substance through the texts produced by schools for parents, for community members, for employing bodies, and in media representations of the strengths and weaknesses of current schooling as public activity.

These issues in the production of texts are particularly significant for educators because it is in the recruitment of textual representations in the conduct and management of educational practices that we see texts typically presenting themselves as undistorted, factual, and usable-for-all-purposes. Texts typically present as comprehensive and in complete good faith in their coverage of the reality at hand. They do not typically contain the grounds on which, or the motivations out of which their choices of perspective and 'purposeful distortion' have been made. Educational texts, visual, printed and electronically mediated, typically seem and claim to speak in one voice, for all possible perspectives and with competence and comprehensiveness. For the most part, they tell A Truth and it is, for the learner, The Truth, unless otherwise signalled.

Analysing texts

There has been an enormous amount of work done from within a variety of disciplines in the development of text-analytic techniques. The task here, rather than attempting to cover this daunting variety of possible qualitative approaches to texts, is less daring: it is to find some approach-paths that are firstly clear and publicly inspectable, and secondly that are compatible with the ideas developed so far in this book.

It is typical to divide approaches to the analysis of text into two large analytic categories: those deriving from linguistics and those from sociology. This usually results in two distinctive sets of analytic techniques, each apparently stand-alone, and each only minimally informed by and informing of the other. Linguistic approaches have typically been concerned with the application of a grammar, itself a theoretically derived taxonomy of language forms and functions; sociological approaches have typically looked at the kinds of ideological and cultural work done by a text, without necessarily offering any detailed taxonomic analysis of textual materials and themselves. Linguists have often criticized sociological approaches for their lack of attention to the structure of the object that they claim to be analysing. Sociologists in turn have often criticized linguistic approaches for the converse reason: that the meanings of texts as cultural objects cannot simply be found in the interiors of a text, and certainly not through a pre-emptive application of grammatical theories.

To organize this chapter, I try to sidestep the problem of simply offering a range of stand-alone approaches that are broadly compatible with a cultural science approach to education. I aim to locate particular analytic moves arising from linguistic and sociological work on texts within a picture that is compatible with the analytic design specifications already laid out in earlier chapters. To do this I use the principal headings that were applied in the previous chapter dealing with the analysis of interviews. First I approach texts as objects that reflect and construct accounts of reality. In keeping with the analytic designs outlined earlier, I approach and illustrate this with four analytic moves, exploring the ways in which crafters of texts render texts sensible and interpretable as cultural objects:

1. locating and documenting the categorizations of persons that are represented in the text;
2. showing how it is that certain attributions are made to these categorizations, in the case of texts, through the attachment of processes (often in the form of verbs) and descriptors (generally in adjectival and adverbial forms);
3. showing how it is that this combination of categorizations and attributions affords a particular line of reasoning that describes, locates, accounts for, explains and elaborates on the topics in the text;
4. documenting the ways in which the author(s) of the text substantiate these categorizations, attributions and explications through the deployment of a variety of linguistic and social resources.

Under this heading we consider as well the text's accounts (including those it assumes or ignores) as reflections of cultural and social order, both a reflection and a rebuilding of ideas, attitudes, relationships and ideologies evident in the cultural context in which the assumed readers live.

The second general approach I take is to consider text as interaction. There are two senses to this:

1. texts are seen as communications with an intended or idealized reader, in which the crafter of the text builds in and makes evident presuppositions concerning the knowledge, disposition, values, and so on, of the reader; and
2. texts can be considered from an interactional point of view by regarding them as platforms for cultural activities. This is the sense in which we can consider texts as objects-in-cultural-action, detailing the ways in which textual materials are used in a variety of educational activities.

Through the object to the account

Much of the study of educational linguistics can be characterized as the search for ways of documenting what texts, as linguistic and symbolic objects, afford a reader. That is, regardless of what it may be that the reader takes from a text or what the underlying conditions for the production and sense of a text may be, many researchers have used a variety of theories of language to document the potential meanings and implications that may be derived from any given crafted object of communication. Note that such linguistic approaches are not essentially theories of reading, writing, or of the uses of text in actual educational activities. Rather they offer a way of looking at the extent of the possible range of ideational, communicational, relational and ideological work that a text *may* offer.

As we saw in the previous chapter, this notion of *work* needs to be taken essentially to be cultural work, in which accounts of some topic are built using recognizable categorizations, attributions and explications that are both available in the culture and that can be reworked, adapted and modified to reflect any particular social setting or activity in which writers and readers are involved. As in the earlier chapter, we begin by examining the central categorizations of persons that are made in a text. In linguistic terms, this means we can begin by examining the human or human-like agents and objects through which a text represents its fundamental ways of carving up the social world. First, we consider and illustrate approaches that begin by the simple method of noting heavy-duty words and formations and proceed to build up the Membership Categorization Analysis from this starting point.

From frequency to accounting

One simple approach to the issue of what it is that texts can offer by way of meaning and interpretation is to study the patterns of word usage. There is a large tradition of studying word usages in texts and corpora of texts for educational purposes. One place to start is to look at the frequencies of certain kinds of words, and to make inferences about what aspects of the texts – their content or structure – may be worth more detailed qualitative follow up. For instance, Freebody and Baker (1985, 1987) reported patterns in the uses of expressive or emotional words in a large corpus of beginning school books, the first reading materials young children get to read in their first year or two at school. One of the findings encountered in the early stages of the analysis of this corpus of materials was the prevalence of children and parents as characters in the stories, along with the complete absence of the word *child*. All references to individual children in the entire corpus were gendered – *girl, boy, girls, boys*. This signpost was taken as an instruction to examine the ways in which generation and gender operated as Membership Categorization Devices through the activities and descriptions of these categories of characters. Some further quantitative analyses (shown in Freebody and Baker, 1987) pursued the question of the emotional or expressive attributes attached to these various categories – what the characters were said to *like*, what they found in it to be *good*, who *laughed* and who *cried*, when they did these things, and so on. Some examples of the findings can be summarized as follows:

1. The term *like* is applied to the case of one person liking another very rarely; it is used by and about parents almost never, and the boy(s)-characters are statistically more likely to *like* objects and events, while the girl(s)-characters tend to *like* animals.
2. The term *good* is much more likely to be used by persons to or about one another than is *like*. Further, the patterns of association of use among characters are: mother(s) call and describe girl(s) as *good*; father(s) call and describe boy(s) as *good*; boy(s) call and describe events as *good*.
3. The term *laugh* has the following statistical associations: boy(s) *laugh* more than girl(s); adult(s) *laugh* at boy(s) and animals, while girl(s) *laugh* at boys and adults. Girl(s) rarely *laugh* and are never laughed at.
4. The term *cry* is never applied to adults; girl(s) *cry* at being lost, hurt or losing objects; boy(s) almost never.
5. Boy characters, and never girl characters, are in the agent position of the following verbal processes: *answer*, *hurt*, *shout*, *think*, and *work*.
6. All verbal processes for which girl characters are in agent position also show boy characters as agents; that is, there are no exclusively girls' actions represented.
7. In the object position of verbal processes, boys and never girls are: *jumped with*, *liked*, *played with*, *talked to* and *walked with*.
8. In the object position of verbal processes, girls and never boys are: *held on to* and *kissed*.

These reading books that children and teachers use in the early years of schooling, at least in the corpus studied by Freebody and Baker, are almost entirely in the form of stories located in the domestic space of the suburban nuclear family. The family, in fact, can be seen as the central organizing Membership Categorization Device for most of these little stories. The physical, intellectual, social and emotional work accomplished by the characters in these stories is divided among the categories afforded by the device Nuclear Family. The adult-characters in these early school reading materials produce almost no expressive talk or activity, and appear to act as agents of surveillance, even when they are not present in the fictive scene. More obviously, the expression of subjective feelings and judgements in domestic settings is firmly cast along gender and generational lines. These patterns of association constitute the unseen texture of, in this case, institutionalized gender and generation relations. They can be seen as a pattern of presentations that constructs a 'virtual' domestic world for use in the classroom.

By using these key references to the various character-categorizations in the text, and by exploring their associations with verbal processes, using, at this point, common-sensical grammatical knowledge, we can begin to develop a set of guidelines as to what may be the key categorizations at work in organizing these texts as cultural products. The prevalence of *children* and the absence of *child* alert us to the significance of both generation and gender as dimensions for the organization of meaning in these texts. Which is to say that the texts appear, just from this analysis of the frequency of key terms, to make much of the difference between adults and children, and the difference between male and female children. The associations noted above also give us hints as to what it is that is made of these differences and how they may become central to the discourses through to which young, novice students need to look. Thinking reflexively again, we can consider that the texts call forth a reader who takes such cultural dimensions to be critical in an understanding of the everyday, common-sensical workings of the culture. When we consider that these books are the first actual school books that most children encounter when they become students, and that these books provide the platforms for much of the work that is done to lead children into becoming readers, then their force as agents of acculturation becomes clear.

But an understanding of the contents of this acculturation can only be suggested by these broad-gauged frequency analyses. To explore how these dimensions operate to allow a firmer platform for commentary about the nature of these books as institutional and cultural products we need to look in a more distinctively qualitative way at the texts themselves, keeping in mind the sign posts that have been offered by the frequency analysis. The following text is an example from a book used in the first year of schooling. It is taken from the corpus studied by Baker and Freebody (1989), and illustrates the follow-up of hints from the frequency analysis summarized above.

EXAMPLE 8.3 *'You can do it, Mary'*

'We have to jump this,' says Peter.
'Come after me. I know how to do it.
Come after me, but keep out of the water.'
Mary says, 'Mummy said that we must keep out of the water.'
'I know she said so,' says Peter,
'but we are not going in the water.
I know how to do this.'
Peter jumps again. 'You can do it, Mary,' he says.
Then Mary jumps. She says, 'Yes, I can do it.
Look at me, Peter. I can do it.'

Clearly, Peter's statements amount to a series of commands and exhortations. Mary's interactional rights and responsibilities consist of a reminder of 'mummy's' command and announcements of her achievement. We might also note that the author's choices consist of the use of the present tense to report ('he says'), and a series of short, grammatically simple declarative sentences, embodying the purpose-built nature of the text and its potential function of reflecting teachers' or parents' work with early or non-readers. The language seems close to oral communication, even when it is the author who 'speaks'.

So we can develop a sense that the portion of the market at which a text such as this is aimed:

- young schoolchildren, capable enough in oral language and familiar with its general patterns,
- but perhaps not yet able or interested to read texts without direct speech,
- in the context of stories that appear at least familiar to them,
- with characters drawn from the same category as themselves,
- doing apparently everyday activities.

But, of course, it is not the schoolchildren that buy such texts. They need to be marketable to the adults working in schools, who make decisions concerning the purchase of reading materials for young students. In that sense, such texts need to reflect activities, dispositions, and values that are familiar and at least not apparently offensive or odd to these adults. As Baker and Freebody (1987) have argued, what needs to be evident are versions of childhood that are at least familiar to the category of people who buy such texts.

Through the interplay of quantitative frequency analysis and Membership Categorization Analysis we can elaborate on the particular ways in which words are used to embody and inflect categorizations made in the crafting of texts such as these.

From grammar to accounting

In the previous section the major signpost for a more detailed pursuit of the qualitative dimensions of the texts was provided by simple frequency analysis. In this section a different starting point is used. Many linguistic researchers begin with a taxonomic theory of some description of how language works and begin by analysing texts in these terms. The point made here, and throughout this book, is that analysis of texts as they are used in educational settings needs to begin with an understanding of education as cultural practice. One of the analytic lines used to develop this in the earlier chapters has been MCA. The particular line taken in this section is that a grammar, in this case Systemic Functional Grammar, can be used in the service of MCA, even though each begins at a distinctive place in its conception of language as social practice.

A variety of linguistic approaches have been well developed in the area of education, but one that is chosen here as an illustration derives from Systematic Functional Linguistics (henceforth, SFL; see Halliday, 1985; Martin, 1992). SFL directs our attention to three sets of 'metafunctions' of language-in-use – the ideational, relational and textual – and to the two contexts in which language-in-use operates – the context of culture and the context of situation. When any instance of language is evident in any situation, SFL approaches its analysis by documenting how the metafunctions are realized, made concrete, in that situation by analysing the three variables related to the metafunctions – the 'field' of the language (the ideational content, what the language is about), the 'tenor' of the language (the relational context, how the language reflects and builds the relationship between the communicators), and the 'mode' of the communication (the textual features of the language that relate to the channel of communication, such as written versus spoken, email versus phone, letter versus website, and so on).

As a simple example to start, consider Example 8.4, a graffito on the wall of a tunnel that passes under a motorway and connects two campuses of an Australian university. The writing is in large red lettering, with florid, extended serifs.

EXAMPLE 8.4 *'against us'*

We train asians to compete against us –

Australians first!!

A first point to notice about this graffito is that it is not surprising or puzzling to us. It is the kind of sentiment commonly expressed in graffiti: it is chauvinist and often counter-cultural, while at the same time laying claim to a cultural congruence and alliance with the reader. We can ask 'what has motivated the choice of a large red letters with extravagant serifs?'; we can also note that this message was written on the tunnel wall between two campuses of the university which has a high enrolment from students living in Asia, and which is in the middle of a large suburban area inhabited by many Australians who have migrated from Asia.

Considering the grammatical structure of the graffito, we note that the term 'we' is in the opening foregrounded agent position, that the competing supposedly done by Asians is directly attributed to our training of them (through the use of an infinitive formation, 'train . . . to compete') rather than a new process at the same clausal level ('train . . . and they compete'); that the theme of the following clausal fragment indicates an exhortatory formation, and that it is to be taken, in the absence of any other indications, to be a parallel to the foregrounded agent of the first clause ('we' equals 'Australians').

We can also ask about the ways in which these grammatical choices on the part of the writer of this text all serve to add to the specification of the categories used and the effects on the alignment of the reader to one or the other of those categories. We have noted that the initial 'we' is grammatically paralleled by the subsequent 'Australians'. The categories we see in this text, therefore, are Asians and Australians. Given the context in which this text is located – a university with foreign people from Asia as students, and a suburb with Australians who have migrated from Asia – the ambiguity built into the contrast between Asians and Australians is clear. The text itself serves to punctuate the difference between those who have membership in either of these categories. Grammatically at least it is therefore impossible, within the world created by this text, to belong to both groups. In this sense the text can be regarded as an instance of the discourse in which nationhood (e.g., Australian) is on a conceptual par with ethnicity (e.g., Asian). In that respect, the text disallows the possibility of a multi–ethnic nation. Note that it reflects this discourse, rebuilds it, affirms it, and directly aligns the reader to it.

We extend the illustration of the possible applications of Systemic Functional Linguistics to educational texts by considering some of the textual materials to which the students in school may be exposed. Recall that the goal here is to use some systematic analytic tools to provide us with a characterization of the choices made by those who produce texts and the consequences for the acquisition of knowledge, the building of relationships, and the maintenance or challenge of dominant ways of thinking about topics in a society. Consider the following key sections from a prominent text on economics for upper secondary school (Tisdell, 1979: 173–9). The topic under discussion is 'less developed countries' ('LDCs'), the ways in which they became that way, and their common features.

EXAMPLE 8.5 *'a reflection of overall poverty'*

Less-developed countries (LDC's) tend to be characterised by the following features:

1. Subsistence living and limited use of markets: Most individuals in less-developed countries use their output for their own family [. . .] and exchange little of their production. [. . .]
2. A high proportion of the workforce in less-developed countries is engaged in agriculture and in other primary industries. [. . .] The manufacturing sector and the tertiary sector in underdeveloped countries are also comparatively small.
3. Technical change in less-developed countries is normally slow and producers often cling to traditional methods. In some circumstances, however, traditional methods may be more appropriate than Western capital-intensive methods. [. . .]
4. Savings are small and the rate of capital accumulation is low. [. . .] those on high incomes in the LDC's are reputed to spend most of their income on ostentatious consumption rather than to invest in productive works. [. . .]

5. Business motivation or entrepreneurship of a productive nature may be lacking. [. . .] Capitalistic entrepreneurship may be lacking.
6. Unemployment, labour-intensive methods, underemployment are common. [. . .]
7. Life expectancy is low, nutrition and health poor. [. . .]
8. High growth rates of the population and a distorted age distribution of the population add to poverty. The higher rate of (population) increase in the LDC's may reflect the less frequent use of birth control techniques. [. . .]
9. Urbanization problems but a proportionately low urban population. [. . .]
10. Lack of social overhead capital. The supply of roads, ports, hospitals, schools, telephone services, water and sewerage facilities is limited. This is a reflection of overall poverty. The ability of the government to raise revenue for public works through taxation is limited. [. . .]
11. Illiteracy is widespread and the technical skills required in modern industry are in short supply.
12. The distribution of income in LDC's is very uneven [. . .]
13. Dualism. [. . .] an urban monetary economy consisting of individuals engaged in Western style industry and a rural traditional barter economy. [. . .]
14. Export dependency on one or two primary products. [. . .] The prices of primary products tend to be very unstable and specialization in such a limited range of primary products (lack of diversification) adds to risk as a rule. [. . .]

We can follow a number of simple steps to begin an analytic commentary on this text, by asking the following questions of it:

1. Who or what is in it? Who or what are the participants? We start here by looking at the nouns or nominal formations.
2. What gets done? What are the verbal processes that the text shows 'getting done?'
3. Are some of the 'doings' . . . the processes . . . shown here as nouns, as things, rather than processes?

One straightforward place to start in considering what it is that this text affords, using SFL as an approach, is to examine who or what it is that are the active or working subjects or objects – the participants – in this text. We can examine both human and non-human participants, and show what kinds of work they do, and what is done to them in a text such as this. This is an initial approach to exploring how the text builds its 'field'. In this particular text, for example, the nature of human participation and the abstract agencies of 'poverty' are central features. The human participants (and the processes associated with them) in this text are:

•   individuals ('use their output . . .'; 'exchange little');
•   the workforce ('is engaged in . . .');
•   producers ('cling to traditional methods . . .');
•   those on high incomes ('are reputed to spend . . .');

- population (its 'high growth rate' 'adds to poverty');
- government ('limited' 'ability to raise revenue . . .').

We can now consider who or what it is that is shown to act in this text – who does the 'doings'? In terms of SFL, this amounts to asking what participants are in the foregrounded agent position of active verbs or processes. Table 8.1 shows the agents and the verbal processes to which they are attached in this text.

TABLE 8.1 *Agents and their associated processes in Example 8.5*

Agent/Categorization	Process/Attribution
LDCs	tend to be
manufacturing sector	are
tertiary sector	are
technical change	is
traditional methods	may be
savings	are
rate of capital accumulation	is
business motivation	may be
entrepreneurship	may be
capitalistic entrepreneurship	may be
unemployment	are
labour-intensive methods	are
underemployment	are
life expectancy	is
nutrition	is
health	is
high growth rates	add to
distorted age distribution	add to
rate of population increase	may reflect
supply of . . . etc.	is
ability of government	is
illiteracy	is
technical skills	are
distribution of income	is
prices	tend to be
specialization	adds to

In Table 8.1 we can see that many of the agents in this textual representation of reality are mainly abstractions and nominalizations – processes that have been grammatically turned into 'things' through the use of nouns, as shown in the first column of the table. Two points can be noticed immediately when we tabulate the agents and the processes they are associated with (through verbs). First, we can see that a few of the agents are references to collectives ('LDCs, manufacturing sector, tertiary sector'), but the remainder are abstractions – ideas or concepts – that are depicted through the grammatical choices of the writers as 'doing' the 'doings' of the text. These abstractions, well removed from explicit human activity, are the moving forces of the processes, as this text depicts them.

A second observation we can make is that the processes do not typically reflect material actions in the world. They consist mostly of forms of the verb to be, sometimes modulated ('tend, may'), with the 'things' sometimes joined to something else ('add'), and sometimes standing for something else ('reflect'). These processes serve to construct a 'static' textual world, a world in which these abstractions and collectivities appear to 'be', independently of active happenings or direct human agency. In terms of the grammar, then, there is not much action in this text – things 'are'.

We can consider the production of abstractions, their representations in texts as agents that can actually do things, and of the representation of the world of the text as a static – a collection of things in space, rather than as active, material processes – all as options exercised in the crafting of the text to substantiate the picture that it portrays, and to give it an apparently independent existential status. In the discussion of substantiation procedures provided in the previous chapter, a number of options were discussed and illustrated: reference to official documents or research, anecdotes, dramatizations through, for example, direct speech, describing the self as experienced and competent, and so on. All these may well be evident in printed, electronic or visual texts as well. Here, however, we explore some additional substantiation resources that are available in the production of textual products. In that respect, we can consider descriptions of linguistic elements in a language as referring in part to the interactional resources that speakers and writers have at their disposal as they go about the more leisurely and typically more deliberate production of printed, electronic or visual textual materials.

So the choices of the authors display agenda that serve to make this an abstract and static description. Abstract notions *act* in this text; but, at the same time, there is little actual action; the processes relate to statements of what is, rather than what happens or what has happened to create this state.

The human participants that are in the agent and theme positions need to be considered not just in terms of their relative infrequency, but also in terms of how they as choices serve to construct the socio-political 'world' of the LDC and how accounts and responses are thus constrained. That is, it is notable that the human participants that appear present the following hierarchical societal composition: individuals, who may be producers, combine into families, into a workforce, into a population, into a country. That, so to speak, is the human taxonomic tree that this text presents. No descriptive terms for people are given that might afford an explanation or response that relies on subgroups within a nation-state contesting or struggling for resources or decision-making power.

This approach gives us a linguistic, vocabulary and grammatical map of what it is that might be gleaned from a text. It clearly relates to the interpretations that the text might make available, but as a purely linguistic approach, it assumes a somewhat idealized view of what it is that text may function to do in the world. It also assumes certain kinds of interpretational work on the part of an idealized reader, by providing the technical vocabulary to document much of what it is that a text might afford the 'Compleat Reader', so to speak. That is, most linguistic approaches assume a default reader, using a text in a default set of circumstances, with a default collection of understood or implicit purposes in reading and analysing a text.

The grammatical and vocabulary moves made in a text do not serve just to provide information or a set of ideas about the topic at hand. As we noted when considering possible maps of the earth, texts operate in a reflexive manner with respect to the relationship between the topic at hand and the reader. A text needs to be produced from a particular vantage point on the facts of the matter, the important ideas about the matter, and the values and norms that are associated, explicitly or otherwise, with the topic at hand (see Gee, 1999). Similarly, a text calls for a reader who shares such vantage points. In that respect we can consider that, while a reader may interpret a text in particular ways, the text also serves, however successfully, to *position* the reader in terms of the key facts, ideas, disposition so, norms and values. This notion of positioning the reader is a central idea in many contemporary approaches to the analysis of texts. Consider, as an example, the following text, drawn from a resource book found in a school library. This example (discussed in Freebody et al., 1991, and drawn from *The Aztecs: A Remarkable Civilisation*, Purdy and Sandak, 1982: 1) shows the first two sentences of a book about the Aztecs. Using the notion of the positioning of the reader, we can begin by considering what presuppositions a reader needs to make this text sensible:

EXAMPLE 8.6 *'The New World'*

The Aztecs were Indian people who controlled an empire in Central Mexico when the Spaniards opened up the New World to exploration, conquest, and settlement. Under Hernando Cortez, the Spanish reached Mexico in 1519, when the Aztec civilization was at its height.

The actual vocabulary and grammatical patterns that make up these sentences can be examined, as can some interesting questions about the major categories that are established here: we see 'Aztecs' (as part of a larger group of Indian people) and the 'Spaniards/Spanish' ('under Hernando Cortez).

What makes these sentences sensible – able to be understood and appreciated by the reader? How is the reader positioned by the categorizations and what is attributed to them? That is: What are the pre-conditions of interpretation that make it possible for a writer to state that the Spaniards 'opened up' the 'New World'? How and for whom is or was this world 'New'? How can the Spaniards have 'opened up' this place 'to settlement', when the next sentence tells us that another civilization was at 'its height' in this place when they arrived, and when the rest of the book is predicated on the idea that the Aztecs had spent centuries developing a 'remarkable civilization'? The critical question here becomes the location, in time, place and culture, of the writers who can deploy such terms in good faith and believing they are telling the truth in an objective manner. These words, in turn, serve to locate a reading position for such a text, in this case a position that regards the continent of America as a 'new world' in the sixteenth century, in spite of the fact that it contained empires, inhabitants, and civilizations before they arrived. In time, place, and culture, therefore, these opening sentences of this book position the reader as viewing the topic of the Aztecs from a European perspective. The language of the text itself is the language of the Spanish who arrived in Central America and who may well have described themselves as 'opening up' that area in these ways. As with our consideration of the maps of the earth, this is not necessarily a criticism of this particular text, but rather a recognition that a text needs to 'stand somewhere', to look from a vantage point, and to embody that vantage point in the grammatical and vocabulary choices that are exercised in its crafting.

Macherey described these aspects of the text analysis in the following terms:

> a true analysis does not remain within its object, paraphrasing what has already been said; analysis confronts the silences, the denials and the resistances in the object – not that compliant discourse which offers itself to discovery. (1978: 150)

That is, while a text has a material history – how, when, why, and in whose interests it was made – it also draws upon a cultural history, a history of inter-pretations, that allows the members of a culture to hear or see it as both sensible and reasonable. The writer offers certain reading positions to us, as 'natural' and 'factual', that in fact ask us to participate in certain beliefs and silences. It is these that the text relies upon for the recognition of its possible meanings, in the broad and multiple senses of that term. Documenting those beliefs, silences, inferences and strategies that texts use to position readers is part of the analytic process; it cannot be relegated to some other domain such as 'subjective interpretation', in particular when we approach the uses of text in education from a cultural science perspective. There is nothing subjective or idiosyncratic to the individual about the ways in which texts draw on cultural understandings and use strategies to silence, marginalize or simply ignore other available interpretive resources and vantage points.

From interpretive frames to accounting

As a final analytic example in this section, we can consider the ways in which the choice of categorizations, the attributions made to them, along with the explanatory or descriptive practices that a text installs, can be further synthesized into a more general statement concerning the interpretive frameworks that a text calls upon. This example is drawn up from the work of Austin et al. (2001), who were concerned to document the versions of childhood represented in a novel for children, and the ways in which these versions were acted out in classroom lessons using the novel. (This latter corpus of data is reconsidered in later sections where we examine the kinds of interactions that text make possible, and the kinds of readings that those interactions produce.) This example concerns a novel used in the upper primary school years in Australia. Clearly, the analysis of an entire novel presents a distinct set of problems for the qualitative researcher. Unlike the contents of the corpus of beginning reading materials as studied by Freebody and Baker (1985; and see Baker and Freebody, 1989), this text is a long and integrated story. The task of beginning to analyse such an extended and integrated text, however, is similar to how we have started so far. Austin, Freebody and Dwyer began by examining the major categorizations of persons and the ways in which attributions are built up of those categorizations through description and through the activities that are attached variously to them. The novel under consideration in this example (*Magpie Island*, Thiele, 1974) concerns a young boy, his father and a bird that becomes stranded on a remote island. Through close MCA of the scenes depicting the son and his father, and of the scenes in which the bird is shown as a young fledgling, Austin, Freebody and Dwyer documented the versions of childhood described and enacted in the novel. In the first instance, MCA provided a description of childhood as it is seen in the text, both through the ascribed and implied attributions of the child characters alone, and in Standardized Relational Pair partnerships with adult characters. Attributions of the child characters were found to include 'gabbling', headstrong and squabbling, contrasted with the calm, serene and tolerant adult attributes, presumably that the child characters had yet to attain.

However, certain interpretive requirements of the novel complicate a simple reading of childhood in terms of these contrasts. There is also a child described by the text, that is the child–reader assumed by the text. As this novel was written and marketed especially for children, and taken into a classroom for children, we ask; What sort of child can read and make sense of this novel? Baker and Freebody (1989) detailed the appropriate interpretive competences of the child-readers called upon, for example, by the interleaving of fantasy and reality commonly found in texts for children (e.g., 'Hose me too!' barked Boxer). In the novel *Magpie Island*, Austin, Freebody and Dwyer found three broad interpretive frames that are called for:

1. *A Realistic Narrative Frame*, requiring the reader to call on the relevances of the real world when making sense of the text (stretches of text with zoological information about magpies, geographical information about the island, and so on).
2. *An Anthropomorphic Narrative Frame*, requiring the reader to call on the relevances of the anthropomorphized world of animals which act, talk, think and feel as humans when making sense of the text.
3. *An Allegorical Frame*, requiring the reader to call on the moral relevances of allegory and parable when making sense of the text.

A further feature of this novel was found to be not only the co-existence of the three frames in the novel, but slippage between them. The novel draws on one and then another, sometimes a whole paragraph will draw on one frame (realistically discussing the habitat and life cycle of an animal for example), and then the next paragraph another (anthropomorphically making analogous links between the life of a bird and that of a human for example, or the bird having human-like thoughts, hopes and dreams). Such slippage assumes particular interpretive competences of its child reader.

As an instance, the novel's finale provides a pivotal example of the slippage between interpretive frames (Austin, 1997, provides an extended discussion of these examples, and the points in Example 8.7 are drawn directly from there). Having returned to the island to find that the Mate and eggs have died and Magpie is alone again, Benny and his father sail away.

EXAMPLE 8.7 *'he saw what his father meant'*

Benny looked back at the cove 'Poor old Magpie. He looks so lonely there – worse than he was before.'
  [Said by the father] 'That's life' 'It's sad and I'm sorry.'
  'Same everywhere. Same with people, even.'
Benny thought for a long time over that.
  'Never mind, Benny. Think of what he stands for. He's a symbol, a talisman. Endurance carved into a silhouette. The everlasting picture of the one against the world. Something for people to get their inspiration from.' . . .
  And then, suddenly he saw what his father meant. Magpie was a dot on a tree, that was a twig on a hill, that was a hump on an island, that was a barrowload of rock. And all around were the vast violent wildernesses of the sea and the mountainous storm clouds lowering in the sky. Solitude. Isolation. Loneliness. Menace. But Magpie was there, and alive. He would live out his whole life there now, defying all the storms and thunderclaps that heaven could turn against him. Sailors and fishermen would slow down their vessels as they went by, and point him out. 'Magpie Island,' they would say, and write it on their maps. He would become a legend as big as a mountain. He would be Crusoe for modern men. He would stir the hearts of lonely people and make stale dreams come fresh again.
  'Goodbye Magpie,' Benny whispered. 'Don't get too lonely all by yourself out there.' . . .
  'Tomorrow's going to be a bright new day.' [said by the father] . . .
But it was dark outside. (47)

The sequence of movement between interpretive frames is this: the novel, through the quoted speech of the father, makes explicit the symbolic and moral interpretation of the narrative. It provides a reading from within an allegorical interpretive frame. Benny, the child character, elaborates that allegorical reading in terms of Magpie as a symbol. The anthropomorphic narrative frame is re-instated. The status of the final reading is ambiguated ('But it was dark outside').

So in this final scene of the novel the text ambiguates its own reading possibilities. Different interpretive frames are referenced from line to line. The novel itself does not establish the allegorical tale as its definitive interpretive frame but as one of a variety of possible interpretive frames.

Austin, Freebody and Dwyer concluded that there is a theory-of-childhood-in-action available in the writing of the novel. Specifically, the child-reader who can make sense of this novel, then, is assumed to be:

1. able to interpret within realistic, anthropomorphic and representational frames;
2. able to 'slip' from one interpretive frame to another in order to read the novel as sensible and coherent; and,
3. tolerant of ambiguity in interpretation, that is accept parallel final renderings of the story, a 'real' ending, a 'sad' ending and a 'symbolic' ending.

The reader of this novel then, is assumed to have considerable interpretive competence and the capacity to accept ambiguity in the final reading of the narrative. We see in the next section how it is that the talk in the classroom, in which the students are discussing this novel, acts upon some and not others of these ideas about childhood, interleaving them with institutional, school-derived ideas about the child-student, in bringing an additional, teacher-sanctioned reading into being.

In making texts, people draw on cultural practices and produce recognizable traces of them. Texts embody these practices, and the traces in the text are brought to life when a cultural member participates in a textual communication. We saw three general approaches to the documentation of the accounts on which texts rely and which they call upon and reinstate. The first of these we arrived at through a frequency analysis of a large corpus of texts; the second we approached through analysis of the many resources that the grammar of language offers and calls upon in the production of texts; in the third, broader interpretive frameworks led to a consideration of character-types in the novel and of the competences and interests of the ideal readership. It is important to keep in mind that the fundamental analytic goal here is to document the accounts that we find: those mutually constitutive categories, attributions, reasoning practices, and substantiation procedures that form the ground-in-common that is a communication. These cultural and linguistic resources simultaneously:

- build up the field of the topic, and the vantage-point from which it is to be viewed;
- construct and position the readership; and
- represent substantiation procedures in three ways: by manipulating the evident agency related to the actions shown in the text; by the abstraction of processes, objects and groups; and by entrenching the ontological status of the topic under discussion (to 'objectify' it), at the same time rendering of the text 'objective', an apparently transparent window onto reality.

These approaches tell us about ways of systematically drawing out the traces of cultural practice that texts embody. They do not, however, constitute a comprehensive qualitative approach to the analysis of texts, simply because we have not yet considered the ways in which texts are actually brought to life in reading practices. It is to this question that we now turn.

Through the object and account to the social practice

The linguistic and cultural resources discussed above, including the interpretive frameworks called upon to understand texts, represent variations on the interactional rights and responsibilities that are acted out between readers and writers. But our discussion to date in this section concerns what certain theoretical approaches tell us about *what text may afford*. They do not tell us *what texts are*, in the sense of cultural science, that is, as part of sets of recognizable cultural practices. If we consider a text as an opening interactional move, they do not tell us what the response is. In education this is a highly significant issue, because much education is about acculturation into ways of reading (McHoul, 1982). This section addresses the issues of how it is that texts are read and used, how they become part of everyday educational practice, and what they afford, though cultural and linguistic information, dispositions and ideologies, when they are taken up, adapted, reflected or reflected in educational practices. As Olson put it:

> Theories of text that ignore the social, institutional context are inadequate, while theories of social structure and authority which simply talk about the exercise of power without seeing how that authority is created and exercised in particular social contexts, such as reading and study, are banal. (1983: 130)

In that sense, we look here at what it is that people *make a text* through their everyday social practices, in particular in educational settings.

We begin this examination by returning to *Magpie Island*. Recall that the novel closes with an image of the central character Magpie alone on an island, with no hope of rescue, having just experienced the death of his mate and eggs. Austin et al. (2002) documented how teachers and students in a year 5 classroom discussed the sadness of this ending:

EXAMPLE 8.9 *'what's he actually telling you?'*

96. T   . . . Umm – do you think the author does that with a purpose what's he trying, he he knows his story is very sad, what do you think he <u>leaves</u> – his readers with a feeling of what. Anita?

97. An Well so they can work out what happens the way, what they want to happen?

98.   T   Yes, there's a feeling there I, I think, Justine.

99.   Ju   Suspension? About//

100. T   //Yes?

101. S   Look what they have done to the magpie kind of thing?

102. T   Y:yes? (.) Ok? Joshua? What do you think there's a feeling of
           at the end? I'd like you to really concentrate and try and think.
           Carol?

103. Ca   Sorrow.//

104. T   //Sorrow? Is there another feeling other than sorrow,
           Toni?

105. To   Well at the end how it says BUT IT WAS DARK OUTSIDE
           and he said it was going to be a bright new day tomorrow, well
           it was gonna like sort of begin all again? The next day?

106. T   Right. Does anyone feel that the author has left the reader

107. S   (   )

108. T   Does the author feel, do you think at least, does anyone feel
           that he's left you with perhaps a feeling of hope?

109. St   Yeah.

110. T   Why, Amy?

111. Am   Beca:ause well umm he says that bit about all the fishermen?//

112. T   //The
           fishermen going past and seeing Magpie. So he is going to
           survive and perhaps [just

113. Am   [Yeah], kind of think
           that//

114. T   //Yeah, I think perhaps there's a slight feeling of hope
           there, I think the author's also trying to tell us something else,
           that people? (3.0) as well as Magpie but I think he's really
           giving us a message about our**selve**s. That we are able to do
           (1.0) what? What are people capable of doing. (4) I think he
           really tries to give us this message **through** (3) the magpie.
           What do you think, even though, I'll phrase it in another way.
           Even though people have losses, and hardships, and dreadful
           periods of sorrow, what's he actually telling you at the end,
           Colin?

115. Col That it doesn't really matter that there are people that do, I
           mean, that do//

116. T   //I'd like you to pay a bit more attention

((and later))

119. Am   Like you shouldn't, I think he might be trying to say that you
           shouldn't feel sorry for yourself you should just try and get on
           with everything?

120. T   I think that you do survive and life goes on, even though at the
           time it seems as black as black. Do you think? Yeah.

There had been a discussion earlier in this lesson which hinged on the notion that novels, especially for children, usually have happy endings. Here we see the teacher working to achieve a happy ending. Magpie's being stranded and alone was achieved as a 'happy ending' using an allegorical interpretation that reads the magpie as a symbol of hope and survival: Toni's restatement of the final words of the novel (turn 105) was reformulated by the teacher into a 'feeling of hope' (turn 108); she then explained this in allegorical terms (turn 114); a few turns later, a student rendered a version of the 'moral' of the story and again the teacher confirmed this allegorical rendering.

Later in the lesson, the teacher and students discussed the 'feeling' that the 'images' in the text evoke. The students talked of the emotional tenor of the conclusion of the novel in terms of sadness, sorrow, disappointment, and depression. The teacher asked for more feelings:

159. T there's also a tremendous feeling of something else at the end I felt.

A few turns later, Toni provided 'hope' (turn 164) which the teacher had suggested earlier in the lesson (turn 108).

164. To Hope? So that it might happen maybe he'll//
165. T   //Maybe he'll be
        happy and survive. Yes.

The teacher interrupted Toni's answer at turn 164 to state her own version at turn 165 'Maybe he'll be happy and survive', explicitly stating her preferred allegorical interpretation of the novel. So the teacher worked hard in the talk to establish a 'hopeful' reading of the text in the face of the students' insistence on more negative, or at least different, readings.

In their study of how picture books were used in the first year of the school in reading lessons, Baker and Freebody drew the following conclusion, which applies equally well to the points made above:

> While the apparent source of an answer lies in the student's background knowledge, in personal preferences, or in the illustrations in the book, the reformulative and evaluative utterances of the teacher can be seen to reveal that virtually all of the retrospectively correct or adequate answers are so found in relation to the teacher's ongoing construction of a reading of the story. . . . We are drawn to the conclusion that it is the teacher's reading and the teachers 'thinking' that are the targets of the students' guesses. It is in this important sense that reading as an organised activity cannot be separated from the relation of teachers and students. (1989: 182)

Similarly, we can examine the ways in which learning and reading practices are effected outside of the classroom. Qualitative research works, in large part, through the juxtaposition of comparable but different events. It is in this sense that the cultural work done in different sites, even while appearing to fall under the same heading (in this case, reading with young children) can be seen to be distinctive. Part of that distinctiveness arises from the ways in which rights and responsibilities in practical social activities orient to and rebuild institutional category pairs such as student–teacher, child–parent. Close comparisons such as these show us the ways in which activities may be labelled in the same way, a label perhaps derived from some theory of education, teaching, or learning, but are nonetheless constitutive at the same time of particular social and cultural arrangements. The context, of the home or the classroom, for example, needs to be thought of as an accomplishment-in-progress, rather than as a frame or, as Drew and Heritage (1992) put it, a 'bucket', around which or in which certain activities occur.

The text-reading event shown in Example 8.10 is taken from Freiberg and Freebody (1995). It is described there as an informal literacy event in the home, and is discussed there because, as the researchers put it, it shows many features, compacted into one event, that they found to be comparable across families when parents and children read and discuss texts as learning-to-read events. The scene is the morning of the birthday of one of the children, all of whom are aged five years or younger. One of the gifts is a book, and the father, who had some teaching experience, took the opportunity to read from it with the children. Examples 8.10(a) and 8.10(b) are excerpts from a longer event.

EXAMPLE 8.10(a) *'we can all see it together'*

1. C Hey Tony have a look at the dino book
2. F Is that a dictionary of dinosaurs, like in alphabetical order?
3. C Yeh it is. 'a' 'a' aliosaurus. Um, there should be ankliosaurus on that page somewhere . . . yeh
4. F Yes you were right. Ankliosaurus
5. C Dad, can you remember some of the names?
6. F Yes I can remember some of the names. Here we'll sit over here and we can all see it together.
7. C But I'm next to daddy
8. F Yes
9. C No you can be in the middle, Renee can be on your lap, Tony can be on one side and I'll be on one side
10. F Okay
11. C That's sort of like ankliosaurus
12. F Well that's albertosaurus
13. M Albertosaurus?
14. F That one there. ALBERTOSAURUS IS A
15. R Which one?
16. F That's an alberto . . . oh no, that's another kind of dinosaur that the albertosaurus is catching to eat. ALBERTOSAURUS IS A LARGE POWERFUL MEAT EATING DINOSAUR . . . ((reading continued)) . . . MILLIONS OF YEARS HAVE TURNED TO STONE. FISH AND PLANT

FOSSILS ALSO EXIST. Okay which one next do you want me to read about?

17. C The one up the top
18. C I want this one
19. C No this one
20. F All right, I'll read ankliosaurus, which is Cal's choice first, and then I'll read aleosaurus which is your choice Renee. Okay ANKLIOSAURUS . . . ((reading continued)) TO ESCAPE FROM PREDATORS. Do you know what a predator is?
21. C Yeh. Meat-eaters
22. F Well they're carnivores, and predators, predators will be meat-eaters yes. They're the kind of dinosaurs that were the chasers.

And later:

EXAMPLE 8.10(b) *'a little bit of a bump on its head'*

52. F Okay which one now?
53. C Ah this one
54. F Okay
55. R No this one
56. F Well that's the one it is. These are the words for the picture here so this here is the picture and these are the words and its ARCHIOPTRICKS. Okay?
57. R (..)
58. F (..) We'll read about archioptricks. ARCHIOPTRICKS WAS . . . ((reading continued)) SUCH AS INSECTS AND LIZARDS.
59. M Cris (..)
60. F (..) SOME SCIENTISTS (..) WAS RELATED TO SMALL DINOSAURS SUCH AS um ((sounds out word)) IF THEY ARE RIGHT THEN ALL BIRDS ARE RELATED TO THE ANCIENT DINOSAURS. So that's (..). Some people think that what look like bird (..) really are feathers, and there's some thought that in fact um their other ancestors (..) that gave rise to birds. Um, we read that one.
61. C Ah
62. F A(..)SAURUS? Okay (..). That's THE OLD NAME FOR A/SAURUS WAS DONKASAURUS. (..) Two different names till someone worked out the fossils were the same. Shall we read it?
63. M (..)
64. F Sorry? Well that's the proper, the first name. A/SAURUS WAS HUGE PLANT EATING DINOSAUR. IT WAS (..) AND COULD WEIGH UP TO THIRTY TONNES. (..) A/SAURUS USED ITS LONG NECK TO REACH THE TREE TOPS WHERE IT GATHERED LEAVES
65. R Dad?
66. F Yes?
67. R Is that the (..)?

68. F That's right. THIS DINOSAUR'S TAIL WAS VERY LONG
         (..). SINCE A DINOSAUR CANNOT BE CALLED BY TWO
         DIFFERENT NAME A/SAURUS WAS CHOSEN. It doesn't have
         to be a dinosaur, nothing can have two different scientific
         names, it can only have one.
69. C Well why did they, why did they keep that name and not the
         other one?
70. F Well the p/saurus was the name it was first given and so um
71. M But Brontosaurus is the name more widely known
72. F Um? Yeh, I guess somehow it got into popular folklore and, and
         its readily recognizable, it's shape and so on (..) why it became
         so popular. Brachiosaurus has a little bit of a bump on its head
         there. Shall I read about Brachiosaurus?
73. R Yes
74. C Yes
75. F Okay. BRACHIOSAURUS WAS SO ((reading and discussion
         continued))

In looking through to the text as it is made a context for social practice, we can begin by noting some of the features of this interaction, keeping in mind the goal of documenting 'the ways in which ordinary actors use or make sense of this visual information in the course of their everyday practical routines' (Emmison and Smith, 2000: 58):

All participants were free to select from within the contents of the book and bid for readings and turns. Thus the children had a range of options and considerable agency in structuring the literacy event. The composition of the text as an object thus allows for various participants to select different sections, and thereby for them to 'take turns' and 'show which bits you like'.

The scene was immediately constituted as a non-teaching session by Father, who opens by asking a genuine question (rather than a quiz- or pseudo-question) about the nature of the book, and organizes that 'we can all see it together'. Father's lack of quizzing throughout signals that what might be learned from the session was not to be heard as accountable later – the learning made it 'educational', but not specifically education about how to read. The text's significance lies partly in the fact that it can be seen by the group and be a focus for talk for the group. Its accounts – descriptions, definitions, explanations and so on – are to be noted but not necessarily remembered.

Note also the number of bids for organizational arrangements made by the children, and the concessions made by Father throughout the event. The children's claims (for where to sit, what next, and so on) had direct consequences on what was read, how and to whom, and so were consequential for the contents and structure of the session.

Nonetheless, Father did a considerable amount of work to bring the text 'alive' as a focus for a particular kind of educational, cultural practice. He interacted with the children:

- about technical distinctions made in the text among various kinds of dinosaurs:

    22.   F Well, they're carnivores, and predators, predators will be meat-eaters yes. They're the kind of dinosaurs that were the chasers.

    60.   F Some people think that what look like bird (..) really are feathers, and there's some thought that in fact um their other ancestors (..) that gave rise to birds.

    121. F They certainly have a lot of physical characteristics that make you think that they could be related. You'd have to know if they lived at the same time and you'd have to look at other characteristics to see how much more they had in common. But that's a good um a good theory to think about first hey?

- about the formatting of the text:

    31.   F So that, so the one there is the big title, right, that's, it's spelt properly, and underneath it they've got the phonetic spelling, so you can look at that to see how you say these other letters up here, then they show you the picture

    56.   F Well that's the one it is. These are the words for the picture here so this here is the picture and these are the words and it's ARCHIOPTRICKS.

- and about elaborations from the text into cultural knowledge:

    45.   F well I don't know if they were so much sharp, but they were certainly very very bony, which means that if anybody tried to bite ankliosaurus they wouldn't be able to because they were really tough

    72.   F I guess somehow it got into popular folklore and, and its readily recognizable, it's shape and so on (..) why it became so popular.

As noted, Father did very little quizzing of the children. Of his 15 questions and one directive throughout the entire session, only one question and one directive could be heard as quizzing:

    20.   F Do you know what a predator is?

    95.   F Can you say it? ((laugh)) Say it, suratosaurus.

Finally, the children's interactional rights and responsibilities included organizing the event around the text–as–object, with Father's around the text as account. He did 'expert reader' with respect to format and content.

Freiberg and Freebody found that, in family interactions around books, learning, reading and writing, whether homework or otherwise, the interactions occurred among people with high levels of shared knowledge and experience. In contrast, they found that the problem was that classroom lessons with books were effected through examples, references and texts that were culturally situated in sites unfamiliar to many students in the classroom. They found in home transcripts that talk 'about-the-world' during home instruction was minimal and generally targeted at helping children to perform the task expediently and accurately.

More generally, Freiberg and Freebody found that children interactively claimed and were accorded a more diverse set of options for behaviour in home events, particularly informal reading, writing and learning events, than in school. In some instances, children were able to protest about the materials ('stupid words') or the parents' ways of handling the event ('my mother/teacher always tells me'). In other events, most clearly homework tasks, the child's interactional rights and responsibilities were restricted, as in school, by the format for completing the task that the parent organized. In these senses, the texts, as they are brought to life in and around practical everyday activities, are constituted differently in the two sites.

Freiberg and Freebody found that, in the classroom and the home alike, the structures of the talk in and around events involving texts sustained the orderliness and category-associated interactional rights and responsibilities that constitute each site – teachers and students, parents and children. The further point is that the texts may be the same objects as those used in both settings, may have the same linguistic affordances and cultural accounts ('same' in the setting of, for example, a theory of linguistics), but that these affordances and accounts are not 'seen through' to enable the same social practices in the two sites, classrooms and homes. A different text is brought to life interactionally. The text as an interactional platform for cultural practice becomes a distinctive viewing site for cultural analysis of ordinary activities on the two sites.

Conclusions

We began this chapter by considering the crucial role of textual materials in education, including the increasing use of electronic and moving texts in the development of policy, administration, and the provision of school resources in education. The approach to texts taken here was to consider them as crafted, representational objects, which evoke a readership of a particular kind, which make representational claims on some aspect of reality and experience, and which entail purposeful choices and distortions as part of those representational processes. The starting point was to consider that texts make representations by looking from somewhere and by both arising from and affording cultural practices of different kinds. The chapter was organized around moves that allow us to look from the object to the account, starting from either simple frequency analyses, putting to work particular grammatical theories developed from linguistics, and developing an account of the interpretive frameworks called upon to look through to the discourse. Second, we looked from the object and the account through to the social and cultural practices that they together afford and enable.

In one sense, a text is anything that can produce a 'reader'. Geographers, geologists and environmental scientists can 'read' landscapes for their histories and their composition, whether crafted by human hands or by geological, meteorological and geographical forces. An object, therefore, is turned into a text by a reader. A reader can look through the object, using the codes on which it relies, through to the meaningful discourses – the sets of ideas – that they represent, and can look through those discourses to the cultural practices afforded by the propositions (knowledge, opinion, ideology) represented in and opened up by the discourses. We can also turn these observations around. Texts call forth certain kinds of readers who can respond to certain objects with understandings of codes, to certain codes with understandings of discourses, and to certain discourses with understandings of cultural knowledges and practices. That is to say, there is a reflexive relationship between texts and cultural members who can read them. The object calls for a certain kind of reader and that kind of reader can render the object into cultural representation – a text. When we can read – a geographical formation, a street sign, a dress code, a graffito, a newspaper article, a document with guidelines for our taxation returns, or an educational text – part of what that means is that we can locate a meaningful version of ourselves in the text as it operates in its surrounding visual, social, cultural and ideological context.

Texts are artefacts that make some representational claim on some aspect of reality. Obviously, no text can capture every possible aspect, affordance or interpretation of any aspect of experienced reality, no matter how straight-faced its claim to comprehensiveness, definitiveness or objectivity. Nor can a text thoroughly determine all of the ways in which it may be read. Even photographs need to be made on the basis of some choices – about the point of view from which the viewer will make the representation, choices to do with the timing of the making of the representation, lighting, angle, depth of field and so on. These choices have consequences for what it is that a text can afford, for what view of reality is presented, and for what aspects are foregrounded, back-grounded, placed in the margins, distorted, short-cut, glossed, or ignored.

Contemporary educational practice is saturated with texts. They are used as learning resources in educational sites; they define and regulate educational practices and arrangements; and they embody the understandings of educators and the communities they claim to serve concerning the purposes, contents and consequences of organized educational activities. It is through texts, therefore, that the reasoning practices that support, or that make thoroughly unremarkable, certain educational activities are legitimated and transmitted from generation to generation. In this sense, we can consider the governing role played by textual materials in contemporary societies. In a comment directly applicable to education, Dorothy E. Smith described traditional, mainstream social and cultural studies as giving us

> a consciousness that looks at society, social relations, and people's lives as if we could stand outside them, ignoring the particular local places in the everyday in which we live our lives. It claims objectivity not on the basis of its capacity to speak truthfully, but in terms of its specific capacity to exclude the presence and experience of particular subjectivities . . . A mode of ruling has become dominant that involves a continual transcription of the local and particular actualities of our lives into abstracted and generalized forms. It is an extralocal mode of ruling. . . . We are ruled by forms of organization vested in and mediated by texts and documents, and constituted externally to particular individuals and their personal and familial relationships. The practice of ruling involves the ongoing representation of the local actualities of our worlds in the standardized and general forms of knowledge that enter them into the relations of ruling. . . . Forms of consciousness are created that are properties of organization or discourse rather than of individual subjects. (1987: 2–3)

Smith has described the role of textual materials in the moral and political regulation of society, partly through its educational activities, as central to an understanding of the relationship between experience and the acquisition and deployment of knowledge in contemporary societies:

> The conditions of our existence are constantly changing. Events enter our immediate experience. If someone intended them, their intention is present only in the event. We cannot track back through them to an author. Buildings are torn down, factories close and open, bombs are dropped, villages are razed, high-rise apartments go up. . . . We do not have to invent a cargo cult because we live it. The break between an experienced world and its social determinations beyond experience is a distinctive property of our kind of society. (Smith, 1990b: 54)

Some of those ruling texts and documents are policies about educational curriculum, teaching guidelines, and assessment and reporting practices – abstracting, generalizing, constructing forms of living and communicating and re-presenting them back to the people about whom they claimed to be in the first place. We saw this process perhaps most powerfully in the text concerning the characteristics of 'less developed countries' in the world. But it is not restricted to texts that have such immediate and obvious consequences for our understandings of sociological and political process. It applies as well to texts about Peter and Mary jumping over a puddle of water, discussions in classrooms about happy endings and the versions of childhood that such discussions sustain and reinforce, graffiti scrawled on pedestrian tunnels, and to the myriad policy documents, syllabus guidelines, advice to parents, and official texts that embody the properties of educational practice, and the norms that relate to it.

The task for the analyst, then, is to produce accounts, using publicly inspectable methods, that document the ways in which objects are structured, reasoned and used in educational settings. As with our analyses of interactions and interviews, such analyses need to entail a series of 'passes' through the data in order to represent in a sequentially reasoned and staged way the various analytic levels with which texts can be approached. A principled understanding of how it is that texts are selected, disseminated and exchanged in and around educational activities draws into high relief the profoundly normative properties of education. Some texts have become central to most institutional educational work – canonical texts – some may come and go, and some will simply never find their way into public or even domestic educational scenes. In that respect, it is inadequate simply to document the interior structure or patterns of particular texts. For an educator, additional crucial questions pertain: How is it that such texts gained their significance and visibility as educational objects in the first place? How is it that they are used everyday as platforms for conduct, and how is it that they both reflect and rebuild knowledge, relationships, and the moral and ideological orders that hold educational activities in place?

DISCUSSION TOPICS, QUESTIONS AND EXERCISES

Texts as objects

1. Choose any text (see definitions this chapter) of an educational nature that matters to you (i.e. is significant for your work, represents an issue you are interested in etc.) and perform the following.

    From frequency to accounting:

    - Identify the spaces where the stories, activities, events in the text are located.
    - Identify the number and type of categories of persons, things, events and activities that are represented in the text.
    - Identify the number and types of physical, intellectual, social and emotional work (i.e. actions performed, emotions expressed etc.) attributed to the categories and persons of things presented in the text.

    From grammar to accounting:

    - Who and/or what is in the text (use of nouns, pronouns etc.)?
    - What gets done (number and type (formation) of clausal themes (verbal processes) in the text)?
    - When (past, present or future action)?
    - Where (place/space, organizational level etc.)?
    - By whom (number, type and distribution of subjects/objects in the agency position (subjects/objects that act)?
    - To whom (number, type and distribution of subjects/objects in the object position (subjects/objects that are acted upon)?

Now consider the following:

(a) What kinds of knowledge do you think is necessary to make sense of the text? For example, does the author's choices of subjects/objects, categories of persons, things and events make sense to you (i.e. they are understandably and recognizably relevant to the issue at hand)? If so, can you suggest a central organizing Membership Categorization Device (MCD) that could be used to group (collect) these? Are there any subjects/objects or categories of persons, things, events, activities you consider relevant to the issue at hand, that belong to or may be collected as part of the central organizing MCD, that have not been presented in the text? Why do you think the author chose to omit these?

(b) Identify any patterns of association between the categories of subjects and objects in the text and the actions, events and processes in the text. How are relationships between the various categories of subjects and objects represented in this text (i.e. how is 'agency' (who/what acts/is acted upon) distributed between the categories of subjects and objects in the text)?

(c) From your analyses, list what you believe are the principle claims made in the text. These may be explicit (such as 'the Spaniards opened up the New World') or implicit (patterns of association revealed by your analysis). Use the list as a platform to speculate about the identity (political, institutional etc.) of the author of the text (what category of 'person' do you think they are?). That is, what category ('type') of person could 'deploy such (claims such as those in this text, in this time place and culture) in good faith and believe they are telling the truth'. Similarly, what kinds of interpretational work is required of the reader to make (good) sense of these claims.

2. A copy of a university textbook contains the following piece of (handwritten) graffito on its inside cover.

This book is garbage.
Don't read it.
           Signed: [the author's name]

Analyse the graffiti using the above approaches and then consider the following:

(a) Who is this comment directed towards?
(b) How do you know this?
(c) Do you think the author actually wrote this graffito? Why?
(d) If so, why would he make a statement such as this?
(e) How then would you characterize the author's action?

Texts as (platforms for) interaction

3. The following is a transcript of two teachers (T1 and T2) and a university researcher (R) involved in a moderation task as part of a project investigating teachers' judgements about (their own and other teachers') students' writing. Here the task for the teachers is to reach a consensus on the grade they would give a particular student's piece of writing.

1. R   (T1) would you like to start? Well I'll make sure everybody gets a turn don't worry
2. T1   That's okay um well the structure looks pretty good ( ) made some good use of variety of vocabulary there um I don't know I personally probably wouldn't like the one sentence paragraph ( ) um but that's the way he's written he might like to sort it out that way um made reasonable use, made some good use of punctuation like the exclamation marks. I would, I would put that above the Benchmark
3. R   And how would you using your own grading?
4. T1   Oh well that depends now I would vary when I look at it. I can look at it that way and say that like 'sound achievement' or I would give it a 6, 7 (out of ten).
5. R   Okay T2 how would you?
6. T2   How would I rate it?
7. R   Um rate it
8. T2   Um he's obviously talking about something that happened so it's a recount. He has the generic structure. I think, (unlike) Jan he's got each new thought that he's got he's made a new paragraph so he has a good idea of paragraphing um and I think I'd put that 'above'
9. R   Okay so you both see it as being 'above' yeah

Consider the actions, interactional rights and responsibilities (see Chapter 6) and organizational arrangements oriented to/displayed by each of the participants in this event and answer the following:

(a)   What kinds of actions (related to the task of grading) do T1 and T2 display a preference for doing? (Hint: what kinds of features of the text do the teachers talk most about?)
(b)   What do they not like doing? How do you know this?
(c)   What actions does R prefer T1 and T2 to do?
(d)   How are the various forms of agency (the rights/willingness to perform the various actions) distributed between the participants?
(e)   How might the forms of agency be constructed around the same task (moderation/justification of grading of a text) conducted in another setting (such as 'staff meeting' or 'parent–teacher interview')?
(f)   From this, what might be said about 'the moral and ideological order that holds (this particular) educational activit(y) (on this occasion) in place'?

9

Studying Education as a
Practical Accomplishment

More educational research?

In concluding his summary of the contribution of Garfinkel to the development of conversation analysis, sociologist Heritage argued that the point of Cultural Science and more specifically of Ethnomethodology is to

> attempt to come more directly into contact with the raw data of human experience and conduct by stripping away the innumerable theoretical and methodological barriers which imperceptibly interpose themselves between observers and the organizationally significant features of social activity. (1984: 311)

Coming directly into analytic contact with the 'raw data' of everyday practice presents special challenges to researchers with an interest in education. The process of 'stripping away' cuts deep into assumptions about what it is to be a member of a society and what that means for efforts to expand the membership possibilities of learners. Precisely because of that difficulty, trying to engage educational practices through direct analytic contact offers both practitioners and researchers the richest opportunities for changing those practices. Equally importantly, it offers a reinvigoration, day after day, of their educative expertise and commitments.

To expand on Heritage's observation, I describe an example (developed more fully in Freebody and Freiberg, 2001) from one of the educational areas in which I work, reading education. This area, particularly reading in early schooling, has been the object of a great deal of empirical study, theorizing and professional advice. It almost goes without saying that it has also been a topic around which there has been much heated debate, at least over the last century (see Huey,

1908). A fundamental empirical and theoretical problem associated with the extraordinary amount of attention that reading has received is this: the accounts available to describe reading have both derived from and reinforced prevalent teaching methods – there are now 'innumerable theoretical and methodological barriers'. These accounts have come to determine what is recognized as 'reading' and thus as 'teaching reading', providing the filter by which certain practices engaged in by parents and other teachers are or are not evaluated as adequate, appropriate, effective, efficient, warranted, or, generally, necessary and sufficient for learning to occur. These accounts have filtered out the 'raw data' of how reading occurs in homes and schools every day, the topic that all this research and theory have aimed to inform. These details are no longer theoretically or empirically available in the research corpus. They are comprehensively mediated and over-written by the coded accounts that have come, in turn, to govern them.

When we explore research on reading, so abundant in the educational literature, we see that researchers' interests have typically been in identifying and arguing for or against idealized types of reading and teaching reading, with these types generally predefined in terms of psychological theories. We can see this process at work in recent influential summaries of reading research. In Adams's (1990) meta-analysis of some 660 studies of early reading teaching and learning, for instance, three of the conclusions are:

> Approaches in which systematic code instruction is included along with the reading of meaningful connected text result in superior reading achievement overall, for both low-readiness and better prepared students.

> Programs for all children, good and poor readers alike, should strive to maintain an appropriate balance between phonics activities and the reading and appreciation of informative and engaging texts.

> Because children have special difficulty analyzing the phonemic structure of words, reading programs should include explicit instruction in blending. (Adams, 1990: 123–8)

Throughout her extensive and influential report, Adams used the terms *code instruction, the reading of meaningful connected text, phonics activities, instruction in blending* and *appreciation of informative and engaging texts* as coded messages, assuming that her readers would appreciate the significance of these conclusions *for* practice and, more importantly, that they would know, directly, transparently and in common, what these codes mean *in* practice. This is in spite of the fact that Adams, like almost all of the studies she summarized, presented no indication of what these terms might specifically refer to in actual practice. As in much of the research literature, it is idealizations that are debated; the practices from which they have been inferred have been overwritten with those idealizations.

Similarly, Snow, Burns and Griffin (1998), in their massive summary of the research on this topic, assumed common understandings of the coded meanings of terms relating to educational practice. Here is a brief sample of their key conclusions:

There is little evidence that children experiencing difficulty learning to read, even those with identifiable learning disabilities, need radically different sorts of supports than children at low-risk, although they may need much more intensive support . . .

Excellent instruction is the best intervention for children having problems learning to read.

Language-rich home, daycare, and preschool environments are important.

Excellent instruction is most effective when children arrive in the first grade motivated for literacy.

If we have learned anything from this effort, it is that effective teachers are able to craft a special mix of instructional ingredients for every child they work with. But . . . there is a common menu of materials, strategies, and environments from which effective teachers make choices. (from Executive Summary)

This extensive report presents some instances of diary-style anecdotes relating to classroom practice, but, as with the advice from Adams, the practices that count as *intensive support, excellent instruction, language-rich environments, motivation for literacy,* and *craft[ing] a special mix of instructional ingredients* are nowhere described in non-idealized terms.

These illustrations indicate the processes of pre-theorization, idealization and translation at work, and suggest how together they can operate to dilute the impact of research on educational practice. In the absence of their treatment of the details of the particular practices that are short-handed by these codes, researchers' conclusions can leave as merely hypothetical the relationship between the debate in which they engage and the practices they claim both to describe and to inform. At the same time as doing this, they reflect and rebuild a particular moral relationship between theoreticians, researchers and those who practice, in this case, reading education with young children. The assistance such a process gives teachers and parents in return remains, at best, generic and ambiguous, and, at worst, speculative.

Researchers have too often settled for analytic formalisms at the expense of an empirical purchase on the detailed texture of reading sessions between adults and young children. An exploration of the details of actual practice has been traded for working with these idealizations and pre-theorizations. The nub of the problem is that the details, the comparabilities and diversities, of what learners, parents and educators do in reading events, are lost to the theoretical and research effort and thus to educators interested in drawing on research for professional development and practical change. Recovering such lost empirical property is an important contribution that qualitative approaches can make.

This example shows how it is that the qualitative researcher's dissatisfaction with the conduct and influence of conventional research is not just a dissatisfaction with research presented through the reporting of quantitative analyses. There is a more substantial issue here than quantitative versus qualitative methods. The deeper dissatisfaction, which can arise from either analytic format, is with research conclusions that hover above the lived reality of the people whose activities are apparently under study.

In most of the accounts we find of everyday educational experiences in the research literature, we sense this hovering – a lack of cultural texture, a glossing and idealization that renders the portrait of everyday educational and social experience almost unrecognizable. The significance of this, as Smith (1987, 1990a, 1990b) has pointed out, is that categories and explanations that relate to human life are, in a sense, 'sold back' to the people whose educational experiences we claim to be describing and explaining. The non-initiated who encounter summaries of research such as those on reading education may feel that they have walked into the middle of an argument whose protagonists have long-standing investments, the relative merits of which they exchange in code. But research can also insert new objects into educational debates, new resources for confirming or questioning the utility and fairness of various forms of investment, or for offering more adaptive investment possibilities. It is important to recognize that debates about education are at the same time contests about social, cultural, economic and ideological processes of which education forms a part.

What matters in educational research?

Educators have never been short of good ideas. Most good ideas have not worked, have worked sometimes and in some places, have been applied where they cannot work, have been either overstated or stripped of their significance and usefulness, have ignored the other good ideas that they needed in order for the original idea to work, have worked to do things that they did not predict, and sometimes have worked to create just as many or even more problems than they solved. The argument concerning any given educational activity, then, informed as it is by accounts and presumptions from the cultural, managerial and governmental formations that surround it and give it meaning and consequentiality, is that it needs to be seen as it lives with other cultural practices. It needs to be studied, therefore, as a working component of a cultural site. The meaning and consequentiality of an educational practice does not travel with it from site to site. Debates about the efficacy, efficiency or social justice of any given practice need to begin with detailed understandings of the activity in question, as it is acted out in a variety of cultural places and times.

I indicated earlier that research should address itself to educational issues that matter. The question of 'what matters?' relates to four distinct roles for research in education, the development of:

1. more powerful theoretical accounts of educational practice;
2. more refined and empirically justifiable methodological approaches to the conduct of research. We can think of the tensions, polarities and choices that face the researcher, many of which have arisen as direct critiques of the others, as epistemological resources – resources-for-coming-to-know – that

redefine the activity of research as increasingly open projects to generate ongoing theory-in-practice;

3. more effective, inclusive and equitable daily practices in homes, schools, colleges, universities and work places; and

4. more effective, inclusive and equitable public policies for the conduct of education.

It is the first two of these aspects of significance that afford researchers some purchase on the development of both practice and policy. If we see research as a way of inserting objects into public discourse in education, then we can see a dialectic interplay between the objects produced by analytic methods and the lived experience of educators. This dialectic is a valuable resource for researchers and educators. We can now approach the everyday activities of people as providing the grounds on which members of a society derive norms for practice, not the other way round. Invoking or complying with a rule is not the same as explaining the behaviours that the rule is taken a priori to govern.

So it is incumbent on researchers to resist not only assessing activities through the use of rules or standards that come from outside the settings in which people act, but also to resist recognizing such activities *in the first place* solely in terms of these exogenous rules or standards. Hester and Francis (2000) have applied this understanding to the conduct of research itself, arguing that the 'just-this-ness' of a social event means that we cannot use a 'standard method', imposing particular analytic dispositions mechanically onto the variety of recognizably, experientially different educational phenomena.

Educational settings themselves – bedside stories, religious lessons, classroom interactions, on the job training, graduate seminars, and all the rest – entail recognizable, reasoned and intelligible accounts of how participants can act in such settings in order to show how their practices constitute orderly educational conduct. So the artful and reasonable practices that people demonstrate every day need to be viewed as sensible within the indigenous setting in which they occur. It is people's practical enactments and re-enactments of these settings – the ways they reflect, adapt, modify or overturn what is known in common by the participants – that build social order, day to day. It is counter-productive to begin either with the presumption that abstract, deterministic rules for social order build and legitimate those everyday practices, or with the premise that human actions are impossibly inchoate or too diverse to be studied.

What is the point of qualitative research in education?

Qualitative research is descriptive in two senses (Silverman, 1993, 1999):

1. It aims to give theoretically adequate descriptions of observable everyday practices, descriptions that can thereby be theoretically productive, and generative of new practices.

2. It aims to study, rather than either naïvely accepting or overwriting, the ways in which people describe their everyday educational experiences.

Further, Silverman advised qualitative researchers in the following terms:

1. do not begin from pre-emptive normative standards of good and bad practice;
2. aim to understand the practices that teachers and learners use and the functions of the communication patterns that are observed;
3. see these patterns of activity (including their activities in an interview) as functional only within particular educational configurations and contexts; and
4. understand those configurations and contexts as part of the requirements of a full documentation of practice.

As I argued earlier, the claim that qualitative methods are necessary because of the inherent complexity of cultural life, or because researchers need to try to capture the quirks and caprices of human behaviour, does not make for a compelling case. Qualitative research can be made more than exploratory, anecdotal or hypothesis-generating. The issue is systematic description, and we could equally well argue that the relationships work the other way around, that quantitative research reports could be just 'suggestive' of actual social practices that would need to be validated through close observation and qualitative analysis.

Earlier I drew on Heap's categorization of research types to argue that we can productively consider two large families of Science: Natural Science and Human Science. Apart from the more obvious distinguishing features of these, it is important to keep in mind an observation made by Schutz (1970) long ago: the natural, physical world of objects, including human bodies, and their structures and associations, presents itself *unaccounted for* to human beings, who must then try to interpret and explain what they see. In contrast, the phenomena of the social world are – continuously, day to day, and generally unnoticed – explained and interpreted by the people who act and produce social order in and through their everyday lives. The participants show one another accounts of what is going on, and routinely display to one another (and thus potentially to us) their senses and explanations of order through their daily activities. This highlights an important point about how researchers in the Human Science traditions are positioned with respect to the phenomena they observe in ways that are, intellectually and morally, different from researchers working in the Natural Sciences. The arguments are that the adequacy of the descriptions and accounts that researchers offer is directly related to the extent to which these descriptions are informed explicitly by the conceptual and analytic approach of the researcher, and that it is adequate description and accounting that offer the most forceful and productive starting points for addressing practical educational questions.

What counts as 'quality' qualitative research?

However blandly they have sometimes been employed, qualitative approaches to the conduct of Cultural Science have the capacity to present educators with the 'shock of the familiar', interrupting their long-developed instincts for accounting for social experience with chains of generalizations about what is 'typical' about people's everyday lives. The rationale for public, institutional education rests on the apparently seamless relationship between the interests of the state, the community and the individual. Education's legitimacy is based on this conjunction; in turn, educators enact it with and for learners. To some extent, society's apparent stability depends fundamentally on the seamlessness, 'naturalness', and singularity of that conjunction. The aim of transformational educational researchers has been to interrupt the seamlessness of this relationship by documenting the details of its unremarked practices and policies, and by questioning the singularity of the ways in which education conjoins state, community and personal interests. But clearly a society in denial of its own complexity, and the ambiguity and inconsistencies of its commitments and practices, will have little interest in all but the most retrospective and comforting research efforts, dismissing, trivializing, familiarizing or commoditizing the products and consequences of research activity.

Qualitative research in education is partly about increasing the repertoire of options for educational activity by attending to the 'seen but unnoticed' sites of daily life and the versions of 'social order in and as locally accomplished human activity' (Hester and Francis, 2000: 19). It is about working to align better these practical activities with the reasoning practices used individually or collectively about them. On occasion, qualitative research in education has been seen as a radical, potentially transformative insertion into educational practice. It is important to recall, however, that positivistic, quantitative research was once seen in precisely the same light, as throwing out a challenge to ways of knowing based on habits of doctrine and superstition, modes of thinking and acting shrouded in the reverence of ethnic, religious, cultural or political heritage. Methods are not of themselves practically, socially or ideologically conservative or transformative. For example, taking the often-suggested option of working collaboratively with teachers in schools can, in some cases, be the best way to ensure that conservative accounts of the data are privileged, and that the professional consequences of research remain comfortably uncritical of practice.

So neither educational nor ideological commitments or outcomes are secured solely by choices of method or methodology. The fundamental danger is that through their work researchers can position themselves as an elite, with their accounts of social experience hovering above the everyday ways and wisdoms of the people who are supposedly the subjects of research. They can thus render those people cultural or ideological 'dopes' by presuming those everyday ways and wisdoms as pre-scripted but unrecognized representations of either an underlying substrate of The Truth or an unseen ideological programme. They can thereby strike an ironic attitude to everyday educational activities, and continue to provide educators either with grey, predictable re-enactments of the Truthful theories with which they began, or with yet more indignant, mock-pious complaints. The positions they advocate can come down to accusations that their opponents are not proper scientists, merely indentured handmaidens of either the apparatuses of the state or of its stubborn and single-minded discontents. Finally their debates can remain about their opponents, rather than about documentations and analyses of educational practice.

So this book has not presented a particular a priori stance on conservative, reformist, critical or revolutionary approaches to education of itself, as a starting point or an assumed ideological disposition. Qualitative studies in education can be, and regularly are used both to critique and to legitimate the practical enactments of education and policy formation, just as surely as to interrupt the conservative urge of educational practice as a public political and economic activity. The issue here is that we cannot have it both ways: we cannot claim the rights accorded to 'the researcher' as someone whose premises and procedures can stand up to public scrutiny, and whose primary interest is in the structure and patterning of actual everyday experiences, at the same time as we pre-empt the kind of project to which analyses of people's lives is to be dedicated.

It is humdrum to say that everyone in a society has an investment in educational activities. It is also obvious that different communities (geographic, ethnic, socio-economic, and so on) may have investments in different, perhaps competing kinds of education. What this means for comparatively disenfranchised groups in a society is that education is a site of struggle over the distribution and recognition of cultural goods and services. The ways in which these goods and services are distributed have significant consequences for the material well-being of members of these groups, and, in some circumstances, for their cultural survival.

What is equally notable from our perspective as researchers, however, is that professional educators and community members alike, along with material investments in education, all have investments in certain ideas and practices about what education is, what it should be, and how it can be productively investigated. It is generally not possible to be an acculturated member of a society without having developed, as part of that cultural apprenticeship, ideas about what is adequate education. These include what the forms and functions of education should be, and what a society should be able to expect from both informal and formal education in return for its material and conceptual investments. Some of these conceptual investments have material correlates; educational researchers and practitioners have careers invested in certain norms of educational practice, theories and research methods and methodologies. So these investments connect with and buttress ideological formations, a set of views about 'the good society' and the various ways it can and should distribute its goods and services.

In the conclusion to his analysis of the sociological, intellectual and political history of statistics ('the mathematics of the State'), Desrosieres (1998) observed that the primordial dialectic driving the conduct of science is this: the 'durably solid forms' of the natural and human worlds must remain always undebated so that human action can proceed, at the same time as they must remain always debatable so that human action can change. We can think of education as one such category of human action: educators need to act as if they were in a space occupied by durably solid forms – learning, tests, grades, syllabuses, motivation, abilities, good and less good outcomes, and all the rest. At the same time, they must behave as if such forms are always debatable, always amenable to more refined or productive understandings and activities.

The forms of qualitative research I have sketched in this book represent an attempt to make that dialectic itself an object of study. In this sense, the study of education enables us to see how 'durably solid forms' begin their existence as cultural forms: it is through educational practice that social activities 'bring off', with and for learners, the visible production of a set of 'durably solid forms' for use in the world – knowledge, procedural capabilities, cognitive processes, interactional repertoires, cultural understandings, and ideological dispositions – ways of being, accounting and acting. Documenting and analysing how educational events serve to bring these off can help educators appreciate the cultural production of educational facts, and allow them the means to provide more powerful and generative objects for the consideration of practitioners and researchers. Such an approach is a declaration of the most radical proposition that can be made about education: that it is built by people's concerted actions, daily, unnoticed and unremarked, and, thus built, can be rebuilt.

From the vantage of the analytic approaches outlined in this book and others like them, the conclusion is not that everyday social and educational experience is intractably complex or messy to the point that it defies documentation. Rather, the approaches I have outlined can lead researchers towards principled ways in which they can marvel, and lead the readers of their research to marvel, at the orderliness, complexity and sophistication with which members of their societies orchestrate their activities for the practical purposes they have at hand – the apparently effortless aesthetic of social life. With detailed documentation and analysis, these complexities can themselves be seen as important 'social, educational facts' that can be acted on and inserted into public debates about educational practice.

The reader as well as the writer of educational research is acting in a world in which there is much at stake for the material conditions of individuals, communities and societies, and for the ways in which they understand themselves. Research about acculturation and education is primordially challenging, because much is also at stake for researchers and readers of research in their interrogations of education. Educational researchers need to re-render those processes that have shaped them as cultural members, as people: the spoken and written texts that have helped give form to their own consciousness, that have structured, interrupted and re-structured their own thoughts, disciplined their own feelings and enlivened their own commitments, such that these processes themselves can become the object of their analyses.

So educational research entails moral effort for researchers and readers. In the evolution of educational ideas and practices, research has not been an ecological imperative. That it goes on with expanding energy and breadth of field attests to the conviction that difficult and long-standing problems to do with learning and growing up need not be seen as intractable obstacles to a society's urges towards more intelligent and just ways of educating people. The conduct of research, and discussions about how it can be done better, together stand for a belief in a society's ability to learn systematically about how to enhance its domestic, professional and institutional conduct. When educational research is driven by curiosity about the ever-changing, always normative, and often unnoticed seedbed of everyday cultural experience and aspiration, then it is above all a discourse of cultural optimism. The point of research is to discover things. The point of educational research is to change the social world by discovering better understandings of its qualities.

References

Action Research International: www.scu.edu.au/schools/gcm/ar/ari/arihome.html

Action Research website:
  http://ousd.k12.ca.us/netday/links/Action_Research/ar.html

Adams, M.J. (1990) *Beginning to read: Thinking and learning about print*. Cambridge, MA: MIT Press.

Adams, N., Causey, T., Jacobs, M.-E., Munro, P., Quinn, M. and Trousdale, A. (1998) *Womentalkin'*: A reader's theatre performance of teachers' stories. *Qualitative Studies in Education*, 11(3), 383–95.

Amidon, E. and Hunter, E. (1967) *Improving teaching: The analysis of verbal interaction*. New York: Holt, Rinehart & Winston.

Apple, M. (1996) *Cultural politics and education*. New York: Teachers College Press.

Atkinson, J.M. (1992) Displaying neutrality: Formal aspects of informal court proceedings. In P. Drew and J. Heritage (eds) *Talk at work: Interaction in institutional settings*. Cambridge: Cambridge University Press: 199–211.

Atkinson, P. (1990) *The Ethnographic imagination: Textual constructions of reality*. London: Routledge.

Atkinson, P. and Silverman, D. (1997) Kundera's *Immortality*: The interview society and the invention of the self. *Qualitative Inquiry*, 3, 304–25.

Austin, H. (1997) Literature for school: Theorising 'the child' in talk and text, *Language and Education*, 11, 77–95.

Austin, H., Freebody, P. and Dwyer, B. (2001) Methodological issues in analysing talk and text: The case of childhood in and for school. In A. McHoul and M. Rapley (eds) *Analysing talk in institutional settings*. London: Continuum International (Cassell/Pinter).

Baker, C.D. (1991) Literacy practices and social relations in classroom reading events. In C.D. Baker and A. Luke (eds) *Towards a critical sociology of reading pedagogy*. Amsterdam/Philadelphia: John Benjamins.

Baker, C.D. (1992) Description and analysis in classroom talk and interaction. *Journal of Classroom Interaction*, 27(2), 9–14.

Baker, C.D. (1997) Membership categorization and interview accounts. In D. Silverman (ed.) *Qualitative research: Theory, method and practice*. London: Sage. pp. 130–43.

Baker, C.D. and Freebody, P. (1986) Representations of questioning and answering in children's first school books. *Language in Society*, 15, 451–84.

Baker, C.D. and Freebody, P. (1987). 'Constituting the child' in beginning school reading books. *British Journal of Sociology of Education*, 8(1), 55–76.

Baker, C.D. and Freebody, P. (1989) *Children's first school books: Introductions to the culture of literacy*. Oxford: Basil Blackwell.

Barnes, D., Britton, J. and Rosen, H. (1969) *Language, the learner and the school*. Harmondsworth: Penguin.

Bernstein, B. (1971) *Class, codes and control. Vol. 1. Theoretical studies towards a sociology of language.* London: Routledge and Kegan Paul.

Bernstein, B. (1975) *Class, codes and control. Vol.3. Towards a theory of educational transmissions.* London: Routledge and Kegan Paul.

Birch, D. (1989) *Language, literature, and critical practice: Ways of analysing text.* London: Routledge.

Boaler, J. (1997) *Experiencing school mathematics: Teaching styles, sex and setting.* Buckingham: Open University Press.

Boden, D. and Zimmerman, D.H. (eds) (1991) *Talk and social structure: Studies in ethnomethodology and conversation analysis.* Cambridge: Polity Press.

Bogdan, R.C. and Biklen, S.K. (1992) *Qualitative research for education.* Needham Heights, MA: Allyn & Bacon.

Bottery, M. and Wright, N. (1996) Co-operating in their own deprofessionalisation? On the need to recognise the 'public' and 'ecological' roles of the teaching profession. *British Journal of Educational Studies*, 44, 82–98.

Burns, R.B. (1990) *Introduction to research methods in education.* Melbourne: Longman Cheshire.

Burns, R.B. (1994) *Introduction to research methods in education* (2nd edn). Melbourne: Longman Cheshire.

Button, G. (1992) Answers as interactional products: two sequential practices used in job interviews. In P. Drew and J. Heritage (eds) *Talk at work: Interaction in institutional settings.* Cambridge: Cambridge University Press. pp. 212–31.

Button, G. and Lee, J.R.E. (eds) (1987) *Talk and social organisation.* Clevedon: Multilingual Matters.

Carr, W. and Kemmis, S. (1986). *Becoming critical: Education, knowledge and action research.* London: Falmer.

Carspecken, P.F. (1995) *Critical ethnography in educational research: A theoretical and practical guide.* London: Routledge.

Christie, F. (ed.) (1990) *Literacy for a changing world.* Hawthorn, Vic: Australian Council for Educational Research.

Clegg, S. (1989) *Frameworks of power.* London: Sage.

Cochran-Smith, M. and Lytle, S.L. (1990) Research on teaching and teacher research: The issues that divide. *Educational Researcher*, 19, 2–10.

Cohen, L. and Manion, L. (1997) *Research methods in education* (4th edn). London: Routledge.

Comte, A. (1842/1970) *Introduction to positive philosophy.* Indianapolis: Boobs-Merrill.

Corey, S. (1953) *Action research to improve school practice.* New York: Columbia Teachers' College.

Delamont, S., Coffey, A. and Atkinson, P. (2000) The twilight years? Educational ethnography and the 'five-moments' model. *Qualitative Studies in Education*, 13, 223–38.

Denzin, N. (1997) *Interpretive ethnography: Ethnographic practices for the 21st century.* London: Sage.

Denzin, N.K. and Lincoln, Y.S. (eds) (1994) *Handbook of qualitative research.* Thousand Oaks, CA: Sage.

Desrosieres, A. (1998) *The politics of large numbers: A history of statistical reasoning* (trans. C. Nash). Cambridge, MA: Harvard University Press.

Douglas, J.D. (ed.) (1970) *Understanding everyday life: Toward the reconstruction of sociological knowledge*. Chicago, IL: Aldine Publishing.

Drew, P. (1992) Contested evidence in courtroom cross-examination: the case of a trial for rape. In P. Drew and J. Heritage (eds) *Talk at work: Interaction in institutional settings*. Cambridge: Cambridge University Press. pp. 470–520.

Drew, P. and Heritage, J.C. (eds) (1992) *Talk at work: Interaction in institutional settings*. Cambridge: Cambridge University Press.

Du Bois, W. (1899/1967) *The Philadelphia negro: A social study*. New York: Bloom.

Durkheim, E. (1901/1938) *Rules of sociological method* (trans. G. Kaplan). New York: Free Press.

Edwards, A.D. and Westgate, D.P.G. (1987) *Investigating classroom talk*. London: Falmer Press.

Edwards, A.D. and Westgate, D.P.G. (1994) *Investigating classroom talk* (2nd edn). London; Washington DC: Falmer Press.

Eggins, S. and Slade, D. (1997) *Analysing casual conversation*. London; New York: Cassell.

Eglin, P. and Hester, S. (1992) Category, predicate and task: The pragmatics of practical action. *Semiotica*, 3, 243–68.

Eisner, E. (1979) Recent developments in educational research affecting art education. *Art Education*, 32, 12–15:

Emmison, M. and Smith P. (2000). *Researching the visual: Images, objects, contexts and interactions in social and cultural inquiry*. London: Sage.

Evaldsson, A.-C. and Corsaro, W.A. (1998) Play and games in the peer cultures of preschool and preadolescent children: An interpretative approach. *Childhood*, 5(4), 377–402.

Fehr, B.J., Stetson, J. and Mizukawa, Y. (1990) A bibliography for ethnomethodology. In J. Coulter (ed.) *Ethnomethodological sociology*. London: Edward Elgar. pp. 475–559.

Fehr, B.J., Stetson, J. and Mizukawa, Y.:
www.bekkoame.ne.jp/~mizukawa/EM/bib/bib-comp.html

Fielding, M. (1997) Beyond school effectiveness and school improvement: Lighting the slow fuse of possibility. *Curriculum Journal*, 8, 7–27.

Freebody, P. (2001) Theorising new literacies in and out of school. *Language and Education: An international Journal*. 15, 105–17.

Freebody, P. and Baker, C.D. (1985) Children's first schoolbooks: Introductions to the culture of literacy. *Harvard Educational Review*, 55(4), 381–98.

Freebody, P. and Baker, C.D. (1987) The construction and operation of gender in children's first school books. In A. Pauwels (ed.) *Women and language in Australian and New Zealand Society*. Sydney: Australian Professional Publications.

Freebody, P. and Freiberg, J. (2000) Public and pedagogic morality: The local orders of instructional and regulatory talk in classrooms. In S. Hester and D. Francis (eds) *Local education order: Ethnomethodological studies of knowledge in action*. Amsterdam/London: John Benjamins.

Freebody, P. and Freiberg, J. (2001) Re-discovering practical reading activities in schools and homes. *Journal of Research in Reading*, 24, 222–34.

Freebody, P., Luke, A. and Gilbert, P. (1991) Reading instruction and discourse critique: Rethinking the politics of literacy. *Curriculum Inquiry*, 21, 235–57.

Freebody, P. and Power, D. (2001) Interviewing Deaf adults in postsecondary educational settings: Stories, cultures and life-histories. *Journal of Deaf Studies and Deaf Education*, 6, 130–41.

Freiberg, J. and Freebody, P. (1995) Analysing literacy events in classrooms and homes: Conversation-Analytic approaches. In P. Freebody, C. Ludwig and S. Gunn, *Everyday literacy practices in and out of schools in low socio-economic urban communities*. Report to the Commonwealth Department of Employment, Education and Training, Curriculum Corporation Vol. 1: 185–372.

Fried, A. and Elman, R. (1968) *Excerpts from life and labour of the people in London*. New York: Pantheon.

Gage, N. (1988) The paradigm wars and their aftermath. *Teachers College Record*, 91, 135–50.

Garfinkel, H. (1952) The perception of the other: A study in social order. Unpublished PhD dissertation, Harvard University.

Garfinkel, H. (1967) *Studies in ethnomethodology*. Englewood Cliffs, NJ: Prentice-Hall.

Gee, J.P. (1999) *An introduction to discourse analysis: Theory and method*. London: Routledge.

Gilbert, G.N. and Mulkay, M. (1984) *Opening Pandora's Box: A sociological analysis of scientists' discourse*. Cambridge: Cambridge University Press.

Gitlin, A. (ed.) (1994) *Power and method: Political activism and educational research*. Critical Social Thought Series. New York: Routledge.

Gitlin, A. and Russell, R. (1994) Alternative methodologies and the research context. In A. Gitlin (ed.) *Power and method: Political activism and educational research*. Critical Social Thought Series. New York: Routledge.

Gitlin, A., Bringhurst, K., Burns, M., Cooley, V., Myers, B., Price, K., Russell, R. and Tiess, P. (1992) *Teachers' voices for social change: An introduction to educative research*. Columbia, NY: Teachers' College Press.

Glaser, B.G. and Strauss, A.L. (1967) *The discovery of grounded theory: Strategies for qualitative research*. Chicago, IL: Aldine.

Goetz, J. and LeCompte, M. (1984) *Ethnography and qualitative design in education research*. New York: Academic Press.

Goffman, E. (1961) *Asylums*. New York: Doubleday.

Goffman, E. (1963) *Behaviour in public places: Notes on the social organization of gatherings*. New York: Free Press.

Goffman, E. (1981) *Forms of talk*. Oxford: Basil Blackwell.

Goodson, I. (1993) The devil's bargain: Educational research and the teacher. *Educational Policy Analysis Archives*, 1, 1–7.

Goodwin, C. and Heritage, J. (1990) Conversation analysis. *Annual Review of Anthropology*, 19, 283–307.

Greatbatch, D. (1988) A turn-taking system for British news interviews, *Language in Society*, 17, 401–30.

Green, J. and Bloome, D. (1997) Ethnography and ethnographers of and in education: A situated perspective. In J. Flood, S.B. Heath and D. Lapp (eds) *Handbook of research on teaching literacy through the communicative and visual arts*. New York: Simon & Schuster Macmillan. pp. 181–202.

Green, J., Tuyay, S. and Dixon, C.M. (2002) Ethnographic research as evidence of meeting the standards in Science, Mathematics and Social Science. Paper presented to the American Educational Research Association Annual Conference, New Orleans.

Green, J., Dixon, C.N. and Zaharlick, A. (in press) Ethnography as a logic of inquiry. In J. Flood, J.M. Jensen, D. Lapp and J.R. Squire (eds) *Handbook of research on English language arts teaching*. New York: Macmillan.

Grundy, S. (1994) Action research at the school level: Possibilities and problems. *Educational Action Research*, 2, 23–37.

Gubrium, J.F. and Holstein, J.A. (1997) *The new language of qualitative method.* New York: Oxford University.

Gumperz, J.J. and Hymes, D. (eds) (1972) *Directions in sociolinguistics: The ethnography of communication.* New York: Rinehart & Winston.

Halliday, M.A.K. (1985) *An introduction to functional grammar.* London: Edward Arnold.

Hamel, J., Dufour, S. and Fortin, D. (1993) *Case study methods.* Newbury Park, CA: Sage.

Harvey, D. (1989) *The condition of post-modernity.* Cambridge, MA: Basil Blackwell.

Heap, J.L. (1980) What counts as reading: Limits to certainty in assessment. *Curriculum Inquiry*, 10, 265–92.

Heap, J.L. (1982) *Word recognition in theory and in classroom practice.* Paper presented to the Ethnography in Education Conference, March, Philadelphia.

Heap, J.L. (1985a) *Applied ethnomethodology: Looking for the local rationality of reading activities.* In Proceedings of the Seventh International Institute for Ethnography and Critical Analysis, Boston, MA, August. pp. 39–74.

Heap, J.L. (1985b) Discourse in the production of classroom knowledge: Reading lessons. *Curriculum Inquiry*, 15, 245–79.

Heap, J.L. (1986) Cultural logic and schema theory: A reply to Bereiter. *Curriculum Inquiry*, 16, 73–86.

Heap, J.L. (1990) A situated perspective on what counts as reading. In C. Baker and A. Luke (eds) *Towards a critical sociology of reading pedagogy.* Amsterdam/Philadelphia: John Benjamins.

Heap, J.L. (1992) Ethnomethodology and the possibility of a metaperspective on literacy research. In R. Beach, J.L. Green, M.L. Kamil and T. Shanahan (eds) *Multidisciplinary perspectives on literacy research.* Urbana, IL: NCTE. pp. 35–56.

Heap, J.L. (1995) Understanding cultural science: A response to Anderson and West. *Reading Research Quarterly*, 30(3), 578–80.

Heap, J.L. (1997) Conversation analysis methods in researching language and education. In N.H. Hornberger and D. Corson (eds) *Encyclopedia of language and education, Volume 8, Research methods in language and education.* Amsterdam: Kluwer Academic. pp. 217–25.

Heath, S.B. (1982) Ethnography in education: defining the essentials. In P. Gilmore and A.A. Glatthorn (eds) *Children in and out of school: Ethnography and Education.* Washington, DC: Center for Applied Linguistics.

Heritage, J. (1984) *Garfinkel and ethnomethodology.* Cambridge: Polity Press.

Hester, S. (1992) Recognizing references to deviance in referral talk. In G. Watson and R.M. Seiler (eds) *Text in context: Contributions to ethnomethodology.* London: Sage. pp. 156–74.

Hester, S. and Eglin, P. (1997) *Culture in action: Studies in Membership Categorization Analysis.* Maryland: University Press of America.

Hester, S. and Francis, D. (1997) Reality analysis in a classroom storytelling. *British Journal of Sociology*, 48, 95–112.

Hester, S. and Francis, D. (eds) (2000) *Local Education Order: Ethnomethodological studies of knowledge in action.* Amsterdam/London: John Benjamins.

Howe, C. (1988) *Peer interaction of young children.* Chicago, IL: Society for Research in Child Development.

Huey, E.B. (1908) *The psychology and pedagogy of reading*, New York: Macmillan.

Hunter, I. (1993) The pastoral bureaucracy: Toward a less principled understanding of state schooling. In D. Meredyth and D. Tyler (eds) *Child and citizen: Genealogies of schooling and subjectivity*. Brisbane: Institute for Cultural Policy Studies.

Hutchby, I. and Wooffitt, R. (1998). *Conversation analysis: Principles, practices and applications*. Oxford: Polity Press (UK and Europe), Blackwell Publishers Inc (USA).

Jalbert, P.L. (ed.) (1999) *Media studies: Ethnomethodological approaches*. Lanham, New York, Oxford: University Press of America and the International Institute for Ethnomethodology and Conversation Analysis.

Jayyusi, I. (1984) *Categorisation and the moral order*. London: Routledge and Kegan Paul.

Jayyusi, L. (1991) Values and moral judgement: communicative praxis as moral order. In G. Button (ed.) *Ethnomethodology and the human sciences*. Cambridge: Cambridge University Press. pp. 227–51.

Jefferson, G. (1984) *Caricature versus detail: On the particulars of pronunciation in transcriptions of conversational data*. Tilburg papers, No. 31. Netherlands.

Jenks, C. (1982) Introduction: Constituting the child. In C. Jenks (ed.) *The sociology of childhood: Essential readings*. London: Batsford.

Jenks, C. (1989) Social theorizing and the child: Constraints and possibilities. In S. Doxiadis (ed.) *Early influences shaping the individual*. London: Plenum Press.

Johnson, B. (1993) *Teacher as researcher*. ERIC Digest # 355205. Washington, DC: ERIC Clearinghouse.

Kant, E. (1781/1955) *The critique of pure reason; The critique of practical reason; The critique of judgment*. Chicago: Britannica Books.

Karnieli, M. (1998) Holistic educational intervention as an action model for the professional development of teacher educators. *Educational Action Research*, 6, 395–412.

Kemmis, S. (1990) Curriculum theory and the state. *Australian Journal of Curriculum Studies*, 22(4), 392–400.

Kemmis, S. (1993) Action research and social movement: A challenge for policy research. *Educational Policy Analysis Archives*, 1, 1–4.

Kincheloe, J.L. and MacLaren, P.L. (1994) Rethinking critical theory and qualitative research. In N.K. Denzin and Y.S. Lincoln (eds) *Handbook of qualitative Research*. Thousand Oaks, CA: Sage.

Knupfer, A.M. (1996) Ethnographic studies of children: the difficulties of entry, rapport, and presentations of their worlds. *Qualitative Studies in Education*, 9(2), 135–49.

Krimerman, L.I. (1969) *The nature and scope of social science*. New York: Appleton-Century-Crofts.

Ladwig, J. and Gore, J. (1994) Extending power and specifying method within the discourse of activit research. In A. Gitlin (ed.) *Power and method: Political activism and educational research*. Critical Social Thought Series. New York: Routledge.

Lee, J.R.E. (1987) Talking organisation. In G. Button and J.R.E. Lee (eds) *Talk and social organisation*. Clevedon/Philadelphia: Multilingual Matters.

Lee, J.R.E. (1991) Language and culture: the linguistic analysis of culture. In G. Button (ed.) *Ethnomethodology and the human sciences*. Cambridge: Cambridge University Press.

Leiter, K. (1980) *A primer of ethnomethodology*. New York: Oxford University Press.

Luke, A. and Freebody, P. (1997) The social practices of literacy. In S. Muspratt, A. Luke and P. Freebody (eds) *Constructing critical literacies: Teaching and learning textual practice*. Cresskill, NJ: Hampton Press.

Macbeth, D. (1991) Teacher authority as practical action. *Linguistics and Education*, 3, 281–314.

Macbeth, D. (1994) Classroom encounters with the unspeakable: 'Do you see, Danelle?' *Discourse Processes*, 17, 311–35.

Macbeth, D. (1996) The discovery of situated worlds: Analytic commitments or moral orders? *Human Studies*, 19, 267–87.

Macherey, P. (1978) *Theory of literary production*. London: Routledge & Kegan Paul.

Martin, J.R. (1992) *English text: System and structure*. Amsterdam: Benjamins.

Maynard, D.W. (1991) On the interactional and institutional bases of asymmetry in clinical discourse, *American Journal of Sociology*, 97, 448–95.

McHoul, A. (1978) The organization of turns at formal talk in the classroom, *Language in Society*, 7, 183–213.

McHoul, A.W. (1982) *Telling how texts talk: Essays on reading and ethnomethodology*. London; Boston: Routledge & Kegan Paul.

McHoul, A. and Watson, D.R. (1978) Two axes for the analysis of 'commonsense' and 'formal' geographical knowledge in classroom talk. *British Journal of the Sociology of Education*, 5(3), 281–302.

Mertens, D. (1998) *Research methods in education and psychology: Integrating diversity with quantitative and qualitative approaches*. Thousand Oaks, CA: Sage.

Mulkay, M. and Gilbert, G.N. (1982) Accounting for error. *Sociology*, 16, 176.

Muspratt, S., Freebody, P. and Luke, A. (2001) Technologies of inclusion, geographies of exclusion: Schooling and literacy in small rural communities. In P. Freebody, S. Muspratt and B. Dwyer (eds) *Difference, silence and textual practice*. New Jersey: Hampton Press.

National Institute on Student Achievement, Curriculum, and Assessment (1999) The Japanese education system: A case study summary and analysis. *Research Today: International Studies*, available at http://www.ed.gov/pubs/ResearchToday/98-3038.html

New Internationalist *Map of the World* (no date) Oxford: New Internationalist Publications.

Olesen, V. (1994) Feminisms and models of qualitative research. In N. Denzin and Y. Lincoln (eds) *Handbook of qualitative research*. London: Falmer Press.

Olson, D.R. (1977) The language of instruction: The literate bias of schooling. In R.C. Anderson, R.J. Spiro and W.E. Montague (eds) *Schooling and the acquisition of knowledge*. Hillsdale, NJ: Erlbaum. pp. 65–89.

Olson, D.R. (1983) Sources of authority in the language of the school. *Curriculum Inquiry*, 13, 129–31.

Ong, W. (1958) *Ramus, method and the decay of dialogue*. Cambridge, MA: Harvard University Press.

Packwood, A. and Sikes, P. (1996) A post modern approach to research. *Qualitative Studies in Education*, 9(3), 335–45.

Pollack, B. (1995) *The experimental psychology of Alfred Binet: Selected papers*. New York: Springer Publishing.

Psathas, G. (1995) *Conversation analysis: The study of talk-in interaction*. Thousand Oaks, CA: Sage.

Purdy, S. and Sandak, C.R. (1982) *The Aztecs: A remarkable civilization*. New York: Franklin Watts.

Putney, L.G., Green, J.L., Dixon, C.N. and Kelly, G.J. (1999) The evolution of qualitative research methodology: Looking beyond defense to possibilities. *Reading Research Quarterly*, 34, 368–77.

Rogers, T.B. (1995) *The psychological testing enterprise: An introduction.* Pacific Grove, CA: Books/Cole.

Rosenau, P.M. (1992) *Post-modernism and the social sciences.* Princeton, NJ: Princeton University Press.

Sacks, H. (1972) On the analyzability of stories by children. In J.J. Gumperz and D. Hymes (eds) *Directions in sociolinguistics: The ethnography of communication.* New York: Rinehart & Winston. pp. 325–45.

Sacks, H. (1992) *Lectures on conversation.* 2 vols. Edited by Gail Jefferson with introductions by Emanuel A. Schegloff. Oxford: Basil Blackwell.

Sacks, H., Schegloff, E.A. and Jefferson, G. (1974) A simplest systematics for the organization of turn taking for conversation. *Language*, 50, 696–735.

Schegloff, E.A. (1991) Reflections on talk and social structure. In D. Boden and D. Zimmerman (eds) *Talk and social structure: Studies in ethnomethodology and conversation analysis.* Cambridge: Polity Press. pp. 44–70.

Schegloff, E.A. (1992). Introduction. In H. Sacks (1992) *Lectures on conversation.* 2 vols. Edited by Gail Jefferson with introductions by Emanuel A. Schegloff. Oxford: Basil Blackwell.

Schegloff, E.A. (1995) Parties and joint talk: Two ways in which numbers are significant for talk-in-interaction. In P. ten Have and G. Psathas (eds) *Situated order: Studies in the social organization of talk and embodied activities.* Washington, DC: University Press of America.

Schutz, A. (1970) *Reflections on the problem of relevance.* New Haven, CT: Yale University Press.

Shkedi, A. (1998) Teachers' attitudes towards research: A challenge for qualitative researchers. *The International Journal of Qualitative Studies in Education*, 11(4), 559–77.

Shulman, L.S. (1996) Just in case: Reflections on learning from experience. In J. Colbert, K. Trimble and P. Desberg (eds) *The case for education: Contemporary approaches for using case methods.* Needham Heights, MA: Allyn & Bacon.

Silverman, D. (1987) *Communication and medical practice: Social relations in the clinic.* London: Sage.

Silverman, D. (1993) *Interpreting qualitative data: Methods for analysing talk, text and interaction.* London: Sage.

Silverman, D. (ed.) (1997) *Qualitative research: Theory, method and practice.* London: Sage.

Silverman, D. (1998) The quality of qualitative health research: The open-ended interview and its alternatives. *Social Sciences in Health*, 4, 104–18.

Silverman, D. (1999) *Doing qualitative research: A practical handbook.* London: Sage.

Sinclair, J. and Coulthard, M. (1975) *Towards an analysis of discourse.* London: Oxford University Press.

Smith, D.E. (1987) *The everyday world as problematic: A feminist sociology.* Boston: Northeastern University Press.

Smith, D.E. (1990a) *Texts, facts, and femininity: Exploring the relations of ruling.* London: Routledge.

Smith, D.E. (1990b) *The conceptual practices of power: A feminist sociology of knowledge.* Boston: Northeastern University Press.

Smith, D.E. (1999) *Writing the social: Critique, theory and investigations.* Toronto: University of Toronto Press.

Smith, J.K. and Heshesius, L. (1986) Closing down the conversation: The end of the qualitative–quantitative debate among educational enquirers. *Educational Researcher,* 15, 4–12.

Snow, C.E.(1997) The development of conversation between mother and babies. *Journal of Child Language,* 4, 1–22.

Snow, C.E., Burns, M.S. and Griffin, P. (eds) (1998) *Preventing reading difficulties in young children.* Washington, DC: National Academy Press.

Speier, M. (1970) The everyday world of the child. In J.D. Douglas (ed.) *Understanding everyday life: Toward the reconstruction of sociological knowledge.* Chicago, IL: Aldine. pp. 188–218.

Stake, R.E. (1995) *The art of case study research.* Thousand Oaks, CA: Sage.

Strauss, A. and Corbin, J. (1990) *Basics of qualitative research: Grounded theory procedures and techniques.* Newbury Park, CA: Sage.

Summers, L. (1994) *Investing in all the people: Educating women in developing countries.* EDI Seminar Paper 45. Washington: World Bank Publications.

Taylor, S.J. and Bogdan, R. (1984) *Introduction to qualitative research methods: The search for meaning.* New York: John Wiley.

Taylor, T. and Cameron, D. (1987) *Analysing conversation: Rules and units in the structure of talk.* Oxford: Pergamon Press.

ten Have, P. (1991) Talk and institution: A reconsideration of the 'asymmetry' of doctor–patient interaction. In D. Boden and D.H. Zimmerman (eds) *Talk and social structure: Studies in ethnomethodology and conversation analysis.* Cambridge: Polity Press.

ten Have, P. (1995) Formatting the consultation: communication formats and constituted identities. In E. Huls and J. Klatter-Folmer (eds) *Artikelen van de Tweede, Sociolinguïstische Conferentie.* Delft: Eburon: 245–68.

ten Have, P. (1999a) An idealized model of CA practices. *Methodological issues in conversation analysis:* www.pscw.uva.nl/emca/mica.htm

ten Have, P. (1999b) *Doing conversation analysis: a practical guide.* London: Sage.

ten Have: www.pscw.uva.nl/emca/resource.html

Thiele, C. (1974) *Magpie Island.* Ringwood, Victoria: Puffin Books.

Tisdell, R. (1979) *Economics in our society: Principles and applications.* Milton, Qld: Jacaranda.

Tizard, B. and Hughes, M. (1985) *Young children learning: Talking and thinking at home and at school.* London: Fontana.

United Nations Convention on the Rights of the Child (1989) http://www1.umn.edu/humanrts/instree/k2crc.htm

Unsworth, L. (ed.) (2000) *Researching language in schools and communities: Functional linguistic perspectives.* London; New York: Cassell.

Vidich, A. and Lyman, S (1994) Qualitative methods: Their history in sociology and anthropology. In N. Denzin and Y. Lincoln (eds) *Handbook of Qualitative Research.* Thousand Oaks, CA: Sage.

Wainwright, D. (1997) Can sociological research be qualitative, critical and valid? *The Qualitative Report,* 3, 1–15.

Watson, G. and Seiler, R.M. (eds) (1992) *Text in context: Contributions to ethnomethodology.* London: Sage.

Wellberg, D. (1985) Post-modernism in Europe. In S. Trachtenberg (ed.) *The post-modern movement.* Westport, CT: Greenwood Press.

Wells, G. and Wells, J. (1984) Learning to talk and talking to learn. *Theory into Practice*, 23, 190–7.

Wells, G. (1981) *Learning through interaction: The study of language development*. Cambridge: Cambridge University Press.

Wells, G. (1985) Preschool literacy-related activities and success in school. In D.R. Olson, N. Torrance and A. Hildyard (eds) *Literacy, language, and learning: The nature and consequences of reading and writing*. Cambridge: Cambridge University Press.

Wiersma, W. (1995) *Research methods in education: An introduction* (6th edn). Boston, MA: Allyn & Bacon.

Willes, M.J. (1983) *Children into pupils*. London: Routledge and Kegan Paul.

Wilson, T.P. (1991) Social structure and the sequential organization of interaction. In D. Boden and D.H. Zimmerman (eds) *Talk and social structure: Studies in ethnomethodology and conversation analysis*. Cambridge: Polity Press. pp. 22–43.

Wootton, A.J. (1997) *Interaction and the development of mind*. Cambridge: Cambridge University Press.

Yin, R. (1984) *Case study research: Design and methods*. Beverly Hills, CA: Sage.

Yin, R. (1989) *Case study research: Design and methods* (revised edn). Newbury Park, CA: Sage.

Yin, R. (1993) *Applications of case study research*. Beverly Hills, CA: Sage.

Yin, R. (1994) *Case study research: Design and methods* (2nd edn). Beverly Hills, CA: Sage.

Yin, R. and Moore, G. (1987) The use of advanced technologies in special education. *Journal of Learning Disabilities*, 20(1), 60.

Zimmerman, D.H. and Boden, D. (1991) Structure-in-action. In D. Boden and D.H. Zimmerman (eds) *Talk and social structure: Studies in ethnomethodology and conversation analysis*. Cambridge: Polity Press. pp. 3–21.

Zimmerman, C.C. and Frampton, M.E. (1935) *Family and society: A study of the sociology of reconstruction*. New York: Van Nostrand.

Zuber-Skerritt, O. (ed.) (1996) *New directions in action research*. London: Falmer.

Index